A CULTURAL HISTORY OF THE EMOTIONS

VOLUME 3

A Cultural History of the Emotions
General Editors: Susan Broomhall, Jane W. Davidson, and Andrew Lynch

Volume 1
A Cultural History of the Emotions in Antiquity
Edited by Douglas Cairns

Volume 2
A Cultural History of the Emotions in the Medieval Age
Edited by Juanita Ruys and Clare Monagle

Volume 3
A Cultural History of the Emotions in the Late Medieval, Reformation, and Renaissance Age
Edited by Andrew Lynch and Susan Broomhall

Volume 4
A Cultural History of the Emotions in the Baroque and Enlightenment Age
Edited by Claire Walker, Katie Barclay, and David Lemmings

Volume 5
A Cultural History of the Emotions in the Age of Romanticism, Revolution, and Empire
Edited by Susan Matt

Volume 6
A Cultural History of the Emotions in the Modern and Post-Modern Age
Edited by Jane Davidson and Joy Damousi

A CULTURAL HISTORY OF THE EMOTIONS
IN THE LATE MEDIEVAL, REFORMATION, AND RENAISSANCE AGE

Edited by Andrew Lynch and Susan Broomhall

BLOOMSBURY ACADEMIC
LONDON • NEW YORK • OXFORD • NEW DELHI • SYDNEY

BLOOMSBURY ACADEMIC
Bloomsbury Publishing Plc
50 Bedford Square, London, WC1B 3DP, UK
1385 Broadway, New York, NY 10018, USA
29 Earlsfort Terrace, Dublin 2, Ireland

BLOOMSBURY and the Diana logo are trademarks of Bloomsbury Publishing Plc

First published in Great Britain 2019
This edition published in Great Britain, 2022

Copyright © Bloomsbury Publishing, 2019

Andrew Lynch and Susan Broomhall have asserted their right under the Copyright, Designs and Patents Act, 1988, to be identified as Editor of this work.

Cover image © The Magdalen Weeping, c. 1525. Found in the collection of the National Gallery, London. (Photo by Fine Art Images/Heritage Images/Getty Images)

All rights reserved. No part of this publication may be reproduced or transmitted in any form or by any means, electronic or mechanical, including photocopying, recording, or any information storage or retrieval system, without prior permission in writing from the publishers.

A catalogue record for this book is available from the British Library.

A catalog record for this book is available from the Library of Congress.

ISBN: HB: 978-1-4725-3578-8
       PB: 978-1-3503-4523-2
       Set: 978-1-3503-4769-4

Series: The Cultural Histories Series

Typeset by RefineCatch Limited, Bungay, Suffolk
Printed and bound in Great Britain

To find out more about our authors and books visit www.bloomsbury.com and sign up for our newsletters.

CONTENTS

LIST OF ILLUSTRATIONS		vi
GENERAL EDITORS' PREFACE		xi
Introduction: Emotional Cultures of Change and Continuity, 1300–1600 *Andrew Lynch*		1
1	Medical and Scientific Understandings *Susan Broomhall*	13
2	Religion and Spirituality *David Lederer*	31
3	Music and Dance *Denis Collins and Jennifer Nevile*	49
4	Drama *Kathryn Prince*	69
5	The Visual Arts *Patricia Simons and Charles Zika*	85
6	Literature *Sarah McNamer*	107
7	In Private: The Individual and the Domestic Community *Jeremy Goldberg and Stephanie Tarbin*	123
8	In Public: Collectivities and Polities *Jelle Haemers*	141
NOTES ON CONTRIBUTORS		157
NOTES		161
REFERENCES		167
INDEX		199

ILLUSTRATIONS

INTRODUCTION

0.1 *Madonna dell'Umiltà* (Madonna of Humility) c. 1470, artist unknown, Italy (Ferrara?), painted wood (Italian poplar), 65.5 × 47.5 × 21.0 cm, National Gallery of Australia, Canberra. 4

0.2 Masaccio, *Crucifixion*, c. 1426, panel, 83 × 63.5 cm, Ministero per i Beni e le Attività Culturali, Museo e Real Bosco di Capodimonte, Naples. 7

0.3 *Casket* (c. 1450). Workshop of the Embriachi, Florence/Venice. Wood, iron, bone, colored woods. National Gallery of Victoria, Melbourne. Bequest of Howard Spensley, 1939 (4120-D3). 11

CHAPTER 1

1.1 Frontispiece to Andreas Vesalius, *De humani corporis fabrica* (Basel, ex Officina Joannis Oporini, 1543). Courtesy of Universal History Archive/UIG via Getty Images. 17

1.2 Portrait of the author, Andreas Vesalius, *De humani corporis fabrica* (Basel, ex Officina Joannis Oporini, 1543). Courtesy of The Print Collector/Print Collector/Getty Images. 18

1.3 Colored portrait of the author, Konrad Kyeser, *Bellifortis*, before 1430, Niedersächsische Staats- und Universitätbibliothek, Göttingen 2° Cod. Ms. philos. 64. Courtesy of Paul Fearn/Alamy Stock Photo. 19

1.4 Putti dissecting a pig in a historiated woodcut letter Q in Andreas Vesalius, *De humani corporis fabrica* (Basel, ex Officina Joannis Oporini, 1543). Courtesy of AF Fotografie/Alamy Stock Photo. 24

1.5 A depiction of the consequences of the plague at Tournai in 1349, in Gilles le Muisit, *Annales*, Brussels, Bibliothèque royale de Belgique ms 13076–77, f. 24v. Courtesy of Photo 12/Alamy Stock Photo. 26

CHAPTER 2

2.1 The virtue Hope allegorically directed toward heaven, juxtaposed with the sin of Despair, depicted as a suicide carried off by a demon. Giotto, Hope, Despair, c. 1305, fresco, each 120 × 60 cm. Arena Chapel, Padua. Images courtesy of Wikimedia Commons and Getty Images respectively. 34

LIST OF ILLUSTRATIONS vii

2.2 The tortures of the damned in hell. Giotto, *The Last Judgment*, c. 1305, detail, fresco, 1000 × 840 cm, Arena Chapel, Padua. Image courtesy of Wikimedia Commons. 35

2.3 Deathbed temptations: pride staved off through faith. *Ars Moriendi*, Netherlands, c. 1460, woodcut. Image courtesy of Wikimedia Commons. 38

2.4 Neither pope, nor king, nor queen, nor cardinal, nor prince sits out the Dance of Death. Bernt Notke, *Danse Macabre*, St. Nicholas' Church, Tallinn, end of the 15th century. Image courtesy of Wikimedia Commons. 38

2.5 "All Aboard": rejoicing fools set sail for the New World under the flag of Dr Greed. Title page to Sebastian Brandt, *Ship of Fools* (Basel, 1494). Collection of the State A. Pushkin Museum of Fine Arts, Moscow. Courtesy of DeAgostini/Getty Images. 44

CHAPTER 3

3.1 Martin Luther playing the lute. Imagined scenario in an engraving by Gustav Adolf Closs (1864–1938). Courtesy of Prisma/UIG/Getty Images. 51

3.2 Anonymous, seated crowned figure surrounded by musicians playing the lute, bagpipes, triangle, horn, viola, and drums. Private Collection via Getty Images. 56

3.3 Amico Aspertini, *Transportation of the Holy Face*, detail, 1507–9, fresco, Basilica of San Frediano, Lucca. Courtesy of Dea Picture Library via Getty Images. 56

3.4 First page of the dance *Amor Costante* from Fabritio Caroso, *Il ballarino* (Venice, 1581). Courtesy of the Library of Congress, Washington, D.C. 59

3.5 An illustration of how a student can learn to perform virtuosic jumps such as the different types of *capriole*, from Cesare Negri, *Nuove inventioni di balli* (Milan, 1604. A re-edition of *Le gratie d'amore*). Courtesy of the Library of Congress, Washington, D.C. 63

CHAPTER 4

4.1 Scant visual evidence of English mystery play staging survives. David Sharp's copper engraving, "Representation of a Pageant Vehicle at the time of Performance," imagines a fifteenth-century performance. From Thomas Sharp, *A Dissertation on the Pageants or Dramatic Mysteries Anciently Performed at Coventry* (Coventry, 1825). Image courtesy of Wikimedia Commons. 71

4.2 Pacino di Bonaguida, *The Crucifixion*, detail, c. 1315–20, tempera and gold leaf on panel, 32 × 17 1/2 in. Fondazione di Studi di Storia dell'Arte Roberto Longhi di Firenze. Courtesy of Getty Images. 72

4.3 Phillippe de Champaigne, *Still Life with a Skull*, 1644, oil on panel, 28 × 37 cm, Musée de Tessé, Le Mans. The painting combines symbols used in *memento mori* painting and in *Hamlet*. Image courtesy of Wikimedia Commons. 80

CHAPTER 5

5.1 Albrecht Dürer, *Melencolia I*, 1514, engraving, 23.9 × 18.7 cm (image), 24.1 × 18.7 cm (sheet). National Gallery of Victoria, Melbourne Felton Bequest, 1956 (3486-4). 87

5.2 Rogier van der Weyden, *Deposition*, c. 1436, oil on wood, 204.5 × 261.5 cm. Museo del Prado, Madrid (P02835). Image courtesy of Getty Images. 89

5.3 Giotto, *Lamentation*, c. 1305, fresco, 200 × 185 cm. Arena Chapel, Padua. Image courtesy of Getty Images. 91

5.4 Niccolò dell'Arca, *Pietà*, c. 1485–90, painted terracotta. Santa Maria della Vita, Bologna. © 2017. Photo Scala, Florence. 92

5.5 Mathias Grünewald, *Crucifixion, with Lamentation*, oil and tempera on limewood; central panels of the closed state of *The Isenheim Altarpiece*, by Mathias Grünewald (painted panels) and Niclaus of Hagenau (wooden sculpture of the open state), 1512–16, 376 × 668 cm. Musée d'Unterlinden, Colmar. Image courtesy of Getty Images. 93

5.6 German (Ulm), *Man of Sorrows*, c. 1465/70, hand-colored woodcut (mounted to detached cover of a lost book), 39.7 × 26.2 cm (image), 40.5 × 26.9 cm (sheet). The Art Institute of Chicago, Waller Fund; gifts of Mrs. Tiffany Blake, Thomas E. Donnelley, Emil Eitel, Carolyn Morse Ely, Alfred E. Hamill, Frank B. Hubachek, Monarch Leather, and Mrs. Potter Palmer, 1947.731. ©2017. The Art Institute of Chicago/Art Resource, NY/Scala, Florence. 96

5.7 Agnolo Bronzino, *An Allegory with Venus and Cupid*, c. 1545, oil on wood, 146.1 × 116.2 cm. National Gallery, London (NG651). Image courtesy of Getty Images. 98

5.8 Albrecht Altdorfer, *Christ on the Mount of Olives*, 1509, pen and white heightening on red-brown grounded paper, 21 × 15.7 cm. Staatliche Museen zu Berlin, Kupferstichkabinett. ©bpk/Kupferstichkabinett, SMB/Jörg P. Anders, No: 00048735. 99

5.9 Hans Rudolf Manuel Deutsch, *The Changing Faces of the Catholic Church*, trick woodcut, 1556. Left, View 1: *A Prelate as a Fool with a Goiter*. Right, View 8: *A Prelate as the Devil*, Graphische Sammlung Albertina, Vienna, Inv. DG2002/209. 102

5.10 Pieter van der Heyden, engraving after Pieter Bruegel the Elder, *The Peasant Wedding Dance*, after 1570, 38 × 43.3 cm. Metropolitan Museum of Art, New York, Harris Brisbane Dick Fund (33.52.29). 103

LIST OF ILLUSTRATIONS

5.11 Titian, *Venus, Cupid and an Organist*, c. 1555, oil on canvas, 150.2 × 218.2 cm. Museo del Prado, Madrid (P00421). Image courtesy of Getty Images. 106

CHAPTER 6

6.1 Giotto, Wrath, c. 1305, fresco, 120 × 55 cm. Arena Chapel, Padua. Image courtesy of Wikimedia Commons. 111

6.2 Lute tablature, "Greensleeves." The Board of Trinity College, Dublin, MS 408, p. 104. 113

6.3 Cologne, Reliquary bust of a young martyr, artist unknown, c. 1310–25, polychromed wood, 27.4 × 23.4 × 11.6 cm. Yale Gallery of Art 1985.42.l. 115

6.4 Lancelot and Guinevere's first kiss, *Lancelot-Graal*, Northeastern France, 1310–15, New York, Pierpont Morgan Library MS M. 805.6, fol. 67r. 119

CHAPTER 7

7.1 The Virgin sits in a comfortably appointed chamber which features an image of St Christopher on paper pinned above the fireplace. Maître de Flémalle (Robert Campin?), *Annunciation*, c. 1415–25, Inv. 3937, Royal Museum of Fine Arts, Belgium. Image courtesy of Wikimedia Commons. 131

7.2 Chambers functioned as spaces for entertaining and for displaying emblems of family pride and personal identity, as shown in this miniature of Queen Isabella of Bavaria in her chamber receiving a manuscript from Christine de Pizan. From the poems of Christine de Pizan, c. 1410–15. Harl 4431 fol. 3, British Library, London, UK/© British Library Board. All Rights Reserved/Bridgeman Images. 133

7.3 The central panel of the *Mérode Altarpiece* (c. 1427–32) by the Master of Flémalle (Robert Campin?) mirrors the sorts of hall furnishings found in urban homes of merchants and prosperous craftsmen. © The Cloisters Collection (1956), The Metropolitan Museum of Art. 135

7.4 Peasant festivities took place inside barns or in the open air, as with this decorous feast depicted in an engraving from the mid-sixteenth century. *The Peasants' Feast or the Twelve Months*, 1546–7, by Sebald Beham. Gift of J. Rockman, 1942 © The Metropolitan Museum of Art. 136

CHAPTER 8

8.1 In 1379, two urban functionaries are killed during a violent revolt in Montpellier, in *Chroniques de France, dites de Saint-Denis*, Paris, after 1380. British Library, MS Roy. 20 CVII, f. 212r. 142

8.2 Eat, drink, and be merry: elite and popular dining culture around 1500, in V. Maximus, *Faits et dits mémorables des romains*, Bruges, c. 1480. Getty Museum, MS 43, f. 50r. — 144

8.3 Peasant armies in fourteenth-century England, Wat Tyler meets John Ball, in J. Froissart, *Chroniques de France et d'Angleterre*, Bruges, 1475–1500. British Library, MS Roy. 18 E I, f. 165v. — 147

8.4 Fifteenth-century procession in a city in the southern Low Countries, in *Spinola Hours*, Bruges, c. 1510. Getty Museum, MS Ludwig IX, 18, f. 48v. — 150

8.5 In 1306, Parisians pillage the house of the royal exchequer, in *Chroniques de France, dites de Saint-Denis*, Paris, after 1380. British Library, MS Roy. 20 CVII, f. 134r. — 154

GENERAL EDITORS' PREFACE

The General Editors, volume editors, and individual authors of this series have many organizations to thank for helping to bring it into existence. They gratefully acknowledge assistance from the Arts and Humanities Research Council (UK); the European Research Council Project, The Social and Cultural Construction of Emotions, University of Oxford, and its Director, Professor Angelos Chaniotis; the Leverhulme Trust; and the Wellcome Trust. Above all, the series has depended on support from the Australian Research Council Centre of Excellence for the History of Emotions (CE110001011). The project was conceived as a key part of the Centre's collaborative research work and has benefited greatly from the generous help of its academic and administrative staff.

The General Editors also express their deep gratitude to the volume editors and authors for their time, expertise and gracious willingness to revise essays in the light of readers' comments. Many other people helped in reading, tracing images, and advising in various ways. Our thanks go to Merridee Bailey; Jacquie Bennett; Sophie Boyd-Hurrell; Frederic Kiernan; Mark Neuendorf; Fiona Sim; and Stephanie Thomson; and to the patient staff at Bloomsbury: Dan Hutchins; Claire Lipscomb; Beatriz Lopez; and Rhodri Mogford. We especially acknowledge Ciara Rawnsley, who as Editorial Assistant for the entire series has tirelessly helped authors and done indispensable and meticulous work on all aspects of the volumes' preparation.

This series is dedicated to the memory of Philippa Maddern (1952–2014) who was an original General Editor, and an inspiring friend, mentor and colleague to many of the contributors.

Introduction

Emotional Cultures of Change and Continuity, 1300–1600

ANDREW LYNCH

What goes to make up a "cultural history" of the emotions? There could be as many answers to that question as there are forms for understanding, expressing, and enacting how emotions have existed in the known world. One starting point might be to note that the question in itself assumes that emotions, as well as culture, have a history. And given that this volume covers the years 1300–1600 CE, in a series stretching from European antiquity to the present, a further assumption must be that they have a long history, meaning that they are seen as continuing and changing elements of life.

Emotions have a "history" in the sense that we find their place in the record of life inextricably entangled with factors of historical difference, across time, place, and culture. To say that they have a cultural history is basically to say that they are generated, experienced, expressed, shared, understood, and later observed and interpreted within cultural contexts, amongst many others. Emotions both help to make up these cultural contexts and are made within them in an endless, always fluid, interactive process. Not all definitions of "culture" have taken this view. Raymond Williams once restricted the word's usefulness to "responses in thought and feeling to the changes in English society since the late eighteenth century" (Williams 1960: v). But, writing more generally, he advocated

> a "social" definition of culture, in which culture is a description of a particular way of life, which expresses certain meanings and values not only in art and learning but also in institutions and ordinary behaviour. The analysis of culture, from such a definition, is the clarification of the meanings and values implicit and explicit in a particular way of life, a particular culture. Such analysis . . . will also include analysis of elements in . . . the organization of production, the structure of the family, the structure of institutions which express or govern social relationships, the characteristic forms through which members of the society communicate.
>
> —Williams 1961: 57–8

It will be clear from the chapter structure in each volume of this series, which includes medicine and science, religion, and private and public life, along with music and dance, drama, the visual arts, and literature that we are taking up the analysis of culture in something like Williams's "social" sense.

It is in that sense also, implying both a broad disciplinary outlook and a concern with the specifics of cultural forms and discourses, social structures, and institutional arrangements, that essays in this volume treat 1300–1600 as a historical section of

European culture. In doing so we are conscious of transgressing long-standing period boundaries—between medieval and Renaissance, or medieval and early modern. We have done this consciously, taking the view that looking at cultural history through emotions offers new opportunities for examining the complexities of historical situations, their patterns of influence and difference, and the nature of change. This volume emphasizes the emotional impact of new expressive forms in art, music, dance, and drama, and their complex ties to court, church, and city. Thinking about emotions in relation to cultural forms casts further light on traditional features of periodic change, like the Reformation, humanism or the rise of the nation state. Yet our essays also show clearly that some major cultural practices of emotion, such as popular demonstrations of discontent with authority, or rituals surrounding childbearing, were prevalent across all the centuries and many of the locations we review. Manuscript production did not cease with the onset of printed books, and printed books spread material that was popular in manuscripts. Similarly, poetic forms such as the sonnet and the neo-Latin epic held sway throughout our period. While we know that there was widespread disruption and disturbance of long-standing ideas, institutions, forms, customs, and ways of life (Salmon 1975; Duffy 1992; Greengrass 2014), there are also evidences of strong cultural continuities.

Clearly, emotional cultures do not march in lockstep with the traditional temporal landmarks of European history; that is part of the value of studying them. Nevertheless emotions, both past and present, have played a large part in establishing modern "feelings" about historical periodization. The period 1300–1600 is a time in which scholarly and confessional discourses, which overlapped with political discourses, oriented themselves toward the past as a different time, and thought about it in terms of communicating across a void or celebrating a liberation. Petrarch, writing to Seneca (d. 65 CE) in the mid-fourteenth century, has been described as "disclos[ing] his awareness of the gap that separates him from his addressee, a gulf which he hopes to bridge—as the very writing of the letter shows—by new practices of reading and writing" (Gur 2015: 141). In the field of art, an idea developed of the great master as an individual, an innovator, surpassing earlier achievements. In 1550, Giorgio Vasari referred to Masaccio (1401–1428) as one who "swept away completely the manner of Giotto" and "gave a beginning to beautiful attitudes, movements, liveliness, and vivacity, and to a certain relief truly characteristic and natural; which no painter up to his time had ever done" (Vasari 1912: 86). These notions empowered new versions of cultural authority, and helped to create an emotional break with the recent past. From the later fourteenth century onwards, artists and architects increasingly hearkened back to the classical world for their aesthetic reference points, while humanist writers in Latin copied classical models and began to study Greek. There was a growing scholarly emphasis on the primacy of original scriptural texts and the early church Fathers, and a project to clear away intervening commentaries. These movements took place alongside attempts, often resisted, to promote the bible to lay people in the vernacular.

In this overarching context, religious reformers spoke of the "darkness" and "superstition" of the immediate past in highly emotive terms, and began to treat their present time as a new beginning, even to invent a new sense of historical time. John Foxe's *Acts and Monuments* (1563) has been seen as symptomatic of "a historical revolution [. . .] so profound that it reversed the western perception of the past within a single generation, from a perception of unity to one of division and difference, from a stillness to a dynamic motion" (Kemp 1991: vi, 104). Foxe is indeed confidently specific on historical eras, repeatedly referring to "these 500 yeares . . . since Sathan broke loose," and is happy "that in these reformed dayes, we seing the prodigious deformities & calamities of those former times, may therfore power oute more aboundant thanks to þᵉ Lord for this his so swete and mercifull reformacion" (Foxe 1563: Book 1, p. 17). James Simpson notes something similar in John Leland's comments on rhetoric: "He claims absolute temporal breaks that form self-enclosed ages, or cultural blocks" (Simpson 2004: 26). One might add that this "dynamic" "revolution" in conceptualizations of time, coupled with the "rebirth" or "flowering" of learning and the arts, was to become a rigid orthodoxy, later reinforced by Enlightenment and other progressivist historiographical discourses. Their combined effects on modern feelings about the past, and especially on the transition from the "medieval" to early modernity, are felt to this day, well after a sense of joyful liberation from the medieval past, or sorrow at its passing, has lost most of its ardor. One task of the essays in this volume is to let the period 1300–1600 suggest some broader possibilities of historical feeling.

In many accounts of the medieval period, the twelfth century stands out as the inventor of the modern emotion of love. It was then, as William M. Reddy writes in *The Making of Romantic Love*, that the idea arose of "a kind of love that could take over one's heart entirely, taming desire-as-appetite, rendering sexual enjoyment innocent, and bringing a marvelous joy" (Reddy 2012: 179). Landmark events in the arts, like the Arthurian romances of Chrétien de Troyes (later twelfth century), the *Roman de la Rose*, composed c. 1230–1275, the Franciscan *laude* of Iacopone da Todi (c. 1230–1306) and the affective "natural" style of Giotto's painting (1270–1337) occurred or took their origins before 1300. By 1300 also, writers in both learned and popular forms had already begun to offer imaginative models for intimate loving relationships between people, or between God and the soul. Through viewing images, reading or hearing lyric poems, meditations, and saints' lives, and through participation in liturgy and other ceremonies, the faithful were already finding new resources to help bind themselves affectively to God, Mary, and the saints. They also learned who were the hateful enemies of God, cut off from his love for ever (Rubin 2009; Bale 2010). The period 1300–1600 cannot be claimed to have instigated these powerful emotive tendencies—the joys and sorrows of intimate love and hate—but it continued, intensified, developed, disseminated, and popularized them with boundless energy. The "praise of passion" was widespread (Strier 2004: 23–42).

Broadly speaking, vernacular cultures of the later Middle Ages are characterized by the high valuation they place on deep feeling. In his treatise *Ego Dormio* the English mystic Richard Rolle, whose works survive in more manuscripts than Chaucer's, inserts an affective Passion lyric and tells readers "If þou wil þynke þis euery day þou shalt fynd gret swetnesse, þat shal draw þi hert vp, and mak þe fal in wepynge and in gret langynge to Ihesu; and þi þoght shal be reft abouen al erthly þynges, abouen þe sky and þe sterres, so þat þe egh of þi hert may loke in to heuyn" (Rolle 1988: 30–1). To Rolle, "thinking" (meditative prayer) is principally a means toward feeling, specifically to divine love-longing. Similarly, a phrase from the Song of Songs, "quia amore langueo" ("for I am sick of love"), becomes the refrain for a lyric, "In a valey of this restles mynde," in which Christ appears as a desolate "Truelove" betrayed by the fickle human soul (Fein 1998: "In a valey"), and for another in which Mary, as universal mother, longingly begs humankind to return her love and find mercy (Saupe 1997: "In a tabernacle"). In Marian art, the love between mother and child—she is literally "in touch" with the divine—becomes recognizably and attainably human (Figure 0.1).

Love is understood as a divinely created impulse, "naturall to every wyght [person]" as a late medieval carol says (Greene 1977: 283). But it is an impulse that must be directed

FIGURE 0.1: *Madonna dell'Umilità* (Madonna of Humility), c. 1470, artist unknown, Italy (Ferrara?), painted wood (Italian poplar), 65.5 × 47.5 × 21.0 cm. National Gallery of Australia, Canberra.

to the right object—in secular romance and lyric to a worthy beloved, and in the sphere of religion to God. Literature and art were called on to provide the right imaginative structures in which these correct orientations could occur, through "emotives" used as deliberate "inputs" to the self (Reddy 2001: 322). A fourteenth-century prayer of the Passion places marginal crosses throughout the text with a preface explaining: "In seying of this orisoun stinteth [pause] and bideth [wait] at every cros and thinketh what ye have seide. For a more devout prayere fond I never of the Passioun, whoso wolde devoutly say itte" (Davies 1964: 120).

Such texts seem designed for forms of private reading and personal utterance, and often gesture to environments and built structures that suit or embody those purposes: "a valey of this restles mynde"; "a tabernacle of a toure"; for William Dunbar "within ane cloister . . . in ane oritorie" (Dunbar 2004: poem 2). Some environments—the springtime wood and the paradisal dream landscape—are shared between religious and secular works, and some texts seem designed to exploit the ambiguity and enjoyable emotional surprise that such sharing can provide for readers: what looks like a *chanson d'aventure*, where the persona goes out in search of a sexual encounter—"Ase y me rod this ender day / By grene wode to seche play"—turns into a Marian praise poem (Saupe 1997: poem 77). The "double coding" and other "crossover" features of some medieval narrative genres, such as romance, saint's life, and moral *exemplum,* and of some narrative themes—pilgrimage, quest, combat—kept secular and religious in continuing dialogue (Newman 2013). Hybrid martyrdom-romances like St. Eustace and St. George from the *Legenda Aurea* (c. 1260), which grew and multiplied in numerous vernaculars, exemplify this emotional porosity (Lynch 2015a).

In such ways, popular religious and secular texts both demanded and modeled the cultivation of an intense interior self, continuing the emotional program begun before 1300. The increasing number and personalization of books of hours, including beautifully illustrated examples, suggests the importance of private devotional practices (Duffy 2005: 233–65). *Le Roman de la Rose,* including its passionate opening section by Guillaume de Lorris (c. 1230), also proliferated in sumptuous illustrated editions and print copies—seven of them before 1500—into the sixteenth century, providing a master narrative for the hopes, fears, joys, and sorrows of love *par amours.* René d'Anjou's masterpiece *Le Livre du cuer d'amours espris* (1457–65) is deeply influenced by the *Roman.* He also wrote *Le Livre des tournois,* a sign of the flourishing continuation and elaboration of the other great theatre of noble emotions—arms. German, Dutch, Italian, English, and Nordic versions of French chivalric romances, including the Tristan story, the *Lais* of Marie de France, Chrétien's works and the Arthurian prose cycles, were continued or originated in the period. The famous later fourteenth-century English romance *Sir Gawain and the Green Knight* is saturated in earlier French works (Putter 1995) and its main characters speak familiarly of "druryes greme and grace" ("love's pain and consolation") (*Gawain* 1967: l. 1507).

Many affective practices of spirituality were communal: for example, Holy Week ceremonies, Passion plays, services held for guild members, and special occasions to give thanks, do penance, or punish offenders of all kinds. Medieval music, religious and other, was written, and understood, to engender and intensify particular emotions (Williams 2005). Through these and many other activities, the cultural history of emotions in our period offers itself to view through the bodies of its people—through weeping, laughing, acclamation, or jeers; in prayers, dances, processions, feasts, funerals, and political demonstrations; and through physical presence and personal witness at everything from assizes and executions to jousts, mummings, and royal entries. "The corporeal and affective were understood and experienced as inseparable" (Harvey 2017: 227), and the body itself was culturally coded in time and place through the emotions that it was encouraged and permitted to display. "Countenance," the direction of the gaze, posture, gesture, and voice were all ideally readable, for good or ill, as signs of inner emotional disposition.

The perceived need for writers and artists of all kinds to "move" readers and audiences toward a correct love, hatred, hope, and fear, and for readers and viewers to be so moved, is a large part of what made emotions such powerful and ubiquitous cultural factors in the period 1300–1600. In the realm of thought, emotions were encountered at every level of discourse and practice from high theology to vernacular proverbs. Both Erasmus and Calvin rejected what they saw as the "frigidity" of academic theology: "knowing for Calvin was frigid if it lacked the involvement of the affections which distinguishes merely knowing from really knowing" (Bouwsma 1982: 205; Essary 2017: 139). The "rhetorical theology" of the period "insists upon a movement of the heart in order for teaching to truly take place" (Essary 2016: 8.) Philip Sidney's *Defence of Poetry* follows a somewhat similar logic: to him, the best poets "imitate both to delight and teach: and delight to move men to take that goodness in hand, which without delight they would fly, as from a stranger, and teach, to make men know that goodness whereunto they are moved"

(Sidney 1988: 87). In numerous poems John Donne stages a fervent wish that prayer and praise of God will, through grace, direct his emotions rightly. Unlike Sidney, Donne sometimes admits a radical distrust of eloquence in emotion, including his own: "I durst not view heaven yesterday; and to day / In prayers, and flattering speaches I court God." Without the constancy in love of God which he sees as impossible for sinful humans with their feverish humoral imbalances, Donne settles for holy dread as his surest motivation: "Those are my best dayes, when I shake with feare" (Donne 2014: Holy Sonnet 19, 495). Yet this movement from words to unspoken bodily affect, in search of sincerity, is itself a literary commonplace, and there was also a long tradition of confusion and distrust concerning whether visible affects like blushing, weeping, and trembling told clear truths about inner emotions (Allen 2005).

Human emotions in general were considered "movements" in that they were particularly associated with physical experiences. The early fourteenth-century author of *Li Ars d'amour, de vertu et de boneurté* readily understood "natural" love and desire in terms of Aristotelian bodily symptoms: "On the basis of physiologic heat and cold occasioned by inner mental or emotional activity he [the author] accounts for blush, perspiration, bleeding, pallor, stretching, yawning, fainting, yellow-hue, fever, weakness, and even death. He also explains how fear, one characteristic emotion of the traditional lover, is engendered by love" (Friedman 1965: 177). Amongst the learned, ideas of emotion were rethought through new professional contexts in universities, academies, and hospitals, and through increased opportunities for dissection and clinical observation. These ideas were taken up and more widely disseminated in printed books, with results that appeared in art and literature, but without necessarily much disturbing traditional cultural understandings. As Mary Lindemann writes, "people tended to refer to bodily processes metaphorically. The language of anatomy and constitution was always laden with broader meanings" (Lindemann 2014: 24).

The poetic notion that love was a drink that caused thirst, a sweet illness, a pleasing pain, a fiery cold and so on was propagated by countless vernacular works, the most influential being Petrarch's *Canzoniere* (1327–c. 1368), and became a standard in lyric versions of love for centuries. In narrative forms, Virgil's *Aeneid* and the *Metamorphoses* and *Heroides* of Ovid, along with many translations and imitations of them, continued to provide a repertoire of physical images and gestures of intense passion for writers throughout the period. Chaucer's Dido, as Aeneas departs

> ... kneleth, cryeth, that routhe is to devyse; ...
> She falleth him to fote, and swowneth there
> Dischevele, with her brighte gilte here,
> And seith, "have mercy! let me with yow ryde!"
>
> —Chaucer 1988: 613, ll. 1311–16

In terms of gesture and bodily affect Chaucer might be describing a female mourner at the foot of the cross, like Rolle's Mary: "Now she wronge her hondes, wepynge and seighynge; now she she cast hir armes abrode; the watyr of hir eyghne dropped at hir fete; she fel in ded swowne ofte tyme for peynes and sorwe" (Rolle 1988: 77); or anticipating the Magdalen in Masacccio's *Crucifixion* (1426) (Figure 0.2), or a real-life penitent weeper such as Margery Kempe (Bale 2015).

Shakespeare's Lucrece in her distress interacts with "a piece / Of skilful painting" showing the fall of Troy, and tries to speak her own grief through the image of Hecuba: "Here feelingly she weeps Troy's painted woes" (Shakespeare 1992: 213, l. 1485). The

FIGURE 0.2: Masaccio, *Crucifixion*, c. 1426, panel, 83 × 63.5 cm, Ministero per i Beni e le Attività Culturali, Museo e Real Bosco di Capodimonte, Naples.

imagined lived experience of emotion is made inseparable from the traditions of art, literature, and history entrusted with both generating and expressing it "feelingly," yet these are also always potentially distrusted as "painted," in the further sense of "feigned," images. Sinon's looks belie his inner treachery as much as Hecuba's reveal her true feelings (Shakespeare 1992: 214–16, ll. 1499–568). The insoluble problem of knowing true feelings from external bodily signs and appearances remained a constant topic throughout 1300–1600. It was inextricably bound up with long-running scientific views that the unseen heart was the principal seat of emotion (Erickson 1997). Both religious texts, following the very extensive reference to the "heart" in Christian scripture and liturgy, and secular texts built elaborate discursive structures around this physiological notion and it features strongly in iconography right through the period, for instance in images of the suffering Christ, the incredulity of Thomas, and the conversion of Mary Magdalen (Benay and Rafinelli 2015: 132, 164; Davidson 2017: 37–110), but also in secular art, and in the use of cardiotaphs—funerary monuments containing the hearts of deceased relatives (Weiss-Krejci 2010). Barbara Rosenwein has compiled a weighty list of "emotions associated with the heart" from a single fifteenth-century French chronicle, involving wonder, sorrow, calm, envy, hatred, happiness, anguish, shame, and anger (Rosenwein 2016: 186–7).

In considerations of human love there was often an important distinction made between whether lovers considered the higher good of the beloved or only desired their own selfish gratification. Some writers found the matter relatively untroubling. In Thomas Malory's *Le Morte Darthur* (1469), a young girl passionately in love with Lancelot, and offering to be either his wife or his mistress, says simply "my belyve ys that I do none offence, though I love an erthely man, unto God; for He fourmed me thereto, and all maner of good love comyth of God" (Malory 1971: 434). As Helen Cooper writes, "[s]exuality, in the Catholic Middle Ages as in the Protestant Renaissance, was taken as a given. What mattered was what you did with it" (Cooper 2004: 220). But the girl's statement occurs in a late descendant of the earlier thirteenth-century Lancelot–Grail cycle, the book in which Dante's Paolo and Francesca are reading when an illicit love overcomes them and eventually condemns them to hell. To Dante, writing 1306/7–1320, this romance tradition of love is a "Galeotto" (Galehaut), the friend who first introduces Lancelot to Guinevere, and therefore stands for the destructive "illusion" of earthly passion that must be rejected, for all its attractions, or rather because of them (Dante 2002: 99, canto 5, ll. 133–7; Scott 2004: 94–5, 259).

Dante's work also serves to introduce the emotion of hatred, which appears as both wrongful and righteous in many forms throughout the period covered by our essays. The pilgrim Dante displays apparent hatred for some of the souls in Hell and great pity for others, but eventually he "has to learn that pity for the damned is an offense against God's justice." "Here . . . pity is quite dead. / Who is more impious than one who thinks / That God shows passion in His judgement?' (Dante 2002: 362, canto 20, ll. 27–30; Scott 2004: 210). How to treat living people was a more complex question. The standard Christian instruction, as expressed by Augustine, was to hate the sin and love the sinner. Chaucer's Parson says simply "Trusteth wel, to love God is for to love that he loveth, and hate that he hateth" (Chaucer 1988: 307–8). But such advice was often complicated by factors of class, race, and religion which branded individuals or groups—heretics, Jews, "infidels," "treacherous" rebels, witches—as inhuman enemies of God. That might in turn justify their persecution for the sake of preserving love and concord in the wider community. John Gower, writing about the Peasants' Revolt of 1381, treated the rebels as animals: "Some of them bray like asses, others bellow like bulls, they grunt, they bark, they howl . . .; the earth is terrified with their sound and trembles at the name of the Jay" [Wat Tyler, the peasants' leader] (Gower 1902: xxxvii). To Martin Luther in 1543, Jews were the implacable enemies of God and Christians alike:

> When you lay eyes on or think of a Jew you must say to your self: Alas, that mouth which I there behold has cursed and execrated and maligned every Saturday my dear Lord Jesus Christ, who has redeemed me with his precious blood; in addition, it prayed and pleaded before God that I, my wife and children, and all Christians might be stabbed to death and perish miserably.
>
> —Luther 2017: 578

In Lyndal Roper's words, Luther "directed the full arsenal of his hatred against the papacy and the Jews" (Roper 2016: 388). "His views were not a medieval relic but a development of it" in the direction of greater intolerance. He no longer saw it as possible to convert Jews. To secure "the Lutherans' providential role in history . . . the Jews had to be pushed aside, discredited, and, if necessary eliminated" (Roper 2016: 395–6).

Luther's attitude to Jews is one extreme outcome of a widespread attitude toward "truth" in the period 1300–1600, increasingly intensified by religious and social change, which had serious emotional repercussions: "In a context in which truth was held to be single and indivisible, the persecution of dissident minorities was logical, rational and legitimate." "To persecute was to display a charitable hatred," exercised on behalf of an imagined true community which in theory could have no legitimate opposition (Walsham 2006: 1–2). Diversity in the world had long been considered to stem from demonic intervention (Barbu 2015: 40–1). Such attitudes meant that identification of differences between members of an ideally single community tended to cause deep emotional disquiet, increasing the supervision of social, political, and confessional orthodoxies and behaviors, and undermining trust in others to employ their senses and rule their own emotions properly. Success and failure in regulating emotions were treated as main markers of religious difference. For Calvin, it has been stated, "reformation" means a "quickening of the heart, the moment when we feel a total confidence in God's word and providential will . . . The human emotions become, through faith, a strength rather than a weakness." Conversely, in the view of the Calvinist François de la Noue, writing in 1589, unreformed Catholic France was "a tree that was dying, its roots exposed and its branches decayed," which suffered "the consequences of ill-disciplined emotions." To him, "indulging their base passions" had turned Catholics into irrational animals (Greengrass 2007: 228–9).

Apart from disputes over religious doctrine, the use and nature of religious images, objects, rituals, and gestures came under intense scrutiny. These were often stigmatized as "idolatry," leading to the destruction of images by some Protestants, their modification in Counter-Reformation worship, and more thorough attempts such as Calvin's to make the Reformed community adopt "a new, scripturally based, theological metaphysics, in which the boundaries between the spiritual and the material were more clearly drawn than ever" (Eire 1986: 3). The idea of "idolatry" was also crucial in determining early European attitudes to the Americas. It has been remarked that in José de Acosta's *Natural and Moral History of the Indies* (1589) the "entire description of the religious customs of the 'Western Indians' rests on the systematic opposition of true Religion, i.e., Christianity, and its inverted, demonic twin, 'idolatry'" (Barbu 2015: 41). On the home scene, even factors like residence at a distance from the main population could inspire angry fear of difference. Alexandra Walsham notes "[e]arly modern society's extreme distrust of mobility." Whether they were feared as aliens, incomers from other counties or parishes, criminals, witches, dissenters, or Catholic recusants, those who came from elsewhere, moved around, or lived apart fell under more suspicion and tended to receive harsher treatment when charged (Walsham 2006: 141–2). At the level of court, political life was often marked by fear, indecision, and doubt. Poetry by Sir Thomas Wyatt alternates between proud expressions of self-sufficiency and deep emotional vulnerability: a sonnet, "The piller pearisht is whearto I Lent," is based on one by Petrarch but possibly references the downfall of Thomas Cromwell, Wyatt's patron, in 1540 (Wyatt 1969: 429–30). It concludes "My penne in playnt, my voyce in wofull crye, / My mynde in woe, my bodye full of smart, / And I my self, my self always to hate, / Till dreadfull death do ease my dolefull state?" Wyatt involves his writing ("penne," "voyce") and whole "state" ("mind"; "body"; "I my self") in the emotional condition he describes, which is clearly also an acute political condition (Wyatt 1969: 238).

Few if any texts in our period represent women *per se* as the hated enemies of God, but many authorities treat them with emotions of fear and loathing. Reading such works, Christine de Pizan (1405) stages herself as "finally decid[ing] that God formed a vile creature when He made woman, and I wondered how such a worthy artisan could have designed to make such an abominable work which, from what they say, is the vessel as well as the refuge and abode of every evil and vice" (Pizan 1983: 5). Books of misogynist jests and insults, sometimes countered by "defences" of women, continued throughout and beyond our period. Christine mentions especially the late thirteenth-century *Liber lamentationum Matheoluli* (*Lamentations of Matheolus*). In 1589, *Jane Anger Her Protection for Women* answered "venerian" misogynists in kind: "some of them wil follow the smocke as Tom Bull will runne after a towne Cowe" (Anger 1589: B2r.). In the religious and political controversy of the period, emotions of anger, resentment, and "zeal" often turned to gendered insult for expression. In *An Apologie of Jhon Philpot. Written for spittyng on an Aryan* (1556), the author fulminates against his opponents: "their forehed is lyke the forehed of a whore, hardned with counterfeted hypocrisy" (Strype 1822: Part 2, No 48, p. 150). In the sixteenth century, fear of female sexuality, linked to fears of physical and religious seduction, made women the focus of an extreme bodily disgust that is harder to find in medieval culture, misogynist as it often is. Edmund Spenser, writing c. 1590, hyper-conscious of the dangers of religious Error, depicts it as a female monster: "Halfe like a serpent horribly displaide, / But th'other halfe did womans shape retaine, / Most lothsom, filthie, foule, and full of vile disdaine" (Spenser 1965: I, i, 14). Duessa, emblem of false religion, is a "filthy foule old woman" in gaudy disguise, "[h]er neather partes misshapen, monstruous" (Spenser 1965: I, ii, 40–1). "Old," and especially "old and female," becomes evil in this apocalyptic religio-historical context. Spenser's obsession with making disgusting images of women (see also Spenser 1965: 1, 8, 47–8) has been described as "inexplicable, unless we keep in mind that he was writing at a time when witch persecutions were at their height" and "jailers would search the bodies of aging women for signs of the devils's mark" (Yarnall 1994: 130).

There were also many more positive emotional attachments to women promoted within the culture of our period, largely praising masculinist versions of female virtue. In Dante's *Commedia*, Beatrice, with other women, both rebukes the narrator and leads him toward knowledge and grace. "Defenses" of women dwelt on heroic figures from the classics and scripture; the triumphs of Judith, Esther, and the Queen of Sheba were frequently depicted in Italian Renaissance bedroom furniture (Tinagli 1997: 31–2). Female martyrs, Catholic and Protestant, were celebrated as proud heroines who scorned the powers of this world and steadfastly kept their marriage vows to God (Broomhall 2005: 67; Lynch 2015b). Women were also often consciously made the focus of "pathetic" scenes, in forms ranging from religious drama on the Slaughter of the Innocents to vernacular epic. In Tasso's *Gerusalemme Liberata* (1581), the death of the Saracen Clorinda, wounded and unrecognized in a combat with her lover Tancredi, is a famously intense emotional moment. As she dies, Clorinda forgives Tancredi—"Amico, hai vinto: io ti perdon . . . perdona / tu ancora" ("Friend, you have won. I forgive you . . . may you forgive me also") (Tasso 1961: 12, 66, p. 298). She asks and receives baptism, and dies happily. But for Tancredi there is a "terrifying anagnorisis"—"Ahi vista! Ahi conoscenza!" ("Ah the sight! Ah the recognition!") (Tasso 1961: 12, 67, p. 298). The scene "combin[es] . . . violent heroic conflict, tragic romance, and religious conversion drama" (Nicholson 1999: 264). Along with poems of suffering love by Petrarch, it would provide perfect text for musical treatment by Monteverdi well into the earlier seventeenth century.

Thinking especially of the religious culture of the sixteenth century and after, Barbara Rosenwein refers to an apparently widespread "melancholic turn" (Rosenwein 2016: 253), and she also suggests that public manifestations of "joy" in our period were often politically managed and unspontaneous (Rosenwein 2016: 182). Certainly, in writing this introductory essay it has seemed easier to find cultural expressions of desire, anger, fear,

FIGURE 0.3: *Casket* (c. 1450). Workshop of the Embriachi, Florence/Venice. Wood, iron, bone, colored woods. National Gallery of Victoria, Melbourne. Bequest of Howard Spensley, 1939 (4120-D3).

disgust, and sadness, or at least solemnity, than of personal joy and happiness. To find the quieter and more intimate emotions of the period one might look to the continuing everyday rituals of birth, baptism, and marriage. Private emotional experience might lie hidden within more formal tokens, like the love-gifts concealed within the caskets presented as part of Italian wedding negotiations (Figure 0.3). "The casket thus facilitated two modes of communicating love: one widely visible and public, the other physical and more intimate" (Martin 2017: 192).

Letters often contain expressions of love and longing between couples, seen in those between the Nuremberg mercantile couple Magdalena Behaim and Balthasar Paumgartner (Ozment 1989). Parents delighted in reporting children's education, development, and prattling in letters to family members (Pollock 1987; Grace 2015). Even in the distress of separation, or perhaps especially then, Huguenot families took pleasure in children's voices and development. Jacques Berot who evidently had the care in England of his grandsons, told his daughter, still in the Low Countries, that her "two sons here are well and grow in size and beauty—little David is most delightful. . . . David asks to be remembered to his mother, brother and sister and kissed me this morning as his remembrance for you."[1] In reporting the affectionate respect of young David for his mother, Berot was able to demonstrate his own attention to the moral and familial education of his grandson, and his insistence on bringing his dispersed generations of his family together through letters and their explicit rhetoric of emotions (Broomhall 2018).

Like the Italian caskets and Berot's letters, cultural practices and products might have mixed and multiple functions. In our period we also see a frequent preference for emotionally heterogeneous cultural products, like the miscellaneous tale collections of Boccaccio and Chaucer, the comic and bawdy elements in mystery plays and moralities, hybrid and parodic forms like Rabelais's *Gargantua*, or John Skelton's requiem for a sparrow, and the opportunities for fun and satire provided even by grim artistic themes like the Dance of Death. Religious culture may have generated melancholy and anxiety but it fostered joy as well. Dante sees the blessed in the circle of Jupiter sparkle with love as they fly "like birds risen from the river's edge," dancing and singing in happiness (Dante 2007: 441, canto 18, ll. 70–81). "Joy" and "bliss" abound in the writing of Julian of Norwich, for whom it is God's will that people "joyen and liken, comfortyn us and solacyn us as we may with His grace and with His helpe into the tyme that we se it verily" (Julian 1994: I, 5, 270–2). Her imagined fellow humans—the "us" she speaks for—live in joyful energy, love, and pleasure. They move and are moved in happiness. For all the many differences in the centuries before and ahead of them, they share something vital with Dante and with Philip Sidney's imagined readers, who through "delight" "know that goodness whereunto they are moved." Emotions fractured the Europe of 1300–1600, but they also united it.

CHAPTER ONE

Medical and Scientific Understandings

SUSAN BROOMHALL

Emotions were a fundamental part of medical and natural philosophical understandings of the human and natural world in the late medieval period and the sixteenth century. They underpinned theories about the corporeal and mental health of humans, animals, and the wider environment; made sense of relationships between these co-inhabitants of the natural world; and informed treatments for perceived imbalances and illnesses experienced by all forms of life. Furthermore, during the period 1300 to 1600, there were deep shifts in how emotions were theorized and practiced in the domains of medicine and natural philosophy in Western Europe. These came as a result of new bodily experiences, innovations in technologies and tools, and concepts of nature and the human that were informed by religious changes and encounters with others around the globe. Yet despite their importance to medieval and scientific thought and practice, emotions have only been haphazardly, and very recently, analyzed in the scholarship of this period. Discussion in these intellectual domains has tended to dwell on emotions as ideas and concepts, rather than analyzing them in modes of practice that informed scientific knowledge production, although it is now widely recognized that these modes were socialized and materialized in important ways. This chapter thus considers emotions within medicine and natural philosophy in a range of ways—as intellectual conceptualizations, as important influences within knowledge-production frameworks, as they were embedded in the bodily practices of medical and natural philosophical systems, and as they were experienced through individual bodies and social communities that included practitioners, their families and households, colleagues, patients, animals, and the natural world.

EMOTIONS IN THE PRODUCTION OF SCIENTIFIC KNOWLEDGE

Emotions were implicated in all stages of the production of medical and natural philosophical knowledge that includes creation, confirmation, innovation, contexts, and exchange. Sociologist Karin Knorr Cetina has emphasized knowledge as a practice that occurs in specific epistemic settings (Knorr Cetina 1999) as does Simon Shapin whose 2010 monograph *Never Pure* reminds us in its subtitle of the need to carry out *Historical Studies of Science as if it was Produced by People with Bodies, Situated in Time, Space, Culture, and Society, and Struggling for Credibility and Authority*. These knowledge practices include important emotional dimensions that structured, processed and communicated information to distinct communities in particular ways.

Conventions for knowledge making in the period were ritually defined by a particular set of emotions performed through processes of discovery. Chief among these was "wonder" and "awe," which had been, since classical times, considered critical to ideas and practices of scientific enquiry and discovery (Daston and Park 2001). Far less charted, as Yasmin Haskell has recently noted, are more de-motivational emotions such as distraction, sloth, and boredom, which were also experienced alongside the inquisitive passions of enquiry (Haskell 2016: 259). Other feelings were typically linked rhetorically to the challenges and struggles of natural philosophical and medical endeavors. From 1300 to 1600, a significant shift occurred in sources of authority from texts to experiences of the human body and its senses. Increasingly, by the sixteenth century, knowledge-making through the body, in such practices as observation and fieldwork, was gaining authority (Ogilvie 2006; Daston and Lunbeck 2011). Brian W. Ogilvie has argued that natural history scholars in the 1530s and 1540s zealously pursued field studies to collect and document botanical matter, highlighting the physical and emotional hardships of their endeavor. Ogilvie notes that the "sober prose of natural history texts disguised this labor, except in the occasional prefatory remark, but it was an important means for the community of naturalists to constitute itself" (1996: 21). Emotional performance and knowledge production were clearly not only intertwined, but the "right" sort of performed emotions were necessary to produce knowledge acceptable to this scientific community.

Medical knowledge was likewise produced not only as an individual author's experience with written texts and corpses for dissection, but through the living and feeling bodies of clients and their extended networks. These were complex, intimate negotiations between practitioners and patients. The latter, and their communities of advising family and friends who also endured the pain of others' suffering, often accessed treatment beyond, or in addition to, professionally trained medical personnel, seeking intercession from saints, through pilgrimage, offerings and prayers, as well as a myriad variety of alternative health practitioners. This produced anxieties of status and authority among some practitioners, but also a sensitivity to emotional expression that would be appropriate in epistolary and face-to-face consultation, both to deliver what might be unwelcome advice and to engender confidence in what was often an uncertain business. Henri de Mondeville, physician to French kings Philippe Le Bel and Louis X, recommended that medical professionals should have any debate and disputes about a patient's illness or treatment in a separate room where they could not be heard by others, and that the eldest or most senior should speak for all in interactions with the patient (Crisciani 2004). Nicolò Falcucci, writing his medical manual at the 1480s, advised that group consultations should include only those who were "animated by good intentions, denuded of envy and rivalry, and who did not seek vain glory" (Crisciani 2004: para. 23). The Strasbourg wound surgeon Hans von Gersdoff suggested in his 1517 *Das Feldbuch der Wundarzney* that those of his profession should be of "a humble disposition and of a chaster nature than other manual workers, because this art and practice touches on human life.... He should have a special love for the wounded persons as for his own body" (Zimmerman and Veith 1993: 214). Although advice in epistolary consultations was typically provided with stoicism, without explicit emotional expression by physicians, the Genevan-born physician Théodore Turquet de Mayerne assured one client that he took seriously the patient's suffering from a melancholy humor and his own obligation to find relief for it, employing strong emotion rhetoric: "I was possessed with careful and troublesome thoughts by reason of the great and dreadful Symptoms described in your last letter" (Weston 2015: 273). Practitioners had to manage their own emotions—fears about illness, frustrations at recalcitrant clients or a lack of clear information about symptoms, and anxieties about professional failures and their moral duties to society—as well as their pain and grief in watching others suffer and die.

Scientific knowledge confirmation was also layered by emotions. It required accreditation by others within particular scientific groups that were exclusive communities of belonging. In 1300, medical faculties within universities were just establishing their claim to be the pre-eminent places for training and transmission of medical knowledge. Over this period, the university community demanded particular forms of documentation of this knowledge both in textual genres and within a manuscript form that they controlled. The elite group of men who formed this latter community limited knowledge access and creation to those who shared their life, social status and educational experience. This instilled a sense of trust in the knowledge developed by others in their community. Moreover, as their knowledge confirmation systems underwent a series of pressures from the turn of the sixteenth century, increasingly, as Peter Harrison suggests, "tests for the trustworthiness of observers stressed social status, education and training, personal virtues, and institutional settings" (Harrison 2011: 124).

The emergence of a range of new technologies and global experiences opened up claims to knowledge production to a far greater range of individuals, of both sexes and different classes. By the sixteenth century, the university-based knowledge confirmation framework was under pressure by those with alternative ideas and concepts, spread widely in print. This created new articulations of emotions among medical and natural philosophical writers, expressing anxieties over control of information among their own community and access to it by others without their shared training and experience. With the 1543 publication of *De corporis humanii fabrica*, the Flemish clinical anatomist Andreas Vesalius challenged one of the classical pillars of medical theory, Galen. Not only casting aspersions on the university medical schools in which he had trained, he also claimed knowledge by direct observation of human bodies, with numerous details of the labour-intensive processes by which he manipulated corpses to reveal the workings of the human body. Dissection involved affective rituals as much as observational and corporeal ones, as Rafael Mandressi has explored, where distinct feeling cultures among professional groups had to be negotiated in the production of anatomical knowledge (Mandressi 2016; Carlino 1999). Vesalius's conclusions were interpreted as an affront to contemporary medical knowledge delivered in the universities. Jacques Dubois (Jacobius Sylvius), renowned anatomist at the University of Paris, and Vesalius's former teacher, returned an emotional salvo denouncing Vesalius's findings in print and calling him "Vaesanus," a mad man (Sylvius 1551). Although Vesalius also had his admirers, attacks from within the medical fraternity continued. In 1562, Francesco dal Pozzo, with thinly veiled personal ambitions, aligned himself with Vesalius's attackers in delivering a stinging rebuke on the insane, mendacious, vile and impudent anatomist who could only read Galen through Latin, not the Greek original as he himself could (Castiglioni 1943: 139). Contemporaries were entirely alert to the deep emotional foundations that underpinned responses to Vesalius's new ideas. Gabriel Cuneus, then Chair of Anatomy at Pavia, in a defense of Vesalius, suggested that Sylvius's response had been strongly motivated by his feelings: "he was seriously perturbed at the writing of Vesalius, who for three years had been his most devoted discipline and diligent student. Many people taunted Sylvius because of these writings." Cuneus concluded that the episode revealed "just how much power truth possesses over a violently enraged and self-tormenting mind" (Castiglioni 1943: 144–5). Renatus Henerus of Lindau, who was a student in Paris in Sylvius's last years, considered his teacher

> completely upset by observing the prestige he had sought had gone to Vesalius, and it became his earnest desire to make everyone thoroughly despise the great and useful labors of [Vesalius] [. . .] we were forced to endure a constant stream of abuse and virtually incessant and furious invective against Vesalius. It wearied our ears and aroused the indignation of many of us.
>
> —O'Malley 1964, 246, n. 92; 247, n. 93

These emotionally driven and laden printed attacks within the scholarly community were largely communicated in Latin, a language that obscured the strong feelings that they voiced from much of the wider populace and held them within a community that, despite divergent views, still shared strong elements of common identity.

Medical and natural philosophical knowledge was created and communicated within particular emotional contexts and sociabilities, forged by family, faith, and friendships. The breakdown of what was understood to be an emotional relationship between the father figure, Sylvius, and his intellectual progeny, Vesalius, was clearly perceived to lie behind their feelings in print. Within bachelor communities of the university and in academic households, students, boarders, and often books and ideas became treasured offspring (Chavasse 2008). Conversely, family members were not infrequently enlisted as part of knowledge communities. At Uraniborg, the Danish astronomer Tycho Brahe envisaged a *familia* in the classical sense of a patronage network informed by ties and obligations as well as emotions, which included inhabitants of his estates as well as artists, architects, builders, graduate students, servants and relatives within his household (Christianson 2000). Among them was Tycho's youngest sister, Sophie, who was renowned among contemporaries for her expertise in horticulture, chemistry and astronomy. The emotional and scientific bonds between brother and sister were widely known through both activities and verse. Tycho wrote a number of poems about Sophie, as his muse Urania, in which he explored his sister's emotional life (Christianson 2000: 256). In his 1594 verse letter, *Urania Titani*, he voiced her challenging romantic situation with the alchemist who would become her second husband, Erik Lange. This was modelled on Ovid's *Heroides*, and referenced contemporary chemical and astrological knowledge, as Urania pleads anxiously, hopefully and erotically with Titan (Lange) to return to her, rather than her rival, alchemy: "I am attracted to you as steel is attracted to a magnet," "my bed is empty because of your science," "I only fear that I will be less attractive to you when you return" (Zeeburg 1994: 999, 1003, 1005).[1] Whether Tycho spoke for Sophie, or perhaps his own feelings for Lange, is unclear. Sophie's own angry complaint about her family's lack of support and commitment to her scientific endeavors fills a long letter she wrote to her sister Margarethe in August 1602 (Mortenson 2017).

Beyond the household, letter writing in Latin increased the range of interested elite men (and some women) who could share the anguish and excitement of emerging medical and natural philosophical ideas. Although exclusive sociability could be experienced in such sites as universities, libraries, and botanical gardens, letters too provided a mechanism for scientific exchange that was embedded with emotions. The core technologies and emotional expressions of the Republic of Letters were already evident in intellectual correspondence transmitted in the fifteenth century (Maclean 2008). Indeed, the humanist community, whose exchanges stretched from philology and archaeology to astrology, astronomy, medicine and botany, imagined themselves following classical traditions, and conceptualized their fellowship of letters in amiable and domestic terms as a gathering of friends exchanging intelligent conversation at dinner in a countryside villa (Van Miert 2014: 271–3). Letters demanded a specific affective rhetoric, with a growing body of epistolary manuals providing advice on how to extol appreciation of a correspondent's friendship and sharing of new insights and information (Van Miert 2014: 275).

Moreover, scientific communities went into print as a group of men linked by shared passions and proclaimed friendships. Laudatory letters, poems and images showed support for the ideas and authoritative identity of the author. In his 1543 *De humani corporis fabrica* (Figure 1.1) Vesalius made full use of the frontispiece to suggest that a whole crowd of male spectators were eager to hear and see him demonstrate his controversial anatomical ideas on the flayed open female corpse before him.

FIGURE 1.1: Frontispiece to Andreas Vesalius, *De humani corporis fabrica* (Basel, ex Officina Joannis Oporini, 1543). Courtesy of Universal History Archive/UIG via Getty Images.

These publications helped to visualize certain groups of men as a community sharing values and ambitions. Tycho Brahe purchased his own printing press and then a paper mill at Uraniborg on the island of Hven to support the publication of his poetic and scientific works, as well as those of his colleagues, correspondents and students. These books, surrounded by verses written by friends and supporters of Brahe and his patrons, helped to project far and wide the *familia* at Uraniborg, and enabled them to participate in a wider community of learning. Other paratextual additions visualized the complex emotions of patronage, linking authors, sponsors and dedicatees in networks of gratitude, hope and obligation, and celebrated the pride and glory of environments in which new ideas flourished. A printed version on parchment of Pliny's encyclopaedia, made for Filippo Strozzi, who had financed Cristoforo Landino's translation and printing of the work (published by Nicolaus Jensen at Venice in 1476), included portraits of Strozzi and his eldest son, Alfonso, opposite the King Ferdinand of Naples to whom Strozzi dedicated the work.[2] Landino, visually located in the humanist environment of Florence with the Duomo shown behind him, appeared on the next page, holding open his masterpiece for the viewer.

As Lisa Jardine has argued in her study of Erasmus, the paratextual apparatus of the book created by authors, editors and publishers could also function to encourage readers

FIGURE 1.2: Portrait of the author, Andreas Vesalius, *De humani corporis fabrica* (Basel, ex Officina Joannis Oporini, 1543). Courtesy of The Print Collector/Print Collector/Getty Images.

to succumb to a media hype that would position authors as charismatic superstars and render their arguments compelling (Jardine 1993: 44). The portrait of Vesalius in his 1543 ground-breaking book on anatomy likewise positioned him as authoritative, a figure of genius at just twenty-eight (his age noted on the base of the table), who was surrounded by both the classical learning and dissected corpse on which his reputation rested (Figure 1.2).

Scientific self-fashioning may have increased with print, but manuscripts likewise depicted authors, although most commonly authors of the classical world. The *Bellifortis* by fourteenth-century Eichstätt-born physician Konrad Kyeser, who made a new career for himself in siege-warfare technologies, bringing together engineering, medical, astrological and chemical knowledge, survives in four early drafts. One complete version was richly illustrated by illuminators—unemployed after Sigismund, king of Hungary, closed the imperial scriptorium—who passed by Kyeser's Bohemian mountain village. In this, perhaps the first, portrait of a living author since antiquity, Kyeser is shown in a green tunic, the color of Jupiter, in whose hour Kyeser had been born (Figure 1.3). Kyeser may even have depicted himself again in the work, as a similar figure is depicted conducting magic rituals, which Kyeser understood as a mechanical art and form of technology (White 1969: 438). Kyeser's work was marked by strong feelings about his personal

FIGURE 1.3: Colored portrait of the author, Konrad Kyeser, *Bellifortis*, before 1430, Niedersächsische Staats- und Universitätbibliothek, Göttingen 2° Cod. Ms. philos. 64. Courtesy of Paul Fearn/Alamy Stock Photo.

experiences on the failed crusade against the Turks, the defeat at Nicopolis in 1396 and his explicit, bitter disappointment with Sigismund, the king who sent him into exile. Kyeser's technological innovations in this work were motivated directly by his feelings of hatred for Sigismund and his passionate desire for better techniques for future military operations.

Emotions were deeply embedded in practices of science production and community formation, where feelings of belonging, friendship, family, exclusivity and anxieties associated with outsider status shaped who could create scientific knowledge and how it would be communicated to others. The impact of print may have re-shaped these communities of knowledge-making and their relationships with authority, as did new tools and techniques that provided mechanisms to challenge who could know of and speak for medicine and natural philosophy, but they did not change the significance of emotions to the processes of scientific knowledge construction.

THEORIZING EMOTIONS

There were significant transformations in ideas about emotion in the period between Aquinas and Descartes and these were shaped by the cultural contexts in which medicine and scientific thought were produced. With the consolidation of medical training in the university domain at the beginning of this period, scholars and practitioners presented their ideas through academic treatises as well as practically oriented advice manuals, both of which began to appear in print by the sixteenth century. These works explored contemporary theories that sought to understand the nature of emotional phenomena, particularly their relation to mind and body processes, and their influence on individuals' health and disease. As Naama Cohen Hanegbi has argued, these theories were shaped by the entry of medicine into the university curriculum, as university-trained practitioners sought ways to assert their chosen study as more than an art of physical manipulation but one that had ethical and moral dimensions as well (Cohen Hanegbi 2016: 59).

Emotions were about bodies and souls in these texts. Most authors maintained the influential Aristotelian understanding of the soul as an embodied entity that could be felt through one's body. This is reflected in the terminology by which medical and natural philosophical theorists explored phenomena for which we use the umbrella shorthand "emotions." This was a diverse terminology that related to emotions' conceptualization as matters of both mind and body, as well as to contemporary theological and devotional ideas (Carrera 2013: 117; Cohen Hanegbi 2017). Emotional and affective experiences were commonly interpreted in medical literature as produced by, or connected to, accidents, or affections, of the soul. However, the specific relationship of these accidents and the visible or felt phenomena of emotions were much debated within the scholarly community (Cohen Hanegbi 2016). Whatever their causative pathways, medical scholars and practitioners certainly understood bodies as the place where emotions were experienced. This was of course what justified their involvement in scholarly and practical discussions of emotions.

Emotions, in medical literature, were discussed for their impact on health and disease. They could be both a positive influence on the mind and body, or lead to destruction and disease. Since Galen, individual bodies had been understood as functioning in a wider environment that affected health. Management of these non-natural elements, including air, food, drink and sleep, was required. Emotions were considered a sixth non-natural factor, which could cause illness as intensive affects or as long-term dispositions (Carrera

2013: 115–16; Cohen Hanegbi 2009: 23–5). These were influenced and experienced in the context of a range of personal and environmental factors, such as diet and lifestyle and by one's unique complexion of qualities and humors (themselves shaped by contemporary cultural constructs about the influence of gender, age, ethnicity, and so on). Melancholy, a troubling form of emotional experience that appeared to be most prevalent among elite men, for example, could become a cause of bodily ill-health and thus exercised the minds of medical professionals (Gowland 2006). As such, physicians needed to both be alert to considerations of a patient's emotional state and look to ways in which they could alleviate potentially harmful emotional factors in devising therapies.

This meant that physicians needed in some respects to care for the soul, since its affections were related to emotional experience. It was a role that medical authors increasingly claimed for themselves over the fourteenth and fifteenth centuries (Cohen Hanegbi 2012: 70–1; 2016: 57–8). Although the soul discussed by physicians was distinct from the immortal soul that primarily concerned theologians, and the intended purposes of their works were usually quite different, many medical authors were also trained in theology at the universities (Yoshikawa 2009: 400). Their views operated within contemporary cultural and religious codes, and the ethics of sensing and feeling were embedded in medieval and scientific thinking (Ziegler 1998; Newhauser 2010: 7). Some authors claimed that medicine could not only affect patients' disposition for bodily health, but also protect their soul and engender what were perceived as socially acceptable emotional traits. The Aragonese religious reformer and physician, Arnau de Vilanova, for example, proposed treatments seeking to develop such emotional dispositions as mercy, piety and benignity that would focus the individual upon a path to salvation (Ziegler 1998: 154). Medical authors not only argued that they could assist in creating a moral individual but that they also had an important role to play in the emotions of pain. By the fifteenth century, a number of physicians merged under one category of pain those emanating from the soul and others derived from physical and emotional experience, between which theologians tended to distinguish (Cohen Hanegbi 2012: 76). Yet medical considerations of pain and suffering themselves took place within understanding of their meaning in religious frameworks. For example, the state of suffering encompassed the sensation of pain but the feelings this provoked could be diametrically opposed, from distress and sadness, to patience and resignation or even joy and ecstasy within a devotional framework (Cohen 2010; Moscoso 2016: 46). This affected what kind of therapy a practitioner might be called upon to offer. Medical ideas about the emotions throughout the period were thus heavily informed by theological and devotional writings and ideas.

The importance of the soul in the formation of emotions persisted throughout the period, but the impact of dissection and the art of anatomy saw emotions also located within specific organs of the body, most commonly the brain or heart, or in some form of communication between them. The heart took precedence in these investigations, informed by the prior ideas of Aquinas, Galen and Aristotle respectively, who situated the origin of emotions there. Spanish anatomist Andrés de Laguna, a student of Sylvius in Paris, offered little challenge to this view in his 1535 *Anatomica methodus*: "If indeed from the heart alone rise anger or passion, fear, terror, and sadness; if from it alone spring shame, delight, and joy, why should I say more? In fact, almost all those perturbations which the Greeks call pathemata have their origin in the heart" (Lind 1975: 281). Nicolas Coëffeteau, writing at the turn of the seventeenth century, likewise proposed that the heat of the heart affected emotional disposition, concluding that animals that have bigger hearts could not hold heat as well and were thus typically more easily frightened, while animals with smaller hearts were more courageous (Coëffeteau 1620: 445). But other organs were also important in providing theorists with locations for emotional phenomena. Jacopo Berengario da Carpi, in his 1522 *Isagogae breves*, opined that the gall bladder "goes to the pylorys of the stomach to aid digestion with its gall. If this duct is large, it makes a man unhappy because of its continuous emission of gall" (Mitchell 2007: 528 n. 155). Vesalius, commenting upon the unusual gall bladder of an oarsman he dissected, observed that "he seems to have been a man of warm and dry temperament; and I made careful enquiry from his close friends as to whether they had ever noticed that he was prone to vomit bile" (Vesalius 2007: 117). The new generation of anatomists that emerged in the sixteenth century increasingly went beyond mere dissection, making their art about final causes of anatomy; that is, the relationship of anatomical parts to the soul (Klestinec 2010: 202–3). Some students complained that these more abstract elements overcomplicated lessons: Baldassar Heseler, for instance, observed Matteo Corti in mid-century Padua and critiqued the time he spent on rhetorical flourishes (Klestinec 2010: 217). However, Fabrizi d'Acquapendente delighted at least two of his students at Padua: Samuele Keller and Johann Wolfango Rabus described listening to Fabrizi in 1578, saying that he had "filled and elevated their souls with many things" (Klestinec 2010: 206). As it had for earlier medical theorists, exploring the connections between emotions, spirits and soul raised the status of late sixteenth-century medicine, this time specifically its sub-field, anatomy.

Medicine also theorized emotions in and through the body in other contexts. In cases of disfigurement and amputation, practitioners could be called upon to create surgical or mechanical substitutes that themselves articulated desires about the normative body and fears of corporeal disintegration (Gagné 2018). The horror of facial disfigurement justified surgeon Gaspare Tagliacozzi's 1597 *De Curtorun Chirurgia per insitionem* on reconstructive facial surgery. He extolled the importance of the face for receiving senses and expressing emotions and as "an indicator of character": "It displays man's dignity . . . it is a true image of our souls and exposes most fully our hidden emotions" (Tagliacozzi 1996: 10). This he explained in anatomical terms, for the

> small offshoots of these arteries ["the external jugular arteries," as he termed them] terminate in the periphery of the face and act as messengers . . . This is especially the case in the case of emotions such as anger and joy . . . with the result that man's hidden emotions are made public by these silent informers. . . . even a minor disturbance of the mind plainly reveals itself in the face. Anger burns in it, fear makes it grow pale, shame reddens it, and grief causes it to waste away. Similarly, sadness clouds it, hope uplifts it, envy pinches it, and joy relaxes it.
>
> —Tagliacozzi 1996: 23

Proceeding to explore each feature of the face in turn, Tagliacozzi considered the eye most significant for the emotions: "In no other conspicuous part of the body (particularly that of man) has Nature supplied greater signs of the state of mind, that is, of temperance, mercy, pity, anger, love, sadness, and happiness, than in the eyes themselves" (Tagliacozzi 1996: 4). Tagliacozzi's work touched on the very ways in which the body made human selfhood, particularly through individual emotional experience and expression in the face.

Other medical and scientific thinkers considered feeling among humans' fellow inhabitants in the natural world. Whether animals had emotions, whether they could choose between emotional responses to stimuli, and whether humans could discern what these sentiments might be, preoccupied a number of theorists. These investigations helped to understand, and confirm, the status of humankind as the pre-eminent living creature in a divinely ordained hierarchy. The Italian theologian and scholastic philosopher Gregory of Rimini, for example, intervened in this long-running debate in which Aristotle, Rabbi Moses ben Maimon and Aquinas had had their say, to argue as a point of difference to their views that animals were capable of more than a simple reflex emotional response to a given stimulus perceived in isolation. He proposed that they could change the course of a passion without it being a response to an external agent, although he distinguished this from the sophistication of human cognition (Perler 2012: 3). The imagined emotions of animals were often anthropomorphized. Contemporary observations of bees and ants by natural philosophers suggested parallels to human patterns of social organization. Spanish apiarist Luis Mendez de Torres proposed in his 1586 *Tractado breve de la cultivation y cura de las colmenas* that bees held a concept of self-sacrifice, in understanding that a single leader to each colony was most convenient, "although it is with much sentiment of theirs, but they overcome the just pain due to the necessity of their love of peace" (Mendez de Torres 2008: 18).[3] Drawing upon a wide range of classical accounts, the Zurich physician and botanist Conrad Gesner provided elephants a lengthy entry appropriate to the majesty with which that quadruped was held, including discussion of their care for the young, partners and the old, as well as what he interpreted as mourning and religious rituals among herds (Gesner 1551: 411–42). In contrast, the essayist Montaigne considered that seeking to understand another animal's emotions and mind was arrogant: "How knoweth he by the vertue of his understanding the inward and secret motions of beasts? By what comparison from them to us doth he conclude the brutishnesse, he ascribeth unto them? When I am playing with my Cat, who knowes whether she have more sport in dallying with me, than I have in gaming with her?" (Montaigne [1603] 1892–3: 277)

Human interest in the potential feelings of non-human inhabitants of this world largely stemmed from the productive value to which such knowledge might be put. Even pets were generally defined by the service that they performed for human feelings, with motifs of animal loyalty to humans found in funerary sculpture and literature. The qualities, humors, and emotional states of animals, whether beasts of war, burden or production, were important to their selection and treatment, in order to be fit for human service (Curth 2016: 337–40). A hierarchy of the nobility of animal feelings also affected ideas of their sociability with each other and how the relevant animals might be housed. Edward Topsell, translating Gesner, opined that "nature hath framed no sympathy or concord betwixt the noble and courageous spirit of a Horse, and the beastly sluggish condition of a Swine" (Topsell 1658: 238). These proposed emotional dispositions frequently reflected human relationships with, and the value of, non-human entities. Silkworms, although insects, were seen as noble creatures. French agronomist Oliver de Serres, in his 1599 manual on the management of silkworms, recommended that they be kept in a sweet-smelling environment, even perfumed, because "not only do your Worms rejoice in agreeable scents, thus they will be comforted in the majority of their illness" (Serres 1599: 87).[4] Such ideas about the feelings of nature could also extend beyond the animal kingdom. The French potter and natural philosopher Bernard Palissy interpreted the behavior of trees in forests according to parallels with human sociabilities and enmities: "I have perceived also how trees at the edge of the forest throw themselves out or incline themselves towards the edge of the lands, as if the other trees were their enemies" (Palissy 2010: 527).[5] Palissy considered "vegetative nature" "sensible and reasonable" (Palissy 2010: 126).[6] He complained that unsustainable branch-cutting left wood "villainously

FIGURE 1.4: Putti dissecting a pig in a historiated woodcut letter Q in Andreas Vesalius, *De humani corporis fabrica* (Basel, ex Officina Joannis Oporini, 1543). Courtesy of AF Fotografie/Alamy Stock Photo.

mauled. Do you think that the trunk that has been thus split and ripped out in various places does not feel the division and exaction that is done to it?" (Palissy 2010: 121–2).[7]

Whatever authors determined about animal and plant feelings, these did not prevent both from being subject to scientific experimentation in service to human desire for knowledge. Animals were even imaginatively visualized in printed works in that role (Figure 1.4). Vesalius conducted a particular canine vivisection in Bologna, encouraging students to feel into the dying dog's heart cavity to sense the movement and heat of the heart, and the sensation of pulse (Cunningham 1997: 114–15). Surgeon, then physician, Realdo Columbo, for a time a close friend of Vesalius in Padua before they too fell out, was interested in the function of voice, and recommended vivisection using "a young dog (a male or a female as you prefer); for when they are cut puppies yell more than old dogs" (Cunningham 1997: 158). If these authors felt compassion, sympathy or love for fellow creatures at the time, such feelings were not rendered explicit in their scientific accounts.

BODIES IN CRISES

Key events of the period—the Great Famine, the Great Bovine Pestilence, and the Black Death—exemplify how natural world phenomena, experienced through bodies, challenged medical and scientific theories and provoked new ones, in specific cultural and emotional contexts. Western Europe in the period 1300 to 1600 experienced some of the most considerable climactic changes observed for many centuries before or since. What is now termed the Medieval Warm Period concluded around 1250 and brought observably cooler temperatures to Europe, which appear to have been sustained until the mid-nineteenth century (Hughes and Diaz 1994). Toward the end of the sixteenth century, Europe was in a noticeably colder phase, often termed the Little Ice Age. Complex belief systems explained observations of climactic variations, natural and political disasters, and emotional tensions of individuals and communities that manifested in witch-crazes, melancholy and suicides (Behringer et al. 2005).

Contemporaries were experiencing unusual and extreme weather events but they were not described in terms of climactic change so much as end times in a religious framework. Natural disasters, and their consequences in famine, poverty and disease, were interpreted through a spiritual lens that revealed divine anger, and sometimes mercy, as powerful regulators of human emotions, sin and weakness. These were long-held templates. The Zurich reformer Heinrich Bullinger was convinced that the miseries of cold weather, hail and floods of the mid-sixteenth century stemmed from such causes, as he wrote to fellow reformer Friedrich Mekum (Myconius) in 1551: "We are depressed by a lack of everything, with which God punishes unbridled drunkenness" (Pestalozzi 1858: 475).[8] This was little different from the chief argument of the English poem *On the Evil Times of Edward II*, written in the early 1320s, that the great famine and bovine pestilence of the preceding years were attributable to God who had signaled through the weather his punishment for the human sin of pride:

> So that for that shrewedom that regneth in the lond,
> I drede me that God us hath for-laft out of His hond,
> Thurw wederes that he hath i-sent cold and unkinde
> [. . .]
> God hath ben wroth wid the world, and that is wel i-sene;
> [. . .]
> For tho God seih that the world was so over gart, [For when God saw that the world was so given to excess]
> He sente a derthe on eorthe, and made hit ful smarte.
>
> —Dean 1996

Contemporary frameworks for understanding these events and the bodies—human, animal, and botanical—that they plunged into crises were socio-cultural, in which the emotions of individuals, communities and the divine were pivotal factors.

A perceived lack of charity, cruelty and breakdown of community bonds characterized a series of catastrophic events that assailed Europe during the fourteenth century. Unusually wet weather in the spring and summer of 1315 led to widespread agricultural failures through 1316 and 1317 that destroyed crops for both humans and livestock and saw Europe experience a catastrophic food shortage that has been termed the "Great Famine," extended in many regions through to 1322 (Kershaw 1973; Jordan 1996). *On the Evil Times of Edward II* recounted the terrifying experience of acute vulnerability:

Tho com ther another sorwe that spradde over al the lond.
A thusent winter ther bifore com nevere non so strong.
To binde alle the mene [poor] men in mourning and in care
The orf [livestock] deiede al bidene [entirely], and maden the lond al bare
   so faste.
Com nevere wrecche [vengeance] into Engelond that made men more agaste.

—Dean 1996

Chroniclers' accounts emphasized shocking consequences for community cohesion and claimed to see some of the strongest emotional bonds falter under the pressure of bodily crisis (Lucas 1930: 364, 375–6). Medical practitioners were equally susceptible to reporting these experiences. Gui de Chauliac, a physician to the popes in Avignon, recounted that in the first plague, "people died without servants and were buried without priests. Father would not visit son, nor son, father; charity was dead, and hope prostrate" (Archambeau 2011: 538–9). All the same, his account of his own plague experience reveals that a community of carers were near at hand. This corresponds with the notarial, municipal and legal evidence explored by Daniel Lord Smail for the plague at Marseille in 1348–9. This material suggests that people continued to gather for bedside vigils for the ill and dying during the plague (Lord Smail 1996). Social institutions and rituals in Marseille were maintained and reconstructed directly after these years, and, indeed, these were likely important aspects of community grieving and healing. Depictions of burials

FIGURE 1.5: A depiction of the consequences of the plague at Tournai in 1349, in Gilles le Muisit, *Annales*, Brussels, Bibliothèque royale de Belgique ms 13076–77, f. 24v. Courtesy of Photo 12/Alamy Stock Photo.

within contemporary manuscripts likewise suggest attempts were made to maintain social and spiritual practices despite the overwhelming number of dead.

The affective experience and emotional consequences of such catastrophic biological events were palpable to contemporaries. The crop failure and famine of both humans and animals after the summer of 1315 was followed closely by another disaster, the Great Bovine Pestilence. By 1319, a panzootic episode was affecting primarily cattle, with further devastating murrains in subsequent decades (Newfield 2009). Some eyewitnesses were concerned with the consequences for human health, such as Simon Eye, the abbot of Ramsay, who recorded in 1319: "since a sudden pestilence has attacked our animals . . . there is a fear that a pestilence among the people is probably coming later" (Newfield 2009: 168). For others, the pestilence reminded onlookers of just how similar human and animal experience and feeling might be. The chronicler of the Cistercian abbey in Newenham, Devon, was pained by the suffering of animals, who were, it seemed, crying out for human assistance that could little aid them: "everywhere they were walking and standing, they were lamenting to those people looking at them, roaring as if in tears because of the harsh pain making them anxious on the inside" (Newfield 2009: 165). Bodies in crises of emotions and nature were both the experiential centers and the consequences of these shocking and remarkable events.

Fear and terror, perhaps also sometimes wonder at the disorder caused by remarkable weather and agricultural events, were always bound up in reports of these events, and emotions too featured in the causation attributed by the populace to these events. For instance, Jewish populations, who were already culturally and socially constructed as "outsiders" to predominantly Christian communities, were blamed as scapegoat cohorts of maleficence, even though spiritual leaders no less than the pope pointed out that their bodies too succumbed to the plague (Cohn 2007). These catastrophic events were perhaps most widely understood as supernatural in origin; that is, as divine emotions exhibited through the natural world. If it was God's wrath that was the causative factor of the weather events that preceded them, solutions also stemmed from the spiritual realm, including processions, flagellation, and prayer. These deeply emotional societal crises that predated the Black Death that would reach Europe by the mid-fourteenth century echo many of the same cultural rationales and practices of fear of divine anger and hopes for redemption. Over time, however, community confidence, hope, and optimism, especially in medical knowledge, increased as mortality decreased during subsequent plague events. This change did not lessen the influence of spiritual frameworks that emphasized divine feelings of wrath and its emotional consequences for human populations. Indeed, these could still go hand in hand at the end of the period. English physician Thomas Phayre maintained in his *A Goodly Bryfe Treatyse of the Pestylence* (1545) that "our corrupt lyvynges have made us more corrupte, so that nowe the lyfe which we leade here is not very pleasaunt [. . .] it is excedyng grievous, sorowfull, and tedious, subject to diseases, infortunes, and calamities innumerable, which for the moost part done increase dayly, ever the iust vengeanunce of God fallyung upon us for our greate abhominations." He advised his reader to look to "cure first the fever pestilential in his soule" (Wear 2000: 278–9, 292).

Moreover, since emotional regulation was understood by both lay people and medical practitioners to underpin health, physicians saw positive emotional dispositions as corporeally protective in such epidemics. Jacme d'Agramont, who wrote the *Regimen for Protection against Epidemics* in 1348, highlighted that "among other influences that must be avoided in such times are especially those of fear and imagination. For from imagination alone, can come any malady. [. . .] No one, therefore, should give up hope or despair, because such fear only does great damage and no good whatsoever" (Archambeau 2011: 556). Likewise, as Samuel K. Cohn Jr has argued in his study of late sixteenth-century plague outbreaks in northern Italy, physicians advised the avoidance of melancholy, and encouraged readers to maintain happiness and social engagement with friends and family in pleasurable activities. Cohn also identifies in the later works a more explicit emphasis on mass emotional experiences for communities who were terrorized by fears. In practice, this led some practitioners to advocate a dismantling of urban public health measures, and others such as the physician Pietro Francesco Arellano of Asti to criticize "the fright of counsellors" and argue for more organized planning campaigns that would overcome the "infinite disorder" "because of fear of this Hydra" (Cohn 2010: 276–7). Similarly, Andrew Wear has suggested that the confident delivery of physicians' advice, increasingly available in print, might have provided a sense of hope and control to communities (Wear 2000: 275–313).

Calamitous events such as the plague also tested physicians' own feelings. Whether medical practitioners had a moral obligation to stay and provide succour to afflicted communities, or could flee with society's elite, was debated not only by those in the profession but by spiritual leaders too (Grell 1993). Martin Luther weighed in on the duties of Christian charity and importance of neighborly love, views echoed by Johann von Ewich. The latter had been appointed the town physician in Bremen in the 1560s when plague had broken out, and argued, in a work that followed much of Luther's earlier thought, that it "greatlie offendeth against the rule of charitie, whosoeuer according to his abilitie doeth not seek and bring some ayde" (Grell 1993: 140). Alternatively, Theodore Beza, who had himself survived an encounter with the plague, authorized flight for self-preservation but added, rather ambiguously, that it should be governed by "the common bond of humaine societie or by any other kind of friendship" (Grell 1993: 138).

The series of catastrophic biological events that marked the period 1300 to 1600 provoked explicit discussion among contemporaries about emotional as well as bodily experiences. These feelings were complex and multiple, confronting and confusing for many, especially within medical and natural philosophical communities whose training and experience gave them only a limited sense of understanding of such events, their cause, meaning and resolution. Descriptive accounts, poems, medical recommendations and advice manuals bore witness to the pain and guilt of both sufferers and survivors, and the grief for lost loved ones in families, fields and communities, and even for lives forever changed. These records also speak of the fears produced by the certain knowledge of God's wrath. Finally, they document evidence of care and charity, and reveal hopes for salvation, mercy and renewal for both individuals and communities through continued social and spiritual engagement.

CONCLUSION

Emotions mattered to the development of medicine and natural philosophy over the period 1300 to 1600. They informed practices of science production and community formation in profound ways that underpinned how medical and scientific understandings about emotions, and the practices that flowed from these, could be created. A desire for authority and acceptance within the academic community influenced how emotions became embedded in scientific discussions, as subjects for investigation in human health experience, as part of treatments for various mental states and corporeal experiences, and attached to individual organs of the body that were attributed with emotional influence. Emotions, and ideas about emotion, similarly determined contemporary perceptions about the appropriate use of human, animal and botanical bodies, living and dead, for medical discovery and developing scientific techniques. Moreover, the emotions of practitioners and their patient communities, from concern to greed, governed appropriate therapeutic techniques for perceived ailments and imbalances, not only in humans, but also in animals and the natural world. It was, after all, through complex feeling relationships with these other inhabitants of the earthly realm, entailed in a divinely ordained dominion over them, that humans understood themselves and their world.

CHAPTER TWO

Religion and Spirituality

DAVID LEDERER

Following the conversion of Constantine I, the Roman Empire embraced Christianity. The Edict of Thessaloniki (380) elevated it to the state religion with a parallel ecclesiastical infrastructure, collocating cathedrals near secular capitols in each administrative diocese. With the collapse of Roman rule in the West, episcopal bureaucracies filled the administrative void. History favored the Bishop of Rome, who transformed Catholic ("Universal") Christianity into the cornerstone of a hierarchical legitimacy embodied in the Corpus Christianum, biblically conceived in Paul's letter to the Corinthians 1:12 and Colassians 1:18. Europeans imagined it as a mysterious union of Christians manifest in the shared consumption of Christ's body in communion.[1] Contemporary organic political theory attributed a corporality and collective consciousness to Christendom, capable of feeling like any sentient being. Today, consensus on the fundamental importance of religion and spirituality from 1300 to 1600 as keys to the emotional regime is nearly as universal.

To make sense of emotions history over such a long period, we engage with enactivism. An enactivist framework offers heuristic tools uniquely suited to this emotional regime. It combines Merleau-Ponty's phenomenology of embodied action with cognitive psychology and affective science to expose dynamic relationships between body and environment: "Western scientific culture requires that we see our bodies both as physical structures and as lived, experiential structures—in short, both 'outer' and 'inner,' biological and phenomenological" (Varela et al. 1991: xvi). Theoretically, cognitive capacities "are rooted in the structures of our biological embodiment but are lived and experienced within the domain of consensual action and cultural history" (Varela et al. 1991: 149). The specific significance of corporeity (Colombetti 2014) for emotions study is etymologically inherent in basic concepts such as "affect" (*ad* + *facere* = to do to; i.e., active exogenous forces eliciting emotional responses) and "emotion" (*ex* + *movere* = to be moved by; i.e., individual passive reactions to exogenous forces).

Rosenwein (2006) explores the extent to which language served to construct emotional communities in the Middle Ages. Emotions are enacted, expressed, performed, and ritualized in response to environment, circulating between the dual experiences of physical and consensual embodiment. By extrapolating from the individual to the social, enactivism's experiential model adapts strategically to emotions history. On the one hand, given the tendency of medieval and early modern contemporaries to stress the allegorical embodiment of society, enactivism highlights their own perceptions. On the other, it allows for the critical conceptualization of modernity as a globally unified concept of temporality since the sixteenth century, one which demystified time across Eurasia through stringent methodologies largely devoid of metaphysical content (Reddy 2016).

Therefore, biological and environmental factors have their role to play in history. Historians regularly apply medical terminology such as crisis and trauma to historical events as metaphors. Contemporaries attributed corruption to the decay of the four basic elements as a matter of atomist physics.[2] From 1300, demographic and economic conjunctures, environmental change and epidemiological catastrophes threatened the Corpus Christianum with factious religious challenges to its emotional regime. By the late sixteenth century, the neostoic Justus Lipsius depicted Christendom's devolution into sectarianism as madness. He diagnosed the horrors of religious wars as epileptic convulsions violently shaking the body politic, symptoms of protracted humoral corruption. One hypercognized emotive trope dominated early corporate expressions of decay: fear.[3] Fear initially buttressed a hierarchical emotional regime, but reactions to spiritual crises ranging from short-term vengeful hatred, egalitarian yet unstable expressions of love, and self-abnegating guilt to sustained anger and resentment ushered in revolutionary religious change.

Some emotions become hypercognized socially, while others remained self-referentially hypocognized. The history of hypercognized fear has a huge literature.[4] Delumeau's two-volume *Fear in the West* (1978) juxtaposes St. Augustine's contempt for the corrupt physical world (*contemptus mundi*) with longing for a metaphysical utopia (*Civitas Dei*) as fear and guilt, dialectic forces driving historical change.[5] Augustinianism, the patristic foundation of Christendom's emotional regime, was still evident in the theology of Martin Luther (an Augustinian monk) and Erasmus (an Augustinian canon). It proffered Christians an emotional anchor in righteous fear of God's judgment.[6]

The Dutch cultural historian Huizinga described the fourteenth century as the waning of the Middle Ages (see Huizinga 2001). On the surface, it commenced with a mundane struggle between the Papacy and France that evidenced changing structural relationships. At a deeper level, prosperity fueled by internal colonization and demographic expansion ended with the saturation of arable land in an economy based on subsistence agriculture. Currency shortages and overpopulation translated into a fall in real wages and rising rents. Political centralization offered rulers one of the few tools left to squeeze holdings, augment treasuries and increase military strength in competition for diminishing resources. Fatefully, in 1294, the hermit Pope Celestine V became the first ever head of Christendom to abdicate.[7] Combined conjunctural factors propelled a downward spiral of spiritual anxiety, destabilizing the emotional regime.

The Curia reacted quickly, elevating Cardinal Benedetto Gaetani to Pope Boniface VIII, despite his role in Celestine's abdication. Evidence suggests he orchestrated the resignation, applying canon law to compose the deed justifying Celestine's renunciation of office. Anecdotes point to sinister machinations: how, in the voice of God, Gaetani whispered each night through a concealed pipe into Celestine's austere cell, admonishing him to resign on peril of his soul until the timorous monk fled in panic to Naples; how, after assuming the tiara, he had Celestine imprisoned until his death. Public accusations stoked apprehensions: the King of France, Philip IV, charged Gaetani with Celestine's murder; in his *Inferno*, Dante alludes to Benedetto's consignment to the eighth circle of hell for simony, the buying of Church office (Norwich 2011: 190–4).

Faced with debts, Boniface VIII institutionalized bureaucratic control in Rome and founded the Sapienzia University to train reliable administrators. He replaced untrustworthy cardinals with relatives and supporters, violently suppressing the rival Colonna family by razing their stronghold at Palestrina. Gaetani envisioned a strategic extension of papal control across Europe. However, his strong-arm tactics failed to sway France, where he met his match in Philip IV.

Philip's moniker, "the Fair," undoubtedly alluded to comeliness rather than justness; opponents dubbed him "the statue" and "the king of iron." In his own quest to extend control over diminishing resources, Philip engaged England in a war, expelled the Jews from France, expropriating their property,[8] and charged the Templars with idolatry, sodomy, and sorcery. Dozens were arrested, tortured, and burned at the stake, and the order's property confiscated. Philip likewise trained a growing bureaucracy of jurists to lessen his reliance on the nobility. Bureaucratization, however, required sharply increased investment.

Philip invoked a 50 percent levy on the clergy, but Boniface retaliated with the bull of *Clericis Laicos* (1296), forbidding the expropriation of Church property under threat of excommunication. The King gathered his counselors and issued his own decree banning the exportation of valuables from his kingdom to Rome. Diplomatically, the Pope circumvented the decree, augmenting revenues through the sale of plenary indulgences to pilgrims during the millennial jubilee in 1300. Negotiations led to concessions on both sides, including Benedetto's intercession in France's war with England.

An uneasy hiatus ended in 1302, when Gaetani unexpectedly issued the infamous bull *Unam Sanctam*. History's most sweeping proclamation of papal power, it unequivocally declared the Pope supreme head of the *Corpus Christianum*: "Therefore, of the one and only Church there is one body and one head, not two heads like a monster... Furthermore, we declare, we proclaim, we define that it is absolutely necessary for salvation that every human creature be subject to the Roman Pontiff" (Papal Encyclicals Online, 2016).

Philip renounced the bull and was duly excommunicated. He hurled charges back at the Pope (idolatry, sorcery, simony, heresy, unnatural sexual intercourse, and the murder of Celestine V) and dispatched his minister Nogaret with 2,000 soldiers to arrest Gaetani. They cornered him at his ancestral home in Anagni and imprisoned the septuagenarian. The vengeful Sciarra Colonna slapped him repeatedly to the ground, threatening to decapitate him, until Nogaret intervened, narrowly averting the Pope's murder. Loyal townsfolk freed Benedetto after three days, but harsh treatment and the humiliating "Slap of Anagni" broke his spirit. He contracted a fever and, within a month, Gaetani was dead. News of the Pope's humiliation and death stunned Christendom. His successor reigned less than a year and in 1305 the Curia elected Clement V, a Frenchman, under pressure from Philip. Clement moved the Curia to Avignon and for sixty-seven years the papacy fell under French control during the Babylonian Captivity. Shock over the fall of the head of Christendom and the relocation of its heart from Rome to Avignon resonated in a move away from spiritual idealization in literature and art.

In humanist literature, Dante condemned Boniface to hell and, in his *De Monarchia*, he demoted the pontiff to a hypocritical mortal whose *Unam Sanctam* devalued him for thrusting the Church into the earthly sphere of petty politics, symbolizing its profanation.[9] Dante's compatriot Petrarch elevated secular affairs to Elysian heights during a journey in contemplation of the human soul on his *Ascent of Mount Ventoux*. Upon reaching the summit, Petrarch opened his copy of St. Augustine's *Confessions* to a passage berating the pursuit of earthly pleasures in favor of the inner search for human virtue. He recalled how even pagan authors overcame emotional adversity by looking within and learned not to fear any cross or prison or sting of fortune.

In art, Huizinga associated the autumnal imagery of late medieval art with perceptions of spiritual decay, suggesting, "Thus the religious emotion always tended to be transmuted into images" (2001: 193). Renaissance painters strove toward anatomically naturalistic emotionality, moving away from the unrealistic grandeur, rigidity, and idealized formality of the dominant Byzantine style. The Virgin, the saints, and even Christ adopted human proportions and realistic expressions of affective states in non-verbal poses. One early Renaissance artist, Giotto di Bondone, pioneered movement, perspective, depth, and suffering in his religious subjects.

How did contemporaries interpret the representation of emotion in Renaissance art? Giotto's frescoes on the walls of the Arena chapel in Padua provide a blueprint. Commissioned by Enrico degli Scrovegni, work on the frescoes coincided with the fall of Boniface VIII. Scrovegni's father Rainaldo had accumulated a massive fortune amidst scandalous accusations of usury. Enrico himself continued to profit as a money-lender. According to contemporaries (Dante also banished Scrovegni's father to the eighth circle of hell), the son repented and hired Giotto to adorn the family chapel with a votive offering to placate divine wrath. The cycle features Christ's Passion, the path to salvation through suffering and Scrovegni donating the Chapel (see Figure 5.3). Along the opposite sidewalls, Giotto contrasted allegorical images of seven cardinal virtues (prudence, fortitude, temperance, justice, faith, charity, and hope) with the seven deadly sins (folly, inconstancy, anger, injustice, infidelity, envy, and despair). Each displayed a novel intensity of feeling—the faces of the vices contorted in anger, shame, and fear (see Figure 6.1), while the virtues sport cheerful, composed, and stalwart visages (see Figure 2.1). The

FIGURE 2.1: The virtue Hope allegorically directed toward heaven, juxtaposed with the sin of Despair, depicted as a suicide carried off by a demon. Giotto, Hope, Despair, c. 1305, fresco, each 120 × 60 cm. Arena Chapel, Padua. Images courtesy of Wikimedia Commons and Getty Images respectively.

ensemble performs a pedagogical function: to instruct worshipers in an emotional code. Over the entrance, Giotto concluded with a vivid scene of the *Last Judgment*, on full view to everyone leaving the chapel—a reminder of the joyful rewards awaiting the just in heaven and the anguished suffering consuming the damned in hell (Figure 2.2).

Giotto's choice of imagery derived from a classical tradition at the heart of patristic emotional theory—literary history's "first sustained personification allegory" (Smith 1976: 3f.); Prudentius's *Battle for the Soul* (*Psychomachia*, c. 405). The verse personified seven virtues as warrior maidens combatting seven demonic vices for mastery over the psyche, re-enacting the moral daily struggle for salvation in the soul of every Christian. The seven virtues/vices provided a basic register of emotional intelligence, an essential component of Christendom's emotional regime.[10] Prudentius's allegory rendered the human soul a psychological battleground to moralize quotidian emotions and enacted behavior. Giotto's iconographic verisimilitude equipped viewers with a pictorial index for the performance of their own emotions, profiling behavioral stereotypes which reverberated Augustinian mind/body dualism of the *contemptus mundi* (see King 2010).

FIGURE 2.2: The tortures of the damned in hell. Giotto, *The Last Judgment*, c. 1305, detail, fresco, 1000 × 840 cm, Arena Chapel, Padua. Image courtesy of Wikimedia Commons.

Other Italian buildings featured *Last Judgment* scenes, such as the Byzantine mosaics over the entrance to Torcello cathedral in the Venetian *Laguna* dating from the eleventh century. However, Giotto's imagery in the Arena Chapel offered three fundamental novelties highlighting the corporeity of emotions. One was material. Giotto employed a fresco technique, painting lifelike scenes directly onto wet plaster, rather than fractured mosaic tiles, facilitating greater plasticity in the depiction of emotionally evocative poses engaged in active behavior and vivid expression, as opposed to stiff portrayals of the Lord, the Virgin, and the saints as titanic impassive icons. The Last Judgment held out rewards for good behavior, simultaneously threatening improper comportment with palpable sanctions for penitents to mull over on their way out of the chapel.

A second novelty was location. The frescoes inhabited a private familial space commissioned by a wealthy money lender, flying in the face of the Church's traditional role as patron of the arts and its prohibition on usury. Scrovegni's commission heralded a new class of patrons who employed famous artists in competition with the Church for emotional capital. These entrepreneurial "individuals" (as the Swiss cultural historian Burckhardt styled them) brazenly instrumentalized art in an age consumed by "religious confusion and general doubt" (Burckhardt [1860] 1960). For Burckhardt, these first modern individuals were as bold and dynamic as the art they commissioned. Tempting as it is to interpret the Arena Chapel as an act of piety, we should not forget that the artistic masterpiece was also a display of financial power completed just two years after Boniface's "Slap at Agnani."[11] Though not directly related, both events epitomize an emerging space for the expression of what Reddy calls "emotional liberty" (2001: 112–37).

Around 1300, climate change from the Medieval Warm Period to the Little Ice Age caused the Great Famine of 1315 to 1317. Malnutrition afflicting large segments of the population lowered resistance to disease. In 1337, the Hundred Years War broke out between France and England. At this critical juncture, an epidemiological disaster of hitherto unseen proportions devastated Europe—the Black Death. Although it is impossible to quantify the suffering with exactitude, at least one third of Europe's population succumbed to bubonic plague between 1346 and 1353 and perished in horrible agony. The Corpus Christianum's physical collapse left lesions in Christendom's emotional regime fully exposed.

Contemporary physicians lacked our comprehension of infectious disease, leaving cruder psychological defence mechanisms to rationalize and adjudicate blame. Even those who survived the devastation of the plague suffered post-traumatic stress on a systemic scale and engaged in a near-delusional search for causes and/or culprits. Popular hatred and lust for vengeance was the result. Some suspected the European Jewry of poisoning wells. Pogroms, particularly virulent in the Rhineland, annihilated dozens of Jewish communities. However, the mechanisms of guilt proved more powerful. Christians began searching their own souls, articulating pangs of conscience for the wrath of a vengeful God (or so it appeared to many) in the guise of illness as a punishment for the breakdown of Christendom and collective sins, manifest in the failure of the papacy.

For example, when Laura de Noves died of the plague at Avignon in 1348, Petrarch wrote of his beloved:

> I thought I should write these words as a bitter reminder of the facts, yet with a certain bitter sweetness, and put them in this place that is so often before my eyes, so that I may realize when I look at them that there is nothing left in the world that should delight me . . . now, with the strongest tie broken, it is time to flee from Babylon.
>
> —Watkins 1972: 199

At the papal court where he toiled as a secretary, Petrarch blamed the plague on the bitter wages of sin as "a sign of the divine anger at human crimes. If those crimes were to end, divine punishment would grow less or milder" (Watkins 1972: 218). Two years later, he blamed the vices of gluttony, laziness, and avarice for the spiritual bankruptcy in Avignon, noting:

> Now I am living in France, in the Babylon of the West . . . Instead of holy solitude we find a criminal host and crowds of the most infamous satellites; instead of soberness, licentious banquets; instead of pious pilgrimages, preternatural and foul sloth; instead of the bare feet of the apostles, the snowy coursers of brigands fly past us, the horses decked in gold and fed on gold, soon to be shod with gold, if the Lord does not check this slavish luxury . . . I have been so depressed and overcome that the heaviness of my soul has passed into bodily affliction, so that I am really ill and can only give voice to sighs and groans.
>
> —Petrarch 1904

On a pilgrimage to Rome during the jubilee of 1350, he suffered a wound to his leg so revolting and unendurable that "I never learned from any corpse the lesson of my own flesh, that man is a vile, wretched animal unless he redeems the ignobility of the body with the nobility of the soul" (Watkins 1972: 202). In an age when religious unity was embodied in an organic conceptualization of society, references to the Babylonian Captivity reflected sufferings of the soul as the wages of sin, afflicting the Christian body with physical corruption.

Against the backdrop of plague and mounting spiritual anxiety, the vigor of the universal Church waned. Although Gregory XI returned the Curia to Rome in 1377, his death witnessed the election of two rival popes, one Roman, another in Avignon. The Schism in the Western Church continued until 1409. The Council of Pisa declared both anti-popes and deposed, electing a new candidate, Alexander V, but the other two rivals refused to recognize the election, leaving three contenders for the throne of St. Peter. Alexander was succeeded by John XXIII; a contentious military figure, his two brothers had hanged for piracy.[12] The Council of Constance resolved the succession in 1417, just as a popular revolt led by the Czech priest Jan Hus erupted in Bohemia. Fear gave way to anger, with Hus denouncing the sale of indulgences as papal greed and leading a successful reform movement. He accepted the Council's invitation to negotiate at Constance under a writ of safe passage, but John XXIII had him arrested and burned at the stake as a heretic. The Council ended the Schism, but the damage to the emotional regime of Christendom ran deep.

In response, the Council produced a behavioral manual on the art of dying, the *Ars Moriendi*. Still heavily Augustinian, the *Ars Moriendi* instructed the laity on how to avoid the vices of greed, pride, suicidal despair, impatience, and loss of faith, allegorized as devils sent to tempt the dying. Composed in 1415, the *Ars Moriendi* gained popularity and went into multiple editions; after the advent of printing, the original manuscript was adorned with evocative woodcuts.[13]

Popular artists expressed skepticism toward authority in a novel genre of popular art: the *Danse Macabre*. The first example appeared as a mosaic in a Paris cemetery just after 1420. The allegorical Grim Reaper played upon hypercognized fears of death preoccupying Christians since the Black Death. The *Danse Macabre* acknowledged a fatalistic view of the last judgment, representing all Christians as equals before death, be they peasants, popes, kings, or queens, further challenging the hierarchy inherent in the emotional regime of the Corpus Christianum (Dreier 2010).

FIGURE 2.3: Deathbed temptations: pride staved off through faith. *Ars Moriendi*, Netherlands, c. 1460, woodcut. Image courtesy of Wikimedia Commons.

FIGURE 2.4: Neither pope, nor king, nor queen, nor cardinal, nor prince sits out the Dance of Death. Bernt Notke, *Danse Macabre*, St. Nicholas' Church, Tallinn, end of the 15th century. Image courtesy of Wikimedia Commons.

The popular French poet François Villon skillfully wove the collective spirit of angst and confusion into verse. His own life reflected the growth of an underclass of beggars, comprising a virtual army of itinerant men and women dislocated by famine, war, the plague, and its privations. They supported themselves through criminal activity and through charity afforded by the performance of good works as a necessary means to salvation. By the fifteenth century, charities in Paris operated a virtual beggars' rota, providing a reliable calendar for the distribution of alms on holy days. The provision of welfare not only enhanced the social standing of benefactors, but also redeposited spiritual credit into the treasury of merit on their behalf, lessening their time in purgatory and providing direct reassurances of salvation.

The poor also resorted to criminal activity, with increasing numbers living on the margins of society. Villon himself was convicted for murdering a priest in a drunken brawl. Later pardoned, he was re-arrested for robbing a church with a gang that included a monk, a university colleague and a professional thief (Geremek 1987: 153–8, 187–90). Tortured and sentenced to hang, he had his sentence commuted to banishment and wandered off the pages of historical record. We do not know how he died, only that he lived a vagrant lifestyle among bandits, drunkards and prostitutes who figure prominently in his poems. Like the earlier *Carmina Burana*, his poetry celebrates the pleasures of the flesh and notes the hypocrisies of the Church and society. Unlike goliardic poetry, however, his work projects anxiety through a dazed series of confused paradoxes (a common technique since Petrarch), as in this excerpt from his "Ballade du concours de Blois":

> I die of thirst where fountains play,
> With chattering teeth, like fire I burn;
> In my own land I'm far away;
> I shiver near a heated urn;
> Nude as a grub, dressed to a turn,
> I laugh through tears, despondent, wait;
> Take comfort in my hopeless state;
> Enjoy myself, and yet am grieved;
> Am strong and lack both strength and weight,
> At once rebuffed and well received . . .
> With need of little, How I strain
> For goods whose price I cannot pay;
> Who soothes me adds but to my pain,
> And tells the truth but to betray;
> He is my friend who fain would say
> The swan is of the raven's band;
> He hurts me most who lends a hand;
> Alike are truth and lies believed;
> I know, but do not understand,
> At once rebuffed and well received.

—Villon 1955: 40f.

Villon's affective confusion inhabited a grey area on the margins in stark contrast to the clear choice between virtues and vices portrayed in the Arena Chapel a little over a century earlier. Emotional disequilibrium gave rise to another variety of popular spiritual expression: female mysticism. Mystics witnessed apparitions and ecstatic visions in legitimized expressions of sacred power, gaining a public voice far exceeding their status.

However, revelatory claims were highly unstable. An early example was Marguerite Porete, who lived and died during the reign of Philip IV; she may have been an irregular beguine, an itinerate lay order loosely affiliated by vows of celibacy. In her *Mirror of Simple Souls*, she enumerated steps to divine union in a dialogue between love, the soul, and reason. For example, love implies salvation can be achieved through faith without works or virtues (Bryant 1984). Pure love idealizes an egalitarian spirituality, leaving the soul to concede:

> Virtues, I take leave of you forevermore,
> My heart will be freer and gayer for it . . .
> I was then in bondage to you, now I am delivered from it,
> I had placed all my heart in you, well I know it,
> For which I lived a while in great fear.
> I have suffered for it many a grievous torment, endured many a pain . . .
> Never was I free but when separated from you;
> I have left your dangers, I dwell in peace.
>
> —Bryant 1984: 213–17

Her ecstatic vision and open contravention of virtues challenged a hegemonic emotional regime stabilized in France under Philip IV and his Avignonese papacy. At her trial for heresy, she was sentenced to burn at the stake in 1310.

Subsequent female mystics navigated a safer course by obtaining institutional approval. Of humble origins, Catherine of Siena survived plague and schism to become arguably the most powerful mystic of the late Middle Ages. She successfully admonished Gregory XI to return the papacy from Avignon to Rome and was later canonized. Catherine argued passionately for ecstatic union with Christ through a nuptial *agape*:

> O mad lover! And you have need of your creature? It seems to me, for you act as if you could not live without her . . . Why then are you so mad? Because you have fallen in love with what you have made! You are pleased and delighted over her within yourself, as if you were drunk [with desire] for her salvation. She runs away from you and you go looking for her. She strays and you draw closer to me: You clothed yourself in our humanity, and nearer than that you could not have come. And what shall I say? I will stutter, "A-a," because there is nothing else I know how to say. Finite language cannot express the emotion of the soul who longs for you infinitely.
>
> —Catherine of Siena 1980: 325f.

As Walker Bynum suggests, Catherine understood ecstatic marriage to Christ not as erotic union, but as physically and emotionally transcendental. The union was not gender-specific, as Christ's humanity provided the liminal key enabling any sinner's corrupt flesh to unite with the divine. Although her hagiographer proclaimed she possessed a wedding band, "Catherine herself, in letter after letter, says we do not marry Christ with gold or silver but with the ring of Christ's foreskin, given in the Circumcision and accompanied by pain and the shedding of blood" (Bynum 1987: 175–80). In Augustinian fashion, she deplored her body as a "dung heap," insisting instead that Christ's love incorporated a transcendent bridge to divine union by means of suffering in an ecstatic path to emotional liberty.

Another popular movement, the Modern Devotion, coalesced in the Low Countries just as the Schism broke out in 1378. *Devotio Moderna* centered upon lay communes, first women, then men, known as Sisters and Brothers of the Common Life. *Devotio* communes followed a safer path than the beguines, willingly subordinating themselves to ecclesiastical authorities. Disillusioned by Church affairs, however, they actively promoted religious reform (*vita activa*) and a return to socially engaged apostolic morality in contrast to the monastic life of contemplation and withdrawal (*vita contemplativa*) directed toward the hereafter.

With the schism resolved at Constance in 1417, another mystic elucidated tenets of the *Devotio* in a self-help guide destined to become the most popular spiritual handbook in Christendom after the Bible; Thomas à Kempis's *Imitation of Christ* (*Imitatio Christi*). Like Catherine, Thomas focused on the body of Christ, his life, death, and suffering among humans as key to salvation. The *Imitatio* promoted an emotional platform of denial, appealing to individual conscience and prescribing exercises to inculcate feelings of guilt, humility, low self-esteem, and self-abnegation as visible re-enactments of Christ's passion. Thomas counselled readers to mortify quotidian desires and avoid affections as the surest route to peace of mind. As with other mystics, the text is steeped in affective appeal, as in à Kempis's meditations on death:

> Happy and wise is he who now striveth to be such in life as he would fain be found in death! For a perfect contempt of the world, a fervent desire to excel in virtue, the love of discipline, the painfulness of repentance, readiness to obey, denial of self, submission to any adversity for love of Christ; these are the things which shall give great confidence of a happy death.
>
> —à Kempis 1999: bk 1, ch. 23, art. 4

Mystics and moralists urged individuals to search their conscience for imperfections of sin and undertake individual self-improvement. The Church also successfully harnessed exhortations to emotional self-discipline in a parallel regime of penance. Penance increased in importance even after the Reformation; Luther retained its sacramental character and, in Catholic regions, record numbers of penitents availed of auricular confession well into the eighteenth century (Myers 1996). Since the yearly requirement to confess established by the Fourth Lateran Council of 1215, the casuistry of moral theology developed into a science of conscience (for an overview, see Tentler 1977). Comprehensive manuals for father confessors developed as part of a process Kittsteiner (1995) dubbed "the formation of the modern conscience."

Yet another mystic, Jean Gerson, worked tirelessly to resolve the Schism in the Church. His fourteenth-century "On the Art of Hearing Confessions" is the most famous manual for father confessors. As a learned physician of spiritual afflictions, the trained father confessor, he wrote, should be familiar with all varieties of sin (Gerson 1998: 367).[14] Carnal sins required his scrupulous attention, as penitents were reluctant to reveal indecency without persuasion. Attributed to Gerson, authorship of the brief, but infamous treatise *On the Confession of Masturbation* (*De confessione mollitiei*) remains uncertain. In a penetrating battery of leading questions, it encouraged relentless interrogation into signs of self-pollution (Tentler 1977: 91–4). "The confessor is warned that if he is not especially skilful and circumspect," he will "rarely be able to draw out" an admission of vice "from the mouths of the infected [infectorum]" (Laqueur 2003: 160–8). If a penitent continued to deny the accusation entirely, the father confessor only had one option left, "expressing amazement and saying that it is not credible," coupled with a plea concerning the dangers of lying in confession (Tentler 1977: 92). Individual guilt and denial proved perennially effective weapons against the decay of Christian virtues by effectively transferring responsibility for self-control onto the individual. However, they were highly contingent upon the actual proclivity of the penitent to feel remorse.

With the rise of modern states, non-religious figures too embraced mysticism. In 1429, a young visionary shepherdess came out of the forests of the Vosges to convince the Dauphin Charles of France to place her at the head of a relief column marching to break the siege at Orléans. Jeanne d'Arc, a military leader legendary as "the Maid" (*la Pucelle*), delivered the heir apparent, the army and the people of France from despair, inspiring hope through her courage on the battlefield. The poet Christine de Pizan praised her miraculous accomplishments in verse surprisingly disparaging of Charles's virtue. In her poem *Ditié de Jehanne d'Arc*, she implied that Charles had "fled in haste from Paris," but now received his father's crown thanks to the Maid, whose prowess was greater than all the great men of the past, braver than any man in Rome, and who channeled the will of God, striking fear into the hearts of her English adversaries.[15] Jeanne's success daringly challenged contemporary perceptions of masculinity and feudal hierarchy to live up to their calling, rallying the Dauphin and his nobles around her popular patriotic call to arms. Her emotive message pulled France from the brink of defeat to ultimate victory in its military struggle with England during the Hundred Years War.

However, her challenge to legally proscribed gender roles also proved her downfall. Detractors publicly accused Jeanne of sorcery; still a charge primarily leveled against men, it did not stick (see Kieckhefer 1989). Subsequently captured by the Burgundians, she was delivered to her English enemies and stood trial before an ecclesiastical court on trumped up accusations of heresy for false prophecy.[16] When these failed, the court initiated charges of cross-dressing. A short tract attributed to Jean Gerson, the *Miraculous Victory of the Maid* (*De Mirabili Victoria cuiusdam puellae*), defended her against the charges, citing exceptional circumstances to justify the adoption of male military attire by the Maid. During her trial, Gerson claimed she continued to don armor to protect her honor against the advances of her jailors. Despite legal opinions from canon law experts, she was burned at the stake in 1431. An ecclesiastical retrial conducted by the Borgia Pope Calixtus III twenty-four years later posthumously overturned the verdict and declared Jeanne a martyr. Canonized in 1920, today she is probably better remembered than any other historical figure of the day as a paragon of virtue and a visionary who challenged hierarchical authority. Not without unease, contemporary religious authorities also recognized the power of her emotive appeal and instituted new procedures to control visionaries based on their experience with Jeanne (see Christian 1981; Kagan 1990; and Sluhovsky 2007).

Prior to the mid-fifteenth century, the transmission of emotional ideals relied heavily on the limited distribution of learned manuscripts, the viewing of individual works of art and oral dissemination in the form of sermons and ballads. Limitations on the distribution and private consumption of knowledge rendered hierarchical control over the emotional regime far less problematic. However, an information technology imported from China brought about a communications revolution: moveable type. The Gutenberg Bible, generally considered the first significant printed book, heralded an information revolution in the 1450s only comparable to the IT revolution of the late twentieth century. Printing literally created mass modern culture. It allowed for the mass production of pedagogical tracts like the *Imitatio*, granting ordinary people unmitigated access to information in private for their own contemplation and interpretation. Ironically, print simultaneously rendered emotional disciplining of subject populations more efficient and uniform while facilitating the spread of sedition just as efficiently and uniformly. Control over the printing press called mass propaganda and modern censorship into existence. Readers could be told how to think and learn to think for themselves as a matter of conscience.

Religious moralists were the first to effectively deploy the new medium's full potential. Through the science of demonology, authors promoted fear in a binary world view of good versus evil in the lurid cumulative concept of witchcraft. Two rival interpretations affected public attitudes toward witchcraft for centuries: the *Hammer of Witches* (*Malleus Maleficarum*, 1487) and, in response, *On Witches and Women Soothsayers* (*De Lamiis et Pythonicis Mulieribus*, 1489). Their influence on the major witch-hunts of the late sixteenth and early seventeenth centuries cannot be understated. Both went into multiple editions; the latest edition of the *Malleus* appeared in 2009 (Mackay 2009). Arguably the most infamous demonological tract of all time, it was written by Dominican Inquisitor Heinrich Kramer, aka Institoris, to refute disbelievers after Hapsburg authorities ended a series of witch trials he conducted in Innsbruck. The *Malleus* focused public attention onto gender and sexuality, shifting medieval attention away from the male sorcerer (e.g. the Templars) onto the modern fixation with the female witch (Kieckhefer 1989). By contrast, the author of *De Lamiis*, Heinrich Molitor, reminded Archduke Sigismund of Austria that his decision to shut down Institoris's operations had been the right choice. Molitor did not deny the existence of witches, but urged caution and held many alleged practices for satanic delusions. *De Lamiis*, written as a dialogue with Sigismund, was the first demonological treatise to employ woodcuts, which generally depicted smiling witches engaged in maleficient magic.[17]

Apart from prurient imaginings of demonic copulations, witches also affected sexuality through evil love magic. Love magic was an ancient trope, also common in the chansons of medieval romanciers. One famous example is the medieval tragedy of Tristan and Isolde. Common love magic was far less dramatic, engaged to forcibly gain sexual and affective control over the object of one's desire. The accused were usually women, in Venice, prostitutes and courtesans suspected of seeking supernatural power over their clients and lovers.[18] As Larner demonstrated, the crime of witchcraft, though sex related, was not sex specific, and men too fell foul of accusations for administering love potions (Larner 1981: 92, 102). Love magic, as the term suggests, was essentially about emotional control. Allusion to the story of Phyllis riding Aristotle, a common cautionary tale in contemporary art, warned men against sexual domination. If some Europeans actually attempted love magic (and evidence suggests they did), it did not include many of the demonic elements elaborated in the *Malleus*. Jealousy played a role in accusations; denunciations were frequently directed by women at other women.

Although printed demonology laid the groundwork for widespread witch-hunting, the climate of fear had abated and the major persecutions of the years from 1570 to 1640[19] remained a century away. By the mid-fifteenth century, Europe witnessed a modicum of economic and demographic recovery, cautiously greeted with rising expectations, but tempered by open calls for religious and spiritual reform. While moralists continued to decry negative behavior in behavioral manuals, they also vocalized displeasure against perceived institutional abuses, as well as the hypocrisy and worldliness of their spiritual leaders, the Renaissance popes. Initially, Christian humanists revived the classical genre of satire, employing humor to criticize abuses and develop utopian programs for reforming the Christian commonwealth.

The late fifteenth-century Alsatian humanist Sebastian Brant rekindled classical satire to create a typology of deviant behavior. His *Ship of Fools* appeared two years after Columbus's discoveries in the New World. Brant allegorized the exploration of the New World as folly, a trope recovered from the classical author Lucien.[20] Brant named his fools' paradise "Narragonia," combining the German word for fool (*Narr*) with Aragon,

Kingdom of Ferdinand II, the monarch who sponsored Columbus's journey. He warned readers that traveling to foreign lands in search of gold was madness when they should instead explore their conscience and enrich their souls to secure eternal salvation. Like Molitor, Brant made effective use of woodcuts in his typologies of deviant behaviors. The 1498 edition sported stunning illustrations by Renaissance artist Albrecht Dürer of Nuremberg. Though some figures were purely allegorical, others clearly depicted familiar gesticulations and facial expressions of lascivious monks, greedy beggars, and gluttonous revelers among a roster of 112 villainous types.

FIGURE 2.5: "All Aboard": rejoicing fools set sail for the New World under the flag of Dr Greed. Title page to Sebastian Brandt, *Ship of Fools* (Basel, 1494). Collection of the State A. Pushkin Museum of Fine Arts, Moscow. Courtesy of DeAgostini/Getty Images.

Folly became a stock trope for religious reformers like Erasmus of Rotterdam, whose *In Praise of Folly* (1511) mocked abuses in the institutional Church and the superstitious credulity of the laity.[21] His protagonist, Folly, allegorically depicted as a woman, excused her opinions apologetically by deferring to her diminished female capacity. Erasmus permitted her to banter in jest about abuses, hiding behind allegorical Folly as a defense against accusations of heresy. Utopianism offered another platform from which moralists could heap opprobrium on religious abuses without endangering themselves. Thomas More's *Utopia*, the most famous since Plato's *Republic*, sought emotional liberty in "Nowhereland," a Christian community united by the injunction to "Love thy neighbor." Like Brant's *Narragonia*, the land of fools, More chose the New World as the location for his *Utopia*, related in a dialogue with the fictional sailor Raphael Nonsenso. As author of a work of nonsense about nowhere, More retained plausible deniability. All three moralists admonished readers to control their emotions and behavior. However, they had gone one step further than previous moralists and mystics, recommending an emotional regime ruled by egalitarian love and self-control rather than hierarchy and fear.

Satire gave way to sarcasm, as a rising tide of popular anger directed at the perceived inability of the universal Church to reform culminated in the Protestant Reformation. The Reformation reconceived the emotional regime. Martin Luther successfully exploited novel print media to target mass audiences with the first modern propaganda campaign. The sarcastic, often scatological Protestant devaluation of the Church availed of the vernacular and employed emotive woodcut imagery "for the sake of simple folk."[22] "Mr Doctor" Martin Luther evoked apocryphal imagery to conjure a righteous fear of God.[23] Of his three theological pillars—salvation through faith, grace and scripture alone (*sola fide, sola gratia, sola scriptura*)—the doctrine of the Word lent itself particularly well to the novel communications technology. Whether he actually nailed his *Ninety-Five Theses* to the door of Wittenberg cathedral on the hallowed eve of All Souls in 1517 or whether this was just another typical piece of Luther-spin is largely irrelevant. In a call for a learned disputation, he reasoned against the sale of plenary indulgences, criticizing Church doctrine on purgatory and challenging papal access to the treasury of merit—an accumulated excess of good works performed by the saints and redistributed to the pious as absolution and indulgences in return for coin. His challenge to the doctrine of the keys of St. Peter, seemingly inadvertent, struck at the heart of the hierarchical emotional regime. The Church lost its pivotal *raison d'être*, the keys of loosing-and-binding sanctioned in Mathew 16:19, which ostensibly granted the pope the power to forgive sin. If forgiveness of sin came directly from God, then the institutional Church was irrelevant in a priesthood of all believers. In his *Ninety-Five Theses*, Luther intimated that the power to forgive sin was unmediated and came directly from God's grace:

> 56. The "treasures of the Church," out of which the pope grants indulgences, are not sufficiently named or known among the people of Christ.
>
> 57. That they are not temporal treasures is certainly evident, for many of the vendors do not pour out such [monetary] treasures so easily, but only gather them.
>
> 58. Nor are they the merits of Christ and the Saints, for even without the pope, these always work grace for the inner man, and the cross, death, and hell for the outward man.
>
> —Luther [1517] 1915

In 1520, Luther angrily attacked perceived papal abuses in three treatises, *On Christian Freedom, On the Babylonian Captivity of the Church* and the *Address to the Nobility of the German Nation*. Echoing Petrarch, he accused the vice-ridden whore of Babylon of enslaving the honest German burgers and nobles, fleecing them like sheep through the sale of indulgences to pay for lavish projects like St. Peter's Basilica in Rome. Individual good works (fasting, pilgrimage, indulgences, etc.) did not assure salvation, only faith, leaving Luther to embrace collective public welfare with the communal injunction to "love thy neighbor." Manifest in the establishment of the first community chest at Leisnig in 1523, the idea of public welfare spread quickly to other cities.

Monumental events like the Reformation unfold not only from doctrinal change, but also from personal e-motivations. Ever since the developmental psychologist Erik Erikson published his psycho-historical biography *Young Man Luther* in 1958, historians have continued to probe the reformer's relationship to his father for clues to his rebellion against the pope. Most recently, the manifold personal and psychological reasons behind Luther's anger and resentment toward the Church are contextualized in a recent biography by Lyndal Roper (2016). Like Erikson, Roper examines Luther's break with his father after several events affected his career trajectory, leading him to abandon the study of law for theology. The competitive nature of male relationships in the rugged mining town of Mansfeld, as well as the intellectual influence of his mother and that of his mentors, chief among them Johann von Staupitz, all influenced Luther's theology. Indeed, Luther waited until Staupitz's death before breaking his monastic oath of celibacy and marrying a former nun, Katharina von Bora, in 1525. Clerical marriage played a considerable role in the development of the modern family modelled along patriarchal lines.[24] Advocated by numerous co-religionists, Luther's cautious decision to embrace clerical marriage facilitated a sexual revolution, toppling the moral ascendency of sacerdotal celibacy and exalting marriage and the family unit as the primary emotional building-block of modern society. Luther commented frequently on his close emotional bond to Katharina and their children, held forward as a shining example by subsequent evangelical reformers. It represented a root-and-branch restructuring of society based upon the modern concept of the loving nuclear family as the most basic productive and reproductive unit in Western society.

The Reformation introduced parallel emotional regimes in Europe, exemplified in differing theological attitudes toward the passion of Christ by Catholics, Evangelicals and Reformed Protestants (Karant-Nunn 2010). Catholic theologians upheld a sympathetic sorrow for Christ's sacrifice on the cross, reasserting their hierarchical authority to dispense absolution for sin in his name. The Counter-Reformation even increased a cultural focus on ostentatious displays in ritual, pilgrimage, processions, and, especially with the rise of the Jesuit order, in art and architecture that accentuated the sensual and the bodily in the ritual of mass celebrating human sacrifice in the Eucharistic devotion of transubstantiation. Church buildings reinforced a pedagogical strategy to inculcate guilty feelings through a message of majesty and authority on behalf of the successors of St. Peter and the doctrine of the keys, emblazoned in the cupola of Basilica in Rome: "*Tu est Petrus*" (Smith 2002).

The Protestant Reformation broke with this tradition. Lutheran affective piety focused on Christ's triumph over death rather than his suffering as a hopeful message to the faithful. The saints and the Virgin lost their ability to intercede, effectively removing the female from celestial forces; mediation between God and the individual believer disappeared and, along with it, the penitential regime, as a vainglorious human attempt to manipulate grace. Rather than relying on art and ritual, evangelicals expressed gratitude to Christ in the Word through song as a joyful and vocal expression of emotional community. By eliminating the celebration of Christ's sacrifice in the mass, evangelicals simultaneously ended the mystical elevation of the body of Christ, albeit retaining a Eucharistic doctrine of real presence. The reformed doctrine of Jean Calvin went one step further, removing all physicality from affective piety. They stripped the altars of icons. Allusions to the passion and the suffering of Christ's body almost completely disappeared. Eucharistic devotion evolved into a simple symbolic memorial, while sermons from the pulpit emphasized human unworthiness and the constant drive for individual repentance, offering no sureties of Christ's forgiveness or the consolations of grace through faith. Thus, reformed churches interiorized their emotional regimes, leaving salvation a matter for each individual believer to face alone.

After 1300, the existing hierarchical regime of emotionality began to crumble. Love confronted fear in tiny spaces of emotional liberty in an environment of guilt, until popular anger and resentment propelled the break-up of Catholic Christendom. Throughout our period, from the slow demise of the embodiment of the *Corpus Christianum* to the rise of an atomized moral conscience during the second Reformation, religious and spiritual interpretations of emotions had a deep and lasting influence on Christian values in Europe, once allegorically embodied as virtues and vices only to become abstract ideological principles of conscience. Religious attitudes to the emotions provided the social glue holding society together and giving communities transcendental meaning, but they also came to represent dialectical sources of tension. Like Luther, individuals could experience emotions in a variety of hypocognized ways; they felt simple joy at births and weddings, experienced sincere sorrow at funerals, happiness at material successes, sadness at personal setbacks, hatred in war, love in family and community life. Certainly, the conditioning of emotionality is never complete and public representations of feeling in allegories, tropes, sermons, books, and woodcuts influenced and was influenced by historical events. Throughout the period, religion and spirituality retained their value as codifiers of emotions as Christian signifiers, although some emotions were politically, socially, and culturally more hypercognized than others. Whatever the perspective, from the late Middle Ages to the Renaissance and culminating in the Reformation, emotions cannot be properly understood without taking religion and spirituality fully into account as interpretive tools.

CHAPTER THREE

Music and Dance

DENIS COLLINS[1] AND JENNIFER NEVILE

INTRODUCTION

For the ancient Greeks, music and dance were not two separate disciplines but part of the larger art *mousike* that also included poetry, drama, declamation, and instrumental music. By the period 1300 to 1600, therefore, the association between music and dance in Western European thought had enjoyed a long history. Dance and music were both seen as having the power to move and to change the emotions of those watching, performing, or listening to it. How this power was achieved in these two arts during the late medieval and Renaissance periods, and the responses of modern scholars in investigating the emotional content of music and dance during these centuries, will be explored in this chapter.

MUSIC

In a survey of research publications during the decade or so up to 2015, Elizabeth Eva Leach, David Fallows, and Kate Van Orden (2015) identify several trends that have occupied the attention of musicologists working within the approximate chronological boundaries of 1300 to 1600. The authors note in particular the impact of innovations in digital technology and online resources, ongoing interactions with music performers and with scholarship outside musicology, and greater interest in encounters between European and non-European musical traditions. Conspicuously absent in this study is any mention of the word emotion. This reflects the slow permeation of emotions research into early music scholarship, notwithstanding the claim frequently encountered in all branches of music research that music can convey or arouse emotions; for instance, Timothy McKinney claims that "the notion that music can convey thoughts and stir emotions is perhaps as old as music itself" (2010: 11).

The situation, however, is more complex than the absence of emotion as a theme of study in its own right might suggest. Emotions are a critical aspect of longstanding topics of enquiry in musicology, even if the emotional dimensions of these topics are not necessarily subject to critical examination. These dimensions are evident in studies on the history and application of modal theory in medieval and Renaissance music, the relationship between music and rhetoric, and the impact of humanism on music. A multitude of studies exists also on text-setting, cadences, and instrumental genres where the importance of emotions is noted, even if often just taken for granted. Appearing in the same year as Leach et al., studies by Stoessel (2015) and Hankins (2015) suggest that emotion may become a more actively investigated topic in early music research. These studies will be considered below.

On the whole, the word "emotion" is infrequently encountered in musicological literature, notwithstanding music's supposedly close connections to emotional states.[2] When it does occur, it is usually coupled with other words such as "affect," "affective," "pathos," "passion," or "expressive," although these terms more often appear by themselves without the word "emotion" alongside them. Laurence Wuidar, for instance, observes that "the musical literature prefers to use the terms 'affect' and 'passion' rather than the term 'emotion'" (2013: opening page), whereas Claude Palisca argues for "affection" rather than "passion" to represent "a permanent or semi-steady state of the mind or feeling, because it does not so much imply suffering as the result of some action" (2000: 291).

The following discussion is structured around the main themes running through musicological research where emotions are acknowledged as an important attribute of the topic under investigation. Attention will be drawn in particular to studies that engage in detail with emotional properties of the compositional or other contextual materials being considered,[3] even if this engagement is generally secondary to the author's analytical, critical, palaeographical, or other purposes.

The organization of musical pitches into eight (later twelve) different octave-bound scales known as modes was a regular feature of musical discourse and practice from antiquity until the seventeenth century when it was replaced by the system of major and minor keys. Cristle Collins Judd states that "the word 'mode' is one of the most richly textured and problematic terms of Renaissance discourse about music" (2002: 364). This assessment can be extended to medieval music theory where the complicated transmission and misunderstanding of Greek modal theory has been a major source for musicological enquiry. The association of modal ethos with emotional states was undertaken by the Greeks, who applied names to each mode and described their supposed emotional characteristics. For instance, the first mode, Dorian, was considered majestic, while the Phrygian (mode 3) was exciting and martial. The names of the modes, and indeed other aspects of Greek modal theory, were confused by medieval writers who otherwise developed a cogent theory of modal organization for the rich and abundant corpus of plainchant (also known as Gregorian chant) that formed the cornerstone of Christian church music. This theory, however, seemed to have been applied to polyphonic music with less success by later medieval and Renaissance writers. As Claude Palisca lucidly summarizes, "the ethical characteristics of the Greek modes were unwittingly assigned to the similarly named Christian ones," while the extra-musical associations of modes were too difficult to detect in polyphonic music because of the lack of "affective profile" in modal polyphony (Palisca 1990: 129).[4]

The major studies of modality include summary assessments of the emotional characteristics of each mode and how these were understood by different constituencies of composers, performers, and theorists in the late medieval and early Renaissance eras. A classic study by Bernhard Meier dwells at length on various examples from repertoire where specific properties of a given mode such as melodic intervals or cadences are emphasized or obscured in order to give prominence to certain aspects of word expression (Meier 1988).[5] In a slightly later study (1990: 182), Meier claims that modes were "vehicles for definite affective qualities" and investigates how other factors besides the text being set to music may have influenced the choice of mode. The very notion of "mode as an *a priori* pre-compositional property of Renaissance polyphony" is questioned in another classic study (Powers 1981: 434). While many musicologists share these concerns about mode in fifteenth- and early sixteenth-century polyphony, there were many published collections of music where the composers' order of presentation of the works proceeds systematically through the different modes. For instance, the ordered collections of psalm settings and spiritual madrigals by the late sixteenth-century Catholic composers Orlando Lasso and Giovanni Pierluigi da Palestrina caused Powers to wonder if such cycles were "an expression of spiritual piety, a symbol of faith rather than an expression of affect" (1981: 449).

A composer's use of mode to underline the message imparted by the text is explored further in Richard Freedman's study of Claude Le Jeune's cycle of Psalm settings known as the *Dodecacorde* published in 1598, though possibly completed about ten years earlier (Freedman 2003). This collection reflects the mid-sixteenth-century revision of the number of modes from eight to twelve (which was not, however, universally accepted). Freedman addresses how Le Jeune's use of melodies from the Genevan Psalter along with polyphony vividly reflects the emotional dimensions of those sacred hymns. Furthermore, Le Jeune appears to have selected carefully those melodies whose poetic language could convey the emotional effects associated by music theorists with each mode. Through this process, Le Jeune demonstrated how the Protestant Psalm tradition was compatible with contemporary polyphonic practice (Freedman 2003: 302–8). Indeed, the uplifting nature of music more generally for Christian congregations was recognized by some key Protestant reformers, most especially Martin Luther (see Figure 3.1), a skilled lutenist and composer in his own right.

Appraisals of mode and emotion can be found also in studies of earlier repertoire: Christian Berger argues that subtle differentiations of modal melodies are key to

FIGURE 3.1: Martin Luther playing the lute. Imagined scenario in an engraving by Gustav Adolf Closs (1864–1938). Courtesy of Prisma/UIG/Getty Images.

understanding how the fourteenth-century composer Guillaume de Machaut manipulated musical structure to suit the text of his balade *Plour dames*. For instance, at one point in the composition a Phrygian cadence occurring in the context of a Dorian mode points "very intensively to the plaintive mood of the text" (C. Berger 2003: 202–4). Jean-Pierre Ouvrard traces the association of the E mode (Phrygian) with "sad, grave, languorous or plaintive" texts in French chansons of the late fifteenth and early sixteenth centuries (Ouvrard 1992: 96). Of particular note is Margaret of Austria's *Album de chansons* for its inclusion of several pieces whose modal associations match Margaret's reportedly chronic melancholy. In addition to the Phrygian mode based on the note E, Ouvrard (1992: 96–9) investigates the mournful associations of the Lydian mode on F, which is also well represented by settings in Margaret's album.[6]

In a study recalling the approach to repertoire by Bernhard Meier, Anne Smith's detailed reading of Adrian Willaert's motet O *magnum mysterium* traces how the composer used mode to demonstrate the text structurally (1992). Amongst the many details brought to light by Smith, we may mention how Willaert used a note foreign to the mode (recognized by being sung to the solmization syllable *fa*) to illustrate the word "mysterium" in this and other works (1992: 125).[7] The music of Willaert (c. 1490–1562) is examined from multiple perspectives in a monograph by Susan McClary that is bounded overall by modal considerations but also delves into "notions of Selfhood, interiority and passions" (2004: 58). Like many other scholars, McClary is puzzled by the contrast between the reverence in which Willaert was held by his contemporaries and the general lack of interest nowadays in performing or recording his music. Amongst its many provocative and engaging discussions of modal repertoire, McClary's text is further remarkable for the degree to which it includes the words "emotion" and "emotional" in its treatment of repertoire examples. This feature, as noted above, is relatively rare in musicological literature. Her analysis of Willaert's settings of Petrarch sonnets abounds with emotional descriptions: Willaert's first setting has "seething hostility and flaunted masochism," while the second "offers a condition of unruffled serenity" (89).

Elsewhere in her study, McClary provides nuanced readings of madrigals by various mid- to late- sixteenth-century composers. See, for instance, her account of Jacques Arcadelt's well-known *Il bianco e dolce cigno* (58–63), especially where she interrogates the "depiction of emotional expression" at the word "piangendo." Sixteenth-century madrigals are well known for their expressive use of word painting through various musical means. Of the numerous studies of this repertoire, three can be mentioned for including consideration of emotional dimensions: Chater (1999) on the *dialogo di partenza*, La Via (2013) on the music of Alfonso Fontanelli, and Newcomb's edition (2003) of madrigals by Luzzasco Luzzaschi. The commentaries by Newcomb on each piece in Luzzaschi's collection include descriptions of emotional effects in a composition overall or for specific passages or words.

Another study that employs the word emotion frequently in its critical engagement with music is a monograph by Anne Walters Robertson on Machaut (2002). In Chapter 3, "Machaut's Motets 1–17,"[8] Robertson observes that the tenor parts of the motets feature "a blatantly emotional affective quality . . . For the most part the tenors record cries of fear, anguish, outrage, despair, and uncertainty, along with expressions of resignation and happiness" (84). Robertson asks if there is "an analogously emotional literature that might have influenced" Machaut's choice of tenors and finds possible answers in contemporary biblical commentaries and mystic writings (84–102). She relates key phrases from Henry Suso's *Little Book of Eternal Wisdom* to the motet tenors, and she notes correlations between Machaut's motets and the lexicon of words and phrases developed in twelfth- and thirteenth-century mystic commentaries on the *Song of Songs*. The result, as Robertson suggests, is that Machaut deliberately arranged his motet tenors to reflect a spiritual journey toward salvation.

While invoking the emotional attributes of their chosen repertoires and probing the wider cultural milieux in which such emotions may have been harnessed for artistic use, neither McClary nor Robertson engages with theories of emotions as developed in non-musicological fields in recent years. By contrast, Jason Stoessel's study (2015) of Johannes Ciconia's setting of a poem by Leonardo Giustinian proposes that both men operated in an emotional community of early humanists at Padua c. 1400. Stoessel draws upon the work of Barbara Rosenwein (2006) and William Reddy (1997) to shape an argument about how Ciconia's setting of *Con lagreme* uses various musical figures that "operate as emotive musical gestures" (85). Stoessel's is perhaps the first study in the field of early music studies prior to c. 1600 that engages with pan-disciplinary theories of emotions.

Another study that will likely be very relevant for future research on music and emotions is by James Hankins (2015) on humanism in Renaissance Italy. Drawing upon the well-established view that humanism successfully harnessed traditional grammatical training in Latin, Hankins reminds the reader that humanists also followed Aristotle in claiming that music could lead young men to virtue, noble feelings and valor (232, 238). Early fifteenth-century humanistic music criticism was Aristotelian in its attempts to distinguish good and bad music (245–6), but analytical concepts drawn from classical rhetoric became dominant in the sixteenth century.[9] Paolo Cortesi's *De cardinalate* (1510) and Raffaele Brandolino's *De musica* exemplified the view that music should be subordinate to the words and that great importance should be placed on the expression of the words and the affections they aroused (248). Hankins points out (249) that one of Cortesi's most important legacies was to gather Aristotle's scattered remarks on the emotional effects of the Greek modes and to derive a typology for music of his own time. Notwithstanding that humanists apparently preferred the affective simplicity of accompanied monodic song instead of polyphony, the wider shift that they brought about in moral, civic, and aesthetic judgments about music had a profound impact on speculative and practical, including polyphonic, musical traditions in the sixteenth century.

Beyond Italy, northern humanists applied classical modes of thinking to the music around them, and they encouraged musicians to set a greater variety of Latin poetic forms, which in many cases were of classical origin and involved texts with emotional aspects such as praise, lament, mourning, or satire (Strohm 2015: 275–7). Although the influence of humanism throughout Europe became increasingly apparent during the course of the sixteenth century, the situation is far from clear in the two decades or so on either side of 1500. Focusing on motet repertoire from this period, Warwick Edwards (2012) probes the extent to which humanistic thought influenced composers' attitudes toward text setting. He finds little systematic discussion amongst humanists or music theorists of the time on the manner in which words were set or performed. Whereas there seems to be a tacit assumption that composers should reflect the sentiments of the text, their works were "evaluated on the basis of musical expression alone" (120). Wolfgang Fuhrmann likewise finds little influence of humanism in psalm settings from c. 1500. Composers of Josquin's generation chose texts conveying very strong emotions that were set in "musical expression of dolorous, woeful, plaintive moods, an innovation almost without precedent in sacred polyphony" (Fuhrmann 2011: 53) The psalm settings by Josquin and his contemporaries may have been indebted to the idea of sublime simplicity as transmitted by St. Augustine, with little trace of humanistic influence on the renewed interest in biblical texts c. 1500. These compositions, Fuhrmann suggests (59, 67–71), "signify an engaged, emotive reading of the text."[10]

Josquin's setting of Psalm 50, *Miserere mei, Deus*, is arguably the finest representative of the tradition of psalm settings. This work has attracted much attention, with Patrick Macey (2000) providing perhaps the most authoritative reading of its rhetorical aspects. Macey's prose is peppered with emotional vocabulary as he outlines the rhetorical structure of this monumental work; for instance, "the plaintive semitone that opens the work," and a "piercing Phrygian cadence on a unison e' at 'humiliatum'" (495, 511). Macey notes that contemporary music treatises give little insight into Josquin's use of these and other compositional effects. Notwithstanding the paucity of contemporary documentation on the specific applications of rhetorical knowledge, other scholars have attempted to trace the influence more generally of classical rhetoric and grammar on writings about music. For instance, Margaret Bent (2010) examines how the contents of music treatises in the fourteenth and fifteenth centuries were often modelled on grammar and rhetoric treatises, while Don Harrán underpins his detailed overview of classical and musical sources for rhetoric with the question "to what extent do didactic, pleasurable or emotional ends direct the theorists in their instructions for composing and performing music?" (1997: 39). Opinion on the extent of the influence of rhetoric remains divided in the literature, with Timothy McGee (2004) expressing serious reservations about the ways in which composers of the late Middle Ages and Renaissance may have adopted rhetorical techniques as formative principles for their compositions.

By the 1540s and 1550s, the influence of humanism was perhaps the most important reason for the subordination of harmony to the passions contained in the words (K. Berger 2006: 308). Berger suggests also that advances in the natural sciences during the sixteenth century led to challenges of traditional views of harmony, especially notions of cosmic harmony that were popular in speculative musical traditions since antiquity. Musical harmonies were traditionally understood in terms of the numerically defined consonant intervals that governed the succession of musical sonorities in a composition. Although earlier writers on music often commented on the agreeableness or pleasure derived from listening to music, they had few means of articulating how exactly these responses came about beyond calculating the acoustical ratios of the musical intervals. Systematic theoretical enquiry into the affective qualities of musical intervals only began in the sixteenth century and was spearheaded by Willaert's distinguished pupils, Nicola Vicentino and Gioseffo Zarlino (McKinney 2010). Humanism provided a mechanism for developing sophisticated critical responses to music based on applications of classical rhetoric, but it should be remembered that the process of change developed over a long period and was manifest in different ways. Rob Wegman (2002) has traced changes in how listeners understood and responded to music in the late fifteenth century. His principal point is that, starting c. 1480, commentators on music moved beyond acknowledging "sweetness" as a praiseworthy and sometimes incomprehensible attribute of music toward a greater understanding of how a musical work may be well composed and therefore be intrinsically meritorious. Wegman draws upon testimony by a range of figures from c. 1400 to the early decades of the sixteenth century, including Nicholas of Cusa, Denis the Carthusian, Paolo Cortesi, and, in particular, the music treatises of Johannes Tinctoris to show a transformation in sensibility whereby music can be both a source of sensuous delight and of knowledge and understanding.

Amongst the vocabulary used by late medieval and Renaissance writers, the word "sweetness" is encountered very frequently with reference to the listener's musical experience.[11] Wegman (2002: 60) suggests that the coupling of sweetness and understanding in discourse about music c. 1500 is symptomatic of a rising sense of professional self-confidence amongst composers for their exclusive and specialized art. Such expression of musical identity is especially evident in the relatively large number of laments for deceased composers written in the late fifteenth and early sixteenth centuries.[12] In these works the deceased composer is named and his individual compositional style sometimes recalled through a complex process of musical citation and paraphrase (Higgins 2007; Meconi 2007; Hatter 2014: 29–30, 104–32). The most famous laments are Johannes Ockeghem's *Mort tu as navré/Miserere* on the death of Gilles Binchois (c. 1460) and Josquin Des Prez's *Nymphes des bois/Requiem* following Ockeghem's death in 1497. The sense of mourning is closely related to melancholy, another emotion that has a rich history of association with music. The late fifteenth-century Neoplatonist Marsilio Ficino is credited with driving the high regard for creative artists as conduits for melancholy in aesthetically attractive works (Tomlinson 1993: 101–44; Boccadoro 2013). A composer very well known for exploiting the musical potential of melancholy affect was the late Elizabethan John Dowland, although there appears to be little Neoplatonist thinking underlining the texts he chose for his settings (Wells 1985). In another study, Robert Toft (1984) shows how Dowland's skillful use of rhetoric permitted the creation of various musical figures that could parallel poetic devices and sometimes also introduce figures not present in the poems.

Musical composition between 1300 and 1600 was primarily vocal, with less emphasis on instrumental writing for the genres that were prominent in secular or religious contexts. Brown and Polk (2001) note that it was not until the late sixteenth century that cathedrals and churches began to hire instrumentalists regularly, while minstrels and their instruments were traditionally held in suspicion for questionable morals by the broader society. Nevertheless, singers and instrumentalists are found frequently in the musical iconography of many periods, often together, as Figure 3.1 above attests. Likewise, Figure 3.2 illustrates a convivial scene that involves several musicians playing a selection of commonly used instruments. In a particularly expressive representation of musical performance, a detail from a fresco by Amico Aspertini (c. 1475–1552) shows a group of choristers reading from a book of music, possibly in chant notation (see Figure 3.3). The remarkable attention to details of music notation is matched by the concentrated expressions of the musicians whose facial features were likely composed to reflect their professional training in the art of singing.

A number of documentary sources offer fascinating insights into emotional connotations of specific musical instruments. Konrad of Megenberg's *Yconomica* (c. 1348–1352) includes references to music amongst its discussion of materials useful for study by the sons of princes (Page 2009). In Chapter 49 of this text (translated by Page as "Showing how diverse kinds of music give rise to different passions"), Konrad goes through a long list of instruments and gives their emotional attributes. For instance, "the trumpet and the shawm excite pleasure of the mind in one who is an ally but depresses the spirits of enemies with sadness," while harps and other kinds of string instruments "incline human minds to the mildness of piety" (Page 2009: 31). The eminent late fifteenth-century music theorist Johannes Tinctoris wrote a history of musical instruments where we can find emotional references in two instances (Baines 2009). His favorite instruments, the viola and rebec (bowed string instruments), "induce piety and stir my heart most ardently to contemplation of heavenly joys" (Baines 2009: 59). A tone of contempt informs his assessment of instruments by people he names as Turks: the "miserable and puny instrument which the Turks with their even more miserable and puny ingenuity, have evolved from the lyre and call the tambura, has the shape of a large spoon" (Baines 2009: 57).

FIGURE 3.2: Anonymous, seated crowned figure surrounded by musicians playing the lute, bagpipes, triangle, horn, viola, and drums. Private Collection via Getty Images.

FIGURE 3.3: Amico Aspertini, *Transportation of the Holy Face*, detail, 1507–9, fresco, Basilica of San Frediano, Lucca. Courtesy of Dea Picture Library via Getty Images.

The discussion in the above paragraphs shows how emotions pervade the subject matter of scholarly discourse about late medieval and Renaissance music. Although musicologists have generally been very adept at incorporating cross-disciplinary modes of thought and approaches to their work, there is as yet a conspicuous gap in addressing emotional attributes of topics as diverse as mode, instrument, identity, or rhetoric. The frequent recourse to emotional vocabulary in the literature is, however, without a theoretical framework for the study of emotions. This could assist existing critical and analytical methodologies for interrogating fundamental ways in which historical writers viewed music and its different cultural, social, and political environments. In short, the field of emotions research offers new and dynamic possibilities for fresh appraisals of topics that have stimulated musicologists' curiosity since the foundations of the discipline.

DANCE

As the lawyer Pierre de Brach explains in his account of the carnival masquerade he composed in 1575 for Diane de Foix, dancing, poetry, and music were equally important in conveying the emotions represented during the course of the masquerade (McGowan 2003: 21). Nevertheless, twentieth- and twenty-first-century early dance scholars, as well as those who undertake historical studies of emotions, have not yet systematically focused on emotions in dance from the fourteenth to early seventeenth centuries. The present analysis on emotion and dance in this period, therefore, is incomplete. It is the start of such an investigation, not a report of a completed—or even substantially completed—one. In this exploration of emotion and dance, the aim is to seek to point out the areas in which dance can help elucidate, or simply contribute to, a history of the emotions, by focusing on what was written in dance treatises on the effect of dance on human emotional states, and by examining what emotions were portrayed by dance performances, and the means dance masters employed to create emotional effects.

If any theoretical standpoint is adopted here then it is the approach put forward by Barbara Rosenwein that recognizes and emphasizes the complexity and variability of emotional life through her theory of "emotional communities" (2002: 842–5). Such a flexible view of past emotional lives seems to be the most appropriate and useful for an investigation into dance and emotion. During the Renaissance dance was ubiquitous across all levels of society, occurring in many different circumstances. Thus the possibility for dance to express a range of emotions depending upon the performance context is obvious. Furthermore, dance was—for the most part—a communal activity. People usually danced with others and in front of spectators. Whether the latter group was only small, as when dancing occurred in an intimate space in private apartments, or if it was large, as in the case of court balls or theatrical spectacles, there were always people watching, judging, and assessing the dance performances. In addition, the boundaries between "performers" and "spectators" were fluid, as very often the same people moved from one group to another depending upon the occasion and type of dance performance. The fact that dance was a communal activity meant that it was an ideal vehicle for displays of emotion, and that the emotional content of the choreographies were complex, and that they operated on multiple levels. The choreographies created by the dance masters represented emotions which occurred on one layer—between performers—but the presence of spectators meant that there was also opportunity for additional layers of emotional exchange between the performers and the spectators.

During the late medieval and Renaissance periods dance was viewed as having the power to change people's behavior and emotions. The *quattrocento* humanist Mario Filelfo, in his ode in praise of the dance master Guglielmo Ebreo da Pesaro, asserts that the effect of Guglielmo's dancing is such that it can influence warriors and philosophers—Maccabeus, Solomon, Socrates, Aristotle, and Plato—and even goddesses such as Diana (Guglielmo 1463: 46r–47v). In sixteenth-century France, part of the motivation behind the establishment in 1571 of the *Académie de Poésie et de Musique* was the expectation by various artists, including Antoine de Baïf and Thibault de Courville, that by combining poetry, music, and dance they would be able to revive "the powerful moral 'effects' on participants' emotions which they believed had been achieved by the Greeks" (McGowan 2008b: 103).[13] Thus, during these centuries dance, through its connection to music and through the continuation of classical beliefs linking outward movement to interior spiritual states, was inextricably linked to emotion and to emotional control.

Ways to Investigate Early Dance and Emotion

Perhaps one of the first problems facing early modern historians wanting to investigate emotion and dance is that the majority of sources on which historians rely are written documents, with which the field of early dance is not well provided. Furthermore, as many other scholars have emphasized, "the relationship between words and feelings is not at all clear" (Matt 2011: 119). Certainly, conduct guides and books on behavior and comportment do provide avenues to investigate dance and emotion, at least in regard to what social norms decreed. Other written documentation that pertain particularly to dance, and which can also provide evidence of the emotional content of individual choreographies and theatrical dance spectacles, are the titles of individual choreographies recorded in the treatises, the *libretti* and *livrets* of such spectacles, and the theoretical writings by dance masters. For example, when one examines the titles of dances recorded in the late sixteenth-century Italian treatises of Fabritio Caroso and Cesare Negri, one finds a high proportion of the dance titles refer to love in some way or another: constant love (see Figure 3.4), prudent love, contented love, the nobility of love, the wonder of love, the flame of love, the snare of love. Negri even named his whole treatise *Le gratie d'amore*—the graces of love. These choreographed dances are almost all for one, two or three couples, and it is clear from their titles that the different emotional states of love that existed between men and women are what the dance masters wanted to explore in their compositions.

In terms of the larger-scale danced spectacles, their *libretti* or *livrets*, together with the costumes, music, stage designs, and machines, all reveal the intentions and messages of the spectacle. Often such messages include statements about the virtue or goodness or strength of a ruler. One illustration of such a message comes from the *livret* of the 1617 *ballet de cour La Délivrance de Renaud*. In this ballet, Louis XIII first appears as the Demon of Fire, and, as Greer Garden points out, Étienne Durand's comments on Louis's appearance as a fire demon were more than just the expected flattery, because in the *livret* Durand was "reminding a wide readership that it was subject to a King who ruled by divine right, and issuing a warning that any further uprisings would not be tolerated" (2010a: 24). Durand's description of Louis XIII makes this clear:

> It was not without reason or alternative that the King wanted to portray the Demon of Fire here, and to cover himself with flames . . . because apart from the fact that His Majesty wanted to have the Queen, his wife, see some representation of the fire that

AMOR COSTANTE
BALLETTO;
IN LODE DELL'ILLVSTR.^MA ET ECC.^MA SIG.^RA DVCHESSA DI SORA.

'HVOMO, & la Dama, standosi all'incontro senza pigliar mano, come si ha nel presente disegno, faranno insieme gratiosamente la Riuerenza graue, con due Continenze: poi l'huomo farà due Passi graui, & vn Seguito ordinario innanzi, incontro alla Dama: laquale farà il medesimo in dietro, principiandoli col piè sinistro; & amendue faranno il medesimo per contrario, cioè la Dama farà li due Passi graui col Seguito ordinario innanzi col piè destro, & l'huomo farà il medesimo in dietro, facendo sempre detti effetti insieme: Dopò pigliaranno la fè destra, facendo insieme due Trabuchetti graui, l'vno alla sinistra, & l'altro alla destra, con due Riprese alla sinistra. Il medesimo faranno pigliando la fè sinistra, principiandoli col piè destro; La Dama farà poi due Seguiti ordinarij volti alla sinistra, & l'huomo ne farà altri due fiancheggiati innanzi, pigliando la man sinistra della Dama, & facendo insieme la Riuerenza graue.

Nel secondo tempo, passeggiando si faranno due Puntate, & quattro Seguiti, & lasciandosi detta mano, se ne faranno altri due volti alla

g 2   man

FIGURE 3.4: First page of the dance *Amor Costante* from Fabritio Caroso, *Il ballarino* (Venice, 1581). Courtesy of the Library of Congress, Washington, D.C.

he felt for her, he also costumed himself this way with the intention of displaying his goodness towards his subjects, his power to his enemies, and his majesty to foreigners.

—Durand [1617: 5v] 2010b: 246

The emotions felt by the spectators watching *La Délivrance de Renaud* must have been varied, depending upon the political affiliations of each individual. Some would be overcome with a feeling of awe at the power and majesty of Louis XIII displayed before them, others might have felt unease or fear at the same display, while others might just have responded with wonder and delight at the impact of the whole spectacular entertainment.

Theoretical writings by the dance masters also reveal beliefs that continued throughout the Renaissance and across Western Europe. In his dance treatise, Guglielmo Ebreo expounds the long-held view that dancing proceeds from music and, like music, has the power to move and to change men and women's emotions (1463: 5r–6r). The late sixteenth-century dance treatise by Thoinot Arbeau repeats the same message ([1596] 1972: 5r–5v). Eleven years later in 1600, Caroso opens his treatise *Nobiltà di dame* with a letter to his readers in which the same view is repeated:

> In the course of our lives virtuous pleasures and solace for the soul are as necessary as displeasing things and travail are harmful ... Among these virtuous pleasures one places the practice of dancing ... since in human interactions and society [dance] rouses the soul to joy, and when those who find themselves oppressed by some trouble, it eases [these troubles] and revives them, and holds at bay every annoying and unpleasant thought. In such a form [dance] is of little importance, [but] since it is joined with poetry and with music, its powers are among those other worthy [arts], and it is a part of those same [arts of] imitation which represent the workings of the soul through movements of the body.
>
> —Caroso [1600] 1980: 1[14]

From Guglielmo onwards, dance masters cited ancient authorities to support their arguments regarding the power of music and dance to affect men and women. In England in the 1620s, the dance master Barthélemy de Montagut repeated the case of David who danced to the sound of his harp in order to calm the fury of Saul. He then continues: "Homer in his *Iliad* calls [dance] a divine occupation, Hesiod an undertaking proper to dissipate cares and Pindar a remedy for the passions of the mind" (Montagut [1619/20] 2000: 101).

In the case of recorded choreographies, another avenue to investigate the emotional content of a dance is through an examination of the floor plans. Such analysis reveals the interaction between individual dancers during the course of a dance. It also highlights any patterns or figures formed by the dancers and the significance and meaning behind such patterns. In an article from 1990, Ingrid Brainard discusses how the "changing relationships of the dancers to one another in the performance space" can create dramatic effect, and how social interaction between individuals is illustrated in the fifteenth-century Italian *balli*. She emphasizes how, "in the proper context, simple forward and backwards motions turn into the image of approach and withdrawal; sideways steps become evasive, half turns disdainful or refusing ... two dancers following one another along the same path create the image of flight and pursuit" (Brainard 1990: 90). Analyzing the changing relationships between the dancers during the course of a choreography is a very fruitful avenue for uncovering the emotional potential of such dances.[15] But this method still presents the modern researcher with challenges, as divining the portrayal of a specific emotion is subject to the interpretation of the written choreographic description and then the interpretive decisions required by a modern reconstruction and performance.

During the fifteenth to seventeenth centuries dance, like garden design and architecture, reflected the numerical order of the cosmos through the design principles of order and proportion. Thus the geometric patterns upon which many of the late sixteenth- and early seventeenth-century choreographies were built, and which were also found in fifteenth-century dances, had divine connotations. By reminding those watching of the nature of God, these geometric figures had a moral effect. In other words, people's emotional state, the state of their soul, could be affected by the movements of the dancers, inducing emotions of religious devotion. The belief that geometric patterns such as the square (a symbol of earth and its elements), the circle (a symbol of heaven and perfection), and the triangle (a symbol of the element of fire, the Trinity, and the path between the earthly and divine spheres), affected those viewing such patterns was a commonplace during this period, as the comments made by John Taylor after he had visited the garden at Wilton in 1623 demonstrate:

> [C]ircular, triangular, quadrangular, orbicular, oval, and every way curiously and chargeably conceited: there he hath made walks, hedges and arbours . . . planting them and placing them in such admirable art-like fashions, *resembling both divine and moral remembrances*, as three arbours standing in a triangle, having each a recourse to a greater arbour in the midst, resemble three in one and one in three.
>
> —Strong 1979: 122; emphasis added

The Personal Level

The emotions expressed by the dances performed at balls, or for private entertainments in the apartments of the elite, as well as the choreographies that formed part of theatrical spectacles, can be divided into two categories: the personal level and the state level. The first category is that of the personal level; that is, emotions experienced by individuals and which pertained to the relationships between individuals. The most obvious emotion in this category, and one that was seen at the time as being expressed by dancing per se, as well as in individual choreographies, is the emotion of joy, happiness or pleasure. Dancing was, at this time, a form of entertainment, especially in impromptu, unstructured, and private situations. The mere act of watching dancing gave pleasure. This was certainly true for Charles IX of France. Brantôme records how one day, while in ill-health, Charles IX ordered all to leave him apart from a few close friends. He then ordered the maréchal de Brissac and Filippo Strozzi, both exceptional dancers, to perform for him, with Strozzi playing the lute while de Brissac danced galliards and *canaries*. Brantôme records how the "king watched for a long time, full of pleasure and contentment at such a spectacle" (McGowan 2008a: 156). More formal dance performances were also a source of pleasure, as is illustrated by the festivities for the 1459 visit to Florence of Galeazzo Maria Sforza which included a dance and banquet in the *Mercato Nuovo*. In a poem describing the event, the joy and happiness felt by the dancers is emphasized by the anonymous author: "Do not ask if they had joyful hearts and if the young ladies kept a straight face, seeing so much respect being shown to them by their partners. That joyful dance seemed like a paradise of dancing angelic hierarchies, and everyone was full of joy and laughter" (Carsaniga 2004: 151–2).[16] At the same time, dance could also express the emotion of sexual attraction and desire, as the same poem illustrates: "I believe that the great and worthy ladies made a thousand fires burn on that day without tinder-box, flintstone, sulphur or wood ... Some dance, others sport, others jest, some stare at people and others are stared at, some are objects of desire, and others desire" (Carsaniga 2004: 152).[17] Even when a choreography was not ostensibly about sexual attraction, this aspect of dancing was still present and was recognized by those who were watching. For example, in 1572 when the French court celebrated the carnival season at Blois, Marguerite de Valois and ten of her ladies-in-waiting all performed a danced joust while costumed as men. Their opponents were all male dancers dressed as women. An eyewitness to this danced spectacle wrote that "they danced ... as though they were making love" (McGowan 2015: 196).

Thus if a ball itself provided the opportunity for the pursuit of one sex by the other, the actual choreographies, the step sequences and floor patterns as created by the dance masters, also aided in the ritual of courtship, as is the case of the sixteenth-century French collection of double branles called the gavotte, a dance which involved much kissing between all the male and female participants (Arbeau [1596] 1972: 93r). In fact, any physical contact between partners however temporary would be an important method of conveying the emotional content of a dance. In an age that was increasingly conscious of rank and social status, which were indicated by a host of subtle signals, no one would be able to ignore such an obvious sign as physical contact between dance partners, even if a choreography did not demand closer contact such as a kiss.

Specific emotions could also be portrayed in a single choreography, as in the *ballo Gelosia* by Domenico da Piacenza, which is an exploration of jealousy. In this dance for three couples, each man in turn weaves his way around the three women assessing each one as he does so. The choreography is performed three times with each man dancing with a new partner in each of the repeats, thus allowing plenty of opportunities for displays of jealousy in the men's approaches and departures from each new partner. On many occasions the virtuosic performances of highly skilled dancers evoked a feeling of amazement in those watching, as in 1546 when Piero Strozzi (one of the best dancers of his age), and other French courtiers stunned those watching with their incredible performance of virtuosic steps and leaps (McGowan 2012: 61). "Sixteenth-century audiences wanted to be dazzled," whether by acrobatic performances of professional dancers, or the dance expertise of courtiers (See Fig. 3.5) (McGowan 2008a: 229). Choreographies were also intentionally created to evoke laughter from those watching, as was the case in 1516 when gentlemen from the court performed comic dances in front of the French king and queen:

> these gentlemen of the king made a comic *moresca*, many of them having come with shirts on top of their doublets, and handkerchiefs on their heads, a coif of netting in front of their faces and peasant-style hose on their legs. And with burning torches in their hands they were dancing *moresche* in front of the king and queen.
>
> —Tamalio 1994: 269[18]

Religious devotion is another emotion portrayed by dancers during this period through the symbolism of the geometric patterns created during the course of the choreographies. A choreography from one version of Guglielmo Ebreo's treatise which is built around a single geometric shape is the *ballo Santomera*. The opening instructions of this dance are for the two women and one man to arrange themselves into a triangle, which is maintained throughout the majority of the dance (Guglielmo n.d.: 36r–36v). Many of the floor

FIGURE 3.5: An illustration of how a student can learn to perform virtuosic jumps such as the different types of *capriole*, from Cesare Negri, *Nuove inventioni di balli* (Milan, 1604. A re-edition of *Le gratie d'amore*). Courtesy of the Library of Congress, Washington, D.C.

patterns of this dance involve the three dancers moving around the perimeter of the triangle, tracing out this shape as they move. The triangular shape is also emphasized and maintained by floor patterns in which the three dancers all move toward each other to meet at the center of the triangle, then turn 180 degrees to return to their starting positions at the vertices of the triangle. Now it is not possible to state precisely what the choreographer of *Santomera* had in mind when devising this dance, but one can assume that the triangle as a symbol of the Trinity would be clear to those watching. For the educated viewer, the sustained presentation of the geometric figure of the triangle would be a visual reminder of the moral imperative to aspire to a closer knowledge of the divine nature.

In Spanish cities especially trained choirboys danced and sang in Corpus Christi processions, both inside the cathedrals and outside on stages erected in the streets around the churches. In this case it was the total dance performance that heightened the effect of religious devotion and rejoicing on the citizens of the city: the space in which the dancing occurred, the choreographic patterns and the performers themselves. The effect that these performances had on those watching by heightening their religious sentiments was recognized and commented upon at the time (Brooks 1991: 184).

Negative Emotions

When one looks at social dance overall during the fifteenth to early seventeenth centuries one can say that generally speaking the emotions expressed by dance were positive ones. Negative emotions such as fear, anger, frustration, despair, sorrow, guilt, envy, or melancholy do not appear in the recorded choreographies. There were some sections of society, however, that regarded the expression of emotions such as love and desire as totally undesirable in dancing. Views on the negative moral effects of dancing during the late medieval and early modern period were nuanced (see Arcangeli 2000 and Nevile 2008a: 295–310), but the expression of desire through dance did form the basis of many of the condemnations of dance during this period, a situation that was acknowledged by the dance masters in their treatises. Guglielmo Ebreo, for example, sought to distance the dance practice he taught from that enjoyed by lower, uneducated classes who were unable to appreciate it (1463: 23r), and who, by their performances, turned an art into "an adulterous and servile affair" and into "a pimp for their shameful lust in order that they can bastardize it, so that they can cautiously enjoy each voluptuous effect that comes from the dance" (6v–7r).

For theatrical dances, however, the situation was not so biased toward the presentation of positive emotions. Negative emotions were portrayed, but often by non-courtly dancers as in the English anti-masque dances from the early seventeenth century. A good illustration of such a portrayal are the anti-masque dances by the twelve hags in *The Masque of Queens* from 1609. The hags are all named and represent vices: their leader was Mischief, and her eleven followers were Ignorance, Suspicion, Credulity, Falsehood, Murmur, Malice, Impudence, Slander, Execration, Bitterness, and Rage. Their dances reflected their evil natures, through perverted and exaggerated movements which were interrupted with blasts of loud music. The music that accompanied their dancing also deviated from the norm, as it contained "short snatches of changing dance metre . . . mixed with long notes lacking any rhythm" (Daye 2014: 196).[19] Thus, both dance and music combined to convey a fearful, destructive picture of disorder and evil. On occasions, members of the elite did appear in less than flattering roles. The French were far more relaxed than the English about members of the court representing negative emotions on stage. One example of their more flexible attitude is that the role of the Demon of Vanity danced by François V, Comte de La Rochefoucauld in *La Délivrance de Renaud*. His costume for this role emphasized his vanity with its "huge feathered wings and, the ultimate symbol of pompous pride, the tail feathers of the male peacock on his head" (Downey 2010: 11).

The State Level

The second category of emotions are those that pertain to the wider society, such as civic pride, social order, and decorum, and those that are present in the relationship between individuals and the state. Social order was very important in early modern Europe, especially in Italy where rituals, ceremonies and deference patterns mattered greatly. Rulers fully understood that the reputation of their state depended as much on social order and protocol as it did on the lavishness of state expenditure and the splendor of official spectacles. One reason for their concern with social order was that the precise but correct gradations of position were a clear sign that their court "reflected not only a traditional social and political order, but also a higher, sacred order" (Lubkin 1994: 67). Dance was an important part of ritual events at this time, and was part of the ordered, formal behavior demanded by these events. Because one of the chief means of indicating rank was by spatial relationships among people, and dance was an art form with spatial relationships at its basis, throughout the Renaissance dance was a significant tool in the presentation of power and rank through rituals and ceremonies. For example, at the celebrations held in Milan in 1491 for the wedding of Ludovico Sforza to Beatrice d'Este (the daughter of Ercole d'Este and Eleonora d'Aragona), Eleonora wrote to her husband the duke, who had remained back in Ferrara, describing these events. Not only did the invited guests enter the hall in order of rank, so too did they dance in the same order. It was not until the women, who were closely connected to the ruling family, had danced that the other ladies of the court descended from the tribunal on which they were sitting to participate in the dancing.

Just as a dance was a clear and obvious expression of the ties which bound an individual to the wider social hierarchy, so was it also an expression of the ties and obligations between individuals within a family. The affirmation of familial ties through dance can be illustrated by the *giaranzana*, a dance performed by all the wedding guests both before and after the wedding ceremony.[20] The dance was performed by a long line of couples, who were put into position according to their order in the family in relation to the husband, and in order of their rank. The dance, which could last for over an hour, was one with complicated patterns and turnings, and it required many "modest, gracious and honourable gestures" (Altieri [c. 1500] 1995: 59). Each couple had to meet and acknowledge every other participant in the dance by taking their hand as a symbol of the happiness at the new marriage, and as a demonstration of joy and gratitude toward all the other members of the family (Altieri [c. 1500] 1995: 58–9).

One clear example of a dance evoking civic pride was the continuation of the ancient Roman custom of dancing the *tripudium* to celebrate a military victory. When peace returned to Padua in 1310 such festive dancing was part of the celebrations. In fact it was specifically mentioned in the speech by the podestà giving thanks for the restoration of peace, which began "by proclaiming that 'your letters of peace brought immense *gaudia* (joyfulness) to our hearts and led to the festive dancing of the *tripudium* with high exultation among the whole populace of Padua'" (Skinner 1999: 25).[21] Thus dancing a *tripudium* was considered to be the correct response of people to good news, and a natural expression of the joy people felt at living in a state of peace under the rule of justice.

Royal entries were also important occasions for a display of civic pride as they were ceremonies in which a city's status and rights, and those of its corporations, were reaffirmed (Russell and Visentin 2007: 16). Dance frequently played a major role in these entries, as is illustrated by the 1570 and 1599 entries into Madrid. The entry in 1570 occurred nine years after Philip II moved his court to Madrid, and the city wanted to emphasize its new status, with the town council going to "great lengths and expense to impress the sovereign and to justify its position as the seat of the court," by commissioning six dances (Cano 2005: 127).[22] The town council also insisted that they preview the dances twenty days before the entry occurred, in order to make sure they were of high enough quality and to allow time for any necessary changes to be made if they were unhappy with them. For the 1599 entry, the town council commissioned nineteen separate dances at a staggering cost of 5,777 ducats, shared between the city itself (one dance), the surrounding villages (four dances) and the guilds and merchants (fourteen dances). The contracts demanded that these dances were "to be very brilliant, as the occasion requires" (Cano 2005: 127).

How Dance Masters Portrayed Emotion: Manipulation of Dance Steps and Music

The variety of steps employed and their combination in a multitude of different sequences is one of the chief characteristics of Renaissance dance, a characteristic not found in medieval dance practices. Therefore it makes sense that the manipulation of individual steps and step sequences, in addition to their arrangement into specific floor plans and figures, was one way in which dance masters of the period created expressive choreographies, although exactly what constituted expressive steps did vary from one dance practice to another. One method of creating expressive steps was by an alteration in the rhythm of a step; that is, to change the total time it took to perform a step and/or to alter the temporal relationship between the individual movements in a step (for further details see Nevile 2003: 145–69). Other methods were the addition of extra movements such as a leap or a turn to a step, the performance of different gestures, and the performance of more difficult and longer variants of certain steps such as in the galliard (for more, see Kendall 2003: 170–90). The emotional content of a dance was also created by the juxtaposition of movement and stillness. In the fifteenth-century Italian dance practice the *posada* (pause) was part of the vocabulary of dance steps, as well as the concept of *fantasmata*. This subtle movement was an infinitesimal pause at the end of a step, and then a resumption of movement in an incredibly light and airy manner.[23] Often it was the combination of multiple choreographic elements in a single dance that created the portrayal of emotions. This is illustrated in the victory dance by Diana and her nymphs over Cupid and his followers from the 1575 masquerade by Pierre de Brach. The joy of the victors is expressed through lively, energetic steps—hops and jumps—gestures like hand-clapping and foot-stamping, a multitude of rapid, ever-changing patterns and figures, and a series of complicated interactions between the dancers.[24]

Dance masters also manipulated the music which accompanied their choreographies in order to increase a desired emotional effect. One method was by rhythmic alteration such as syncopation when the same musical material previously heard returns later in a dance, as in the *ballo Pizochara* (see Nevile 2004: 27 for further details). Another method used, particularly in theatrical spectacles, was altering the instrumentation employed at particular moments, as in the anti-masque dances from *The Masque of Queens*. Even in social dances the combative and aggressive nature of choreographed battle dances was enhanced by the music. For example, in the anonymous *balletto La Battaglia* for three couples (*La Battaglia* n.d.: 2r–5r), the music has repeated notes on the same pitch to sound like drums, and long elaborations of the tonic sonority to resemble trumpet calls, as well as an entire section taken from Clément Janequin's chanson *Escoutez tous, gentilz galoys* (*La guerre*).[25]

Conclusion

During the three hundred years from 1300 to 1600 dancing was seen as a means of conveying emotion, both between individual dancers and also between performers and spectators. The commonly held belief that dance had the power to move and to change people's emotions was stated in dance treatises from the fifteenth century onwards. In this period dance, through its connection to music and through the continuation of classical beliefs linking exterior movements of the body to the state of a person's soul, was inextricably tied to the expression of emotion at a personal level and at the wider state level. The choreographies created by the dance masters were vehicles for the expression of emotions, not only in theatrical spectacles such as de Brach's 1575 masquerade, where much emphasis is given in the description to the performers' emotions as depicted by their gestures, facial expressions, and bodily movements (Dawkins 1969: 11), but also in the social dances enjoyed at balls and impromptu gatherings.

CHAPTER FOUR

Drama

KATHRYN PRINCE

Drama is a productive site for analyzing medieval and early modern emotions. More than a literary text written in a particular genre, drama is the written trace of a performance (or, at least, of an intended performance) drawing together the multiple intersecting emotional communities of its spectators, performers, playwright, fictional characters, and originating theatrical culture. Drama demonstrates that emotions are, as Monique Scheer (2012) has theorized, a practice: in performance, emotions are practiced by their mobilization, naming, communication, and regulation in full view of the audience and in ways designed to be intelligible to that audience. Laughter, tears and applause are only the most perceptible signs of spectators' emotional responses. In its capacity to illustrate emotional practices, drama is also, in one fundamental respect, unique: the actors are practicing emotions not their own, but nevertheless, if all goes well, these counterfeit emotions will elicit genuine emotional responses in the audience. Textual insincerity, which Barbara Rosenwein identifies as a theoretical possibility in literary emotions (2006: 28–9), is always present in drama because of its implied performance by actors; drama therefore enables an especially nuanced reading of the emotional work of words. The conventions governing interactions between an actor's fictional and real feelings, between the fictional world of the play and the real world of the spectators, and between the act of spectatorship and the practice of living, are historically and culturally contingent. Attending to emotions produces a theater history in which these interactions are distinguishing features of different theater-making cultures. Understanding the practice of emotions in relation to late medieval and early modern drama can enrich not only the theater history of these periods but also emotions history, particularly because the techniques of performance have a way of escaping the theater. After all, as the medieval German drama scholar Eckehard Simon observes in *The Theatre of Medieval Europe*, drama "was the only form of 'literature' practiced in churches and market squares, on the streets and in houses. Poems, romances and chronicles were heard in several dozen courts by perhaps a few thousand members of the gentry. Theatre, however, was for everybody" (1991: xviii).

"Theater," in the period covered here, ranges from the sprawling, outdoor performances of the Easter, Passion, and Corpus Christi plays enacted by casts of dozens or hundreds of amateurs in towns across Europe to farces written for the amusement of a small côterie, and from the allegorical abstraction of *Everyman*, with its *dramatis personae* of personifications, to the intense interiority of *Hamlet*'s soliloquizing hero. The focus here is on vernacular drama, though liturgical drama sung in Latin persists though this period, in some countries quite significantly. The rise of the vernacular tradition serves as a useful starting point for a period that includes such diverse forms as the mysteries and morality plays prevalent across Europe, the birth of *commedia dell'arte* in Italy and revenge tragedy in England, the dawn of the Dutch and Spanish Golden Ages, and the theatrical debut of Shakespeare's *Hamlet*, the play that serves here as an extended case study and touchstone.

SACRED AND SECULAR SPACES

"The theater," as a concept denoting a particular kind of space as well as a category of performing art, is not quite applicable to early drama before the construction of purpose-built theaters in the sixteenth century or, at least, the repurposing of existing structures as permanent designated spaces for performance. Before the sixteenth century, and into and past it, theatrical performance happened in spaces more usually employed for other purposes. Liturgical drama borrowed from the holiness of the sacred spaces in which it was performed, whereas "mysteries" (Corpus Christi, Easter, and Passion plays), with the same general cast of characters and plot, extruded this sacred element from the church into secular, public, outdoor spaces. Before the first real theater spaces were created, village greens, town squares, inns, and great halls served as temporary performance venues. English scholars, beginning with Glynne Wickham's *Early English Stages* (1959), have tended to use space rather than theme as the organizing principle in categorizing medieval plays; specifically, it is useful to understand the genres of medieval drama in terms of indoor versus outdoor performance because the boundary between them is more tenable than that between secular and religious drama. The holy and the profane are often mingled in a single play, as Simon notes: "In Easter and Passion plays the marketplace quack with his surly wife and sassy servant sells ointment to the Marys walking to Christ's sepulchre," while in the secular Carnival plays biblical episodes like "Daniel saving Susanna, Saint George slaying the dragon, and the priest Theophilus pacting with the devil" provided merriment with a religious undertone (2008: 12). While Wickham's reasons for focusing on space as an organizing principle are not primarily related to the emotions, the result is fortuitous for emotions scholars because it both sidesteps a problem of classification—the evidence does not support a distinction between "secular" and "religious" emotions—and underscores the ways in which spaces can influence emotions.

While a pageant wagon might boast lavish costumes and props furnished by the guild responsible for performing part of a mystery cycle, these wagons had fairly limited scenic resources in which to create a sense of their settings; their meaning was achieved partly as a result of their movement through space rather than their organization of it. An alternative to the pageant wagons, place-and-scaffold staging, used space strategically: drawing on practices developed in the meaningful spaces of the Christian churches where the liturgical plays were performed, medieval place-and-scaffold performances constructed a semiotically rich vista in which the characters' journey from this world to the afterlife was inscribed in movement that had both literal and metaphysical dimensions. Robert Weimann has suggested, drawing on the earlier work of Richard Southern, that the place and scaffold each convey particular kinds of meaning, with the locus, or place, nearly co-extensive with the real world of the spectators it abuts, while the platea, or scaffold, more often represents a specific, fictional location (1978: 73–85, 196–246).

These notions of real and fictional are not unproblematic, as Erika Lin (2006) has recognized in her sustained interrogation of Weimann's influential theory. One solution, drawing on French drama scholarship, is to triangulate between Weimann's locus and platea and Alan Knight's useful distinction between real and fictional in *Aspects of Genre in Late Medieval French Drama* (1983). Knight distinguishes between plays that inhabit the real world as it was seen in the medieval period (including, therefore, biblical elements)

FIGURE 4.1: Scant visual evidence of English mystery play staging survives. David Sharp's copper engraving, "Representation of a Pageant Vehicle at the time of Performance," imagines a fifteenth-century performance. From Thomas Sharp, *A Dissertation on the Pageants or Dramatic Mysteries Anciently Performed at Coventry* (Coventry: 1825). Image courtesy of Wikimedia Commons.

and those that inhabit an imaginary one governed, for example, by folly (farces) or fairness and reason (morality plays). These distinctions, though perhaps somewhat counterintuitive when approached with modern skepticism about biblical truth, help to illuminate some of the emotional tendencies of these genres, and to clarify some of the latent elements of Weimann's locus and platea: the locus, seen in the light of Knight's genres, would be the site of biblical, historical, and other accepted kinds of truth, while the platea would be the site of imaginative spaces governed by moral laws better or worse than those of the real world. As Knight explains, farce is an "ethical jungle in which only the shrewd are fit for survival" (1983: 53), inferior to the real world, while in morality plays "there is always a higher power to punish the wicked and reward the good" (54).

FIGURE 4.2: Pacino di Bonaguida, *The Crucifixion*, detail, c. 1315–20, tempera and gold leaf on panel, 32 × 17 1/2 in. Fondazione di Studi di Storia dell'Arte Roberto Longhi di Firenze. Courtesy of Getty Images.

These spatial semiotics are apparent in the extensive, unparalleled documentary records relating to late sixteenth-century performances of the *Lucerne Passion Play*. The city clerk Renward Cysat, the director and, earlier, a performer, documented the staging, scenography, casting, and every other conceivable element of the cycle's performance. In Cysat's sketch of the place-and-scaffold set for the 1568 performance, the scaffolds appear to be arranged so that God is in the East looking down on the action below, flanked by the scaffolds for groups of virtuous characters, with the Devil opposite him in the West in front of a gaping hell mouth and surrounded by scaffolds for the wicked (Simon 2008: 18). Cysat's extensive notes about the performance of the *Lucerne Passion Play* indicate his thoughtful use of reality effects on the platform, such as a purpose-built stream and a fountain stocked with fish to be caught, but more astonishing *coups de théâtre* on the scaffold, such as a flock of doves released (or, to his frustration, not quite released) at the moment of Christ's birth. Together these effects suggest that the mobilization of curiosity, surprise, and wonder may have spatial affiliations, at least in medieval place-and-scaffold staging. If Weimann is correct, some of the semiotics of locus and platea remain discernible in early modern performance, informing the emotional practices of plays written for the early playhouses. An alternative semiotics of space became possible once playwrights and their companies began to operate within purpose-built early modern theaters; together, playwrights, actors, and audiences learned to make these spaces mean, as Tim Fitzpatrick demonstrates with extensive textual evidence in *Playwright, Space, and Place in Early Modern Performance* (2011). Although Fitzpatrick focuses on the playhouses of Shakespeare's company, his argument about the semiotics of space, if not the actual details of the conventions governing meaningful doors and movements through them, can be usefully applied to other early modern theaters across Europe.

EMOTIONAL PRACTICES

Identifying the conventions that shape emotional practices relating to a play's characters, actors, spectators, playwright, genre, and originating culture is the basis of emotions analysis. Drama from this period draws on rhetorical techniques also employed outside the theater, often by the same people: France's *Basochiens* were lawyers as well as satirists, and their texts are redolent of legal practice, while Shakespeare's early plays have an odor of schoolroom encounters with Plautus and Seneca. Although drama ultimately relies on more than the written text to enact its emotional labors of mobilization and regulation, textual analysis is a crucial component of emotions analysis. Early modern actors' mnemonic techniques and the connection between classical education and dramatic composition underpin Robert Cockcroft's analysis of "rhetorical affect" in early modern drama (2003). While Cockcroft devotes very little attention to *Hamlet* in his wide-ranging and detailed book, a rhetorical analysis of Hamlet's "to be or not to be" speech based on his methods, and drawing also on the considerable existing rhetorical analysis of this play that is not explicitly emotions-oriented, clearly illustrates that *Hamlet* draws amply on rhetorical structures and techniques that Cockcroft identifies as affective:

> To be, or not to be: that is the question;
> Whether tis nobler in the mind to suffer
> The slings and arrows of outrageous fortune
> Or to take arms against a sea of troubles
> And by opposing end them.
>
> —Shakespeare 2013a: 3.1.56–60

These opening lines of the monologue use antithesis ("To be, or not to be") and a rhetorical question ("that is the question"), metaphor ("slings and arrows of outrageous fortune," "a sea of troubles") and the beginning of a plan ("by opposing end them"). In the next section of the speech, Hamlet begins to articulate the goal that this plan tends toward:

> ... To die—to sleep,
> No more; and by a sleep to say we end
> The heartache and the thousand natural shocks
> That flesh is heir to: tis a consummation
> Devoutly to be wishd.
>
> —Shakespeare 2013a: 3.1.60–4

Employing metaphor again, Hamlet repeats "to die: to sleep" in order to develop it further: death both is and is not like sleep. This repetition implies an evolution in his thinking; he is inviting the listener along on an exploration. He also introduces another rhetorical strategy, inclusion, to create the impression of a fellowship between himself and his listener. These are evident in the use of "we" and "us":

> . . . To die, to sleep;
> To sleep, perchance to dream—ay, there's the rub:
> For in that sleep of death what dreams may come,
> When we have shuffled off this mortal coil,
> Must give us pause—there's the respect
> That makes calamity of so long life.
>
> —Shakespeare 2013a: 3.1.64–9

As a literary text, Hamlet's "To be, or not to be" soliloquy appears to be entirely engaged with communicating Hamlet's complex emotional response to his father's death and mother's remarriage to the murderer, in a way that is rhetorically compelling. This act of communication happens only in the emotional community shared by the actor and the audience; within the conventions of the fictional world, Hamlet is speaking only to himself and therefore cannot be understood to be communicating these feelings to anyone. The purpose of rhetorical affect is to move the listener, but within the fictional world Hamlet moves only himself. Within the bounds of the fiction, Hamlet's emotional practices are less about communicating emotions than about mobilizing them; in the fiction, Hamlet is articulating these feelings to make himself more fully feel them. Once he has mobilized his feelings, Hamlet regulates them by referring to the Christian prohibition against suicide and the related notion of conscience; the arrival of Ophelia, at the end of the soliloquy, imposes an additional form of regulation:

> For who would bear the whips and scorns of time,
> Th'oppressor's wrong, the proud man's contumely,
> The pangs of dispriz'd love, the law's delay,
> The insolence of office, and the spurns
> That patient merit of th'unworthy takes,
> When he himself might his quietus make
> With a bare bodkin? Who would fardels bear
> To grunt and sweat under a weary life,
> But that the dread of something after death,
> The undiscovered country from whose bourn
> No traveller returns, puzzles the will,
> And makes us rather bear those ills we have
> Than fly to others that we know not of?
> Thus conscience does make cowards of us all,
> And thus the native hue of resolution
> Is sicklied o'er with the pale cast of thought,
> And enterprises of great pitch and moment
> With this regard their currents turn awry
> And lose the name of action. Soft you now,
> The fair Ophelia! Nymph, in thy orisons
> Be all my sins remember'd.
>
> —Shakespeare 2013a: 3.1.70–90

The distinction between Hamlet mobilizing and regulating his own emotions alone in Elsinore and communicating them to an audience in London, and thus the distinction between the world real to the characters and the one real to the spectators, implies the existence of different emotional communities, each with their own conventions. Moreover, it implies the acceptance that Hamlet has an inner life, or, as he expresses it, "that within which passes show" (Shakespeare 2013a: 1.2.85). This inwardness emerges in the early modern period, not only in early modern England, but also, perhaps even more acutely, in Spain. This fascination with interiority emerges for reasons having to do as much with religious turmoil and medical investigation as with theatrical pleasure, as Katherine Eisamann Maus (1995), Gail Kern Paster (1993, 2004) and Debora Shuger (1990) among many others have analyzed.

While inwardness is an issue of theoretical and philosophical concern in the early modern period, and an urgently practical one in the context of the Spanish Inquisition, introducing it as a dramatic technique poses a serious problem for theatrical performance: how can an actor signal inwardness to an audience? Somewhere between the surface-only characters of *Everyman* and the inward-looking Hamlet, this emerges as a technique, though to see this inwardness as Shakespeare's innovation, as Harold Bloom does in *Shakespeare: The Invention of the Human* ([1998] 1999), is to discount the effect of onstage prayer in the medieval mysteries. In early modern drama, the soliloquy seems to arise from the need to address inwardness onstage. According to the conventions apparent in early modern plays, a character speaking in soliloquy is speaking sincerely, though as we have seen the soliloquy convention does not eliminate the difficulties introduced by the purposes these speeches serve in and out of the fictional world.

EMOTIONAL COMMUNITIES

Taking into account these early modern cultural and theatrical contexts can illuminate the particular emotions being practiced in *Hamlet* by more fully developing the emotional communities that Shakespeare and his earliest audiences inhabited. Shakespeare is not co-extensive with his culture, and descriptions of what E. M. W. Tillyard once famously called the "Elizabethan World Picture" can never be the full picture of what Shakespeare thought and felt, but they can offer some sense of the different emotional communities that intersect to create Shakespeare's individual habitus. Both Pierre Bourdieu (1990: 52–65) and, drawing on him, Monique Scheer (2012: 201–3) suggest that habitus is a productive way of considering the various influences that shape how an individual responds to the communities that surround him. Because Shakespeare has been such a prominent figure in the Western canon, shelves of books like Tillyard's have patiently developed a detailed portrait of various aspects of those communities, but all playwrights inhabit multiple intersecting emotional communities than can illuminate their emotional practices. Introductions to critical editions of medieval and early modern plays usually provide some useful biographical and cultural context about religious and political affiliations, collaborators and coteries, and family networks; familiarity with the playwright's habitus offers only a limited understanding of the emotional practices in a play, however, since most playwrights are able to imagine emotional communities to which they do not belong.

Cultural context can be advantageous in the case of anonymous plays. While *The Somonyng of Everyman* (first published both anonymously and without its title around 1515) is not amenable to biographical criticism, some knowledge of the emotional communities of its time can shed light on its emotional practices. *Everyman* is one of a cluster of related plays that appear to be adapted from the Dutch play *Den Spieghel der Salicheit van Elckerlijc* (*The Mirror of Bliss of Everyman*) attributed to Peter van Diest (1496), itself drawing on an earlier Buddhist text that had been translated and circulated in Europe as a parable about false friendship (see Conley 1969). Comparative literary analysis has shed light on the relationship between *Everyman* and *Elckerlijc*; since both focus on Everyman's emotions as he confronts his own mortality, the particular ways in which they move their protagonist from fear to acceptance, an analysis of their emotional practices would, in theory, illuminate differences in emotional practices, potentially helping, perhaps, to identify characteristically English or Low Countries practices. However, because the entire English morality play genre is limited to five extant examples including *Everyman*, and because these examples have their own intertextual and intercultural affiliations, it is in practice quite impossible to find an English baseline against which to calibrate the emotions of *Everyman*. *Everyman* is, in fact, part of the way in which the emotions of medieval morality plays are understood; it turns out that as a genre the English morality play is inextricably connected to the *Rederijke*, or rhetorician, tradition of the Low Countries through this play. Rhetoric is, of course, a significant aspect of medieval and early modern drama.

CONCEPTUAL BLENDING

Understanding the complex nature of the dramatic text, with its intersecting emotional communities, is only one step in analyzing the emotional practices of drama. The multisensory nature of theatrical performance lends itself to complex emotional effects, and these are apparent, indeed, inevitable, in the drama of this period. Once the priests relinquished the performance of the *Quem quaeritis* ("whom do you seek") of the Easter liturgy to their congregations, European theater was community theater and, in many respects, it remained so throughout this period, even alongside the professional acting companies that were eventually formed in the sixteenth century.

Mysteries, the most widespread form of drama in the late medieval period, involved large numbers of amateur performers whose identities and affiliations, particularly guild memberships, remained recognizable. As Pamela King suggests, in the *York Corpus Christi Plays*, in which different guilds took responsibility for different sections of the cycle, the spectator is not only focused on the characters of Pilate and Christ, but on the particular nature of this Pilate and this Christ: the "Butchers' Pilate and the Butchers' Christ on the Cross," in contrast with the "Tapiters' or Tilemakers' Pilate or the just-disappearing Pinners' Christ" (2000: 161). The procession of the pageant wagons meant that different theatrical moments were simultaneously visible and audible to audiences who cared to direct their attention away from the wagon directly ahead of them; this simultaneity is an even more marked feature of the place-and-scaffold performances, which could stage simultaneous action in several playing spaces at once, with an effect akin to the triptych employed in painting at this time. Just as in a triptych the three paintings are separate but relate to one another thematically, so moments enacted on separate scaffolds might reflect a deeper meaning when beheld together.

This kind of triangulation of meaning is always present when an actor is performing a character, since the actor and the character are both, in some sense, present on stage. The relationship between the emotions and sensations of the actor and those of the character has been negotiated and understood in different ways by different theater-making cultures, many of them analyzed in Joseph Roach's *The Player's Passion: Studies in the Science of Acting* (1993). Roach focuses primarily on the physiology of actors' emotions, situating performance techniques within each period's scientific understanding of the body and its passions, and his analysis begins with the seventeenth century. While this approach is illuminating in regard to early modern drama, the notion of mimesis grounded in Aristotle and practiced in early modern acting would have been of little use to an actor attempting to get in touch with the feelings of God or Five Wits in *Everyman*, or to a spectator seeing different neighbors playing Christ on a succession of pageant wagons.

If medieval spectators were always or at times aware of the person playing the character—the local butcher and tapiter and tilemaker each taking their turn at playing a version of Pilate or Christ—such was also the case for a spectator watching a leading actor like Richard Burbage or Will Kemp in Shakespeare's time, each man's previous roles and reputation blending with his performance. Shakespeare built that blending into his plays: in *Hamlet*, Polonius's remark that he once played the role of Julius Caesar reminds at least some alert spectators that the actor playing Polonius really did also play Caesar. In medieval theater, that blending was more likely to be between life and art, but in both cases awareness of the actor behind the character bleeds through and brings with it emotions that may belong to an entirely different context.

That bleed-through is a variety of conceptual blending, a term used in cognitive linguistics to explain how human thought processing occurs in relation to the semantic ambiguity of metaphorical language. While cognitive science and the history of emotions are not always compatible, and while the term is used here without reference to the neurobiological processes that it entails in cognitive science, conceptual blending is a useful term to explain a mechanism employed in drama that has also been variously described as oscillation, allegory, or upsurges of the real. As Amy Cook explains in her application of conceptual blending theory to Shakespeare, it is the "projection of information from two or more input spaces to a blended space, such that the blended meaning contains information and structure from more than one space," with a result that is "not a combination or a blurring of two ideas, it is a complicated network evoked and integrated to create a new idea" (2010: 11). When Shakespeare critic Norman Rabkin (1977) borrows from the art historian E. H. Gombrich to explain how Shakespeare's *Henry V* oscillates between incompatible and irreducible views of its hero in his often-cited "Rabbits, Ducks, and *Henry V*," what he is describing is a form of conceptual blending that allows the audience to interpret Henry's actions as both heroic and Machiavellian, both sincere and manipulative, and to form a view of the play that, while never resolving these incompatibilities, allows them to coexist. Similarly, the allegorical characters in medieval drama, such as those in *Everyman*, are dependent on conceptual blending; the actor performing Good Deeds or Fellowship or Strength is serving both a representational and a metonymic function. That the audience should attend to the play with this conceptual blending is explicit in the prologue, spoken by a messenger:

> I pray you all give your audience
> And hear this matter with reverence,
> By figure, a moral play:
> *The Summoning of Everyman* called it is,
> That of our lives and ending shows
> How transitory we be all day.
> This matter is wondrous precious,
> But the intent of it is more gracious
> And sweet to bear away.

> The story saith: Man, in the beginning,
> Look well and take good heed to the ending,
> Be you never so gay!
> Ye think sin in the beginning full sweet,
> Which in the end causeth thy soul to weep,
> When the body lieth in clay.
> Here shall you see how Fellowship and Jollity,
> Both Strength, Pleasure and Beauty,
> Will fade from thee as flower in May;
> For ye shall hear how our heavenly king
> Calleth Everyman to a general reckoning.
> Give audience and hear what he doth say.
>
> —Bruster and Rasmussen 2009: Pro. 1–20

After this prologue, God and Death discuss their plans to make an example of Everyman, reinforcing the allegorical nature of this play. This prologue is unique to the English text; in *Elckerlijc*, God gets the opening lines; the English translator has chosen to reinforce the allegorical structure and underscore the conceptual blending.

This oscillating way of understanding medieval drama is entirely consistent with medieval ways of theorizing the experience of watching a play, Jill Stevenson argues in her influential and compelling book *Performance, Cognitive Theory, and Devotional Culture* (2010). For Stevenson, the point of conceptual blending in the context of medieval drama is to infuse the everyday with the divine, resulting in a particular kind of affective piety that results from the physiological and psychological after-effects of watching human bodies perform in holy plays and sacred processions make their way through secular spaces. The actor's body and the space of performance are especially susceptible to what the theater phenomenologist Bert O. States and the theorist of postdramatic theater Hans-Thies Lehmann have described as incursions of "the real" into the theatrical illusion (States 1985: passim; Lehmann 2006: 99). While this intrusion of "the real" into the experience of a dramatic fiction is primarily associated, for States and Lehman, with contemporary theater, their theorizations of the relationship between the fictional and the real are useful in understanding some of the mechanisms that create oscillations in audience's experience of early theater. A spectator's awareness of the neighbor's usual identity within his performance of Pilate or Christ, or the town square's usual uses within its appropriation as a performance space, creates these incursions. The prologue to *Henry V*, with its direct appeal to the audience's imagination, is a case study in the kind of conceptual blending that occurs when a fictional world is mapped onto a real space, but in this case a theater building. It seems that in *Henry V* Shakespeare needs to work to create the conceptual blending that, in medieval theater, was inevitably present:

> O for a Muse of fire, that would ascend
> The brightest heaven of invention,
> A kingdom for a stage, princes to act,
> And monarchs to behold the swelling scene!
> Then should the warlike Harry, like himself,
> Assume the port of Mars, and at his heels,
> Leashed in like hounds, should famine, sword and fire
> Crouch for employment. But pardon, gentles all,
> The flat unraised spirits that have dared

On this unworthy scaffold to bring forth
So great an object. Can this cockpit hold
The vasty fields of France? Or may we cram
Within this wooden O the very casques
That did affright the air at Agincourt?
O, pardon, since a crooked figure may
Attest in little place a million,
And let us, ciphers to this great account,
On your imaginary forces work.
Suppose within the girdle of these walls
Are now confined two mighty monarchies,
Whose high upreared and abutting fronts
The perilous narrow ocean parts asunder.
Piece out our imperfections with your thoughts.
Into a thousand parts divide one man
And make imaginary puissance.
Think when we talk of horses, that you see them
Printing their proud hoofs i' th'receiving earth;
For 'tis your thoughts that now must deck our kings,
Carry them here and there, jumping o'er times,
Turning th'accomplishment of many years
Into an hour-glass: for the which supply,
Admit me Chorus to this history;
Who prologue-like your humble patience pray,
Gently to hear, kindly to judge, our play.

—Shakespeare 2013b: Pro. 1–35

While the prologue does little to convince the spectators that the onstage world is realistic, this is not its objective. By drawing attention to the dual presence of fictional and real persons, places, and things within the "wooden O" of the theater space, the prologue achieves something that, though Shakespeare's contemporaries would not have recognized the term, seems to be a variety of conceptual blending. The specific mention of the "scaffold," here the forestage area closest to the audience, suggests, also, an alignment between the Chorus's world view and the spectators, if Weimann is correct about the survival of locus and platea semiotics.

THE ACTOR'S DILEMMA

A particular form of conceptual blending, Julia Kristeva's "eruption of the Real," is discernible in all genres of late medieval and early modern drama. Kristeva theorized that art, including theater, is one way in which cultures deal with the emotions associated with the functions of the human body that we prefer to avoid, such as defecation and dying, respectively favorite subjects of medieval secular and religious drama (Kristeva 1982: 3). While morality plays like *Everyman* and *Elckerlijc* name, communicate, mobilize, and regulate the emotions associated with death, moving from fear and regret toward acceptance, medieval farces also move toward acceptance, but from a pathway that begins with disgust and shame, as in the case of the French *Farce of the Fart* (*Farce nouvelle et fort joyeuse du Pect*) (in Enders 2011: 65–85) or the *Farce of the Woman Whose Neighbor*

FIGURE 4.3: Phillippe de Champaigne, *Still Life with a Skull*, 1644, oil on panel, 28 × 37 cm, Musée de Tessé, Le Mans. The painting combines symbols used in *memento mori* painting and in *Hamlet*. Image courtesy of Wikimedia Commons.

Gives Her an Enema (*Farce d'une Femme a qui son Voisin baille ung clistoire*) (in Enders 2011: 194–218), both obviously dealing with the bodily functions; one of the earliest extant German plays, the *St. Paul (Swabian) Neidhart Play* (circa 1370), includes, as its inciting incident, the courtier Neidhart's humiliation when he inadvertently proffers, as a gift to his mistress, excrement instead of a flower; most German *Fastnachtspiele* are about excrement and other embarrassing emissions of the human body. *Memento mori* imagery and what Susan Morrison (2008) has memorably called "fecopoetics" are characteristic structures of feeling in the medieval period, both of them concerned with practicing the emotions connected to the abject human body in ways connected to rhetorical affect. There are cultural variations about what gets the farcical treatment, as a Dutch example shows: while defecation is a typical subject elsewhere, the six *sotternieën* in the Dutch Van Hulthem manuscript satirize unruly women and the men they fool, and are bound into the manuscript with four serious plays about love, the *abele spelen*.

Hamlet is, of course, rhetorically obsessed with the human body, especially its decay and death. The abject is the source of the powerful image-clusters that Shakespeare uses to mobilize emotions, so powerful that Yorick's skull and the notion of something "rotten in the state of Denmark" (Shakespeare 2013a: 1.4.90) have wafted out of the play into the popular imagination as surely as the stench of Polonius's decaying body that, farcically, Hamlet imagines will become perceptible if the courtiers fail to locate his body before they "nose him as you go up the stairs into the lobby" (Shakespeare 2013a: 4.3.35–6).

AFFECTIVE PIETY AND PATHOPOEIA

Abjection can elicit a range of emotions including disgust, compassion, and, in the case of Hamlet's jest, amusement tinged, tragically, with pity and fear. When drama mobilizes empathy for Christ's suffering body, for example in the mysteries performed in towns across medieval Europe, abjection is associated with an emotional practice that medievalists, following Caroline Walker Bynum's introduction of the term, have referred to as affective piety. Beyond mobilizing spectators' emotions toward religious ends, the affective piety present in these plays, Herman Roodenberg has suggested, evolved into a sophisticated emotional practice of pathopoeia, a "conscious crafting of the believers' emotions" (2014: 44).

One problem addressed within this emerging medieval pathopoeia is the grief of the Virgin Mary, and, more particularly, its potential to distract attention from the suffering of Christ. As Roodenberg notes in relation to the Low Countries (2014) and Katharine Goodland suggests in relation to the York, Chester, N-Town, and Towneley–Wakefield cycles (2005a and 2005b), Mary's grief is both an aesthetic and a religious problem. The difficulty is not only with women's mourning, though all four extant English cycles depict situations in which women other than Mary are exhorted, by men, to control their lamentations on religious grounds: there is a consolation in the Christian notion of heaven that these women, in their spectacular grief, are ignoring. Excessive mourning is a challenge to the Christian faith in an afterlife, but Mary's grief is also aesthetically challenging because it shares the stage with Christ's abject body and diverts attention from it.

Despite attempts to control their expressions of grief, other excessively grieving women, including Mary Magdalene, Martha, and the mothers of the slaughtered innocents, are able to engage in elaborate weeping, lamenting, and rending their hair and garments, all their emotional excess eventually leading to divine intervention. When Christ's suffering body is the spectacle, the Virgin Mary's manifestations of grief, Goodman suggests, become artistically problematic. Even though her grief corresponds to the pattern set up by these other women in which unfettered lamentation is rewarded, the particular ways in which the medieval Mary communicates her grief detract from the affective work of Christ's suffering. In order to shift the emphasis from Mary to Christ, these plays employ a set of rhetorical strategies that ritualize, aestheticize, and contain her grief.

The eventual evacuation of Mary from this dramatic tradition in England after the Reformation, despite the perseverance of the cycles themselves in revised form, only completes the erasure begun for pathopeiac and dramaturgical reasons in order to increase the affective piety experienced through a more sustained focus on Christ's suffering. There is, perhaps, an echo of the medieval mystery in the three lamenting women of Shakespeare's *Richard III*, whose grief follows the medieval dramaturgical tradition and succeeds in toppling the play's anti-hero. Given the connections between the historical Richard III and the city of York, this is a tantalizing intertext drawing together the emotional communities of the fictional medieval York of Shakespeare's play and the city's real culture captured in the York cycle when it was transcribed at some point in the 1460s or 1470s.

Productive as that intertextual reading might be, on the post-Reformation English stage the epitome of female grief is not the lamenting women of the mysteries but Hecuba. When Hamlet laments his own overly temperate emotions in response to his father's murder, he invokes the Trojan queen, or, more precisely, a traveling actor's depiction of her, as the symbol of his shortcomings. Remembering that moving performance of Hecuba's grief enables Hamlet to mobilize his own, but, as the plot of *Hamlet* illustrates, grief can become vengefulness. Indeed, it is through the conscious mobilization of his grief by remembering the touring actor's Hecuba that Hamlet hopes to locate his own dormant vengefulness. *Hamlet*'s generic affiliation with revenge tragedy perhaps occludes the extent to which the mobilization of grief is also associated, through the figures of grieving women, with justice and divine intervention, a connection that the denouement suggests when Hamlet relinquishes his revenge quest to the workings of Providence.

If *Hamlet* is connected to the medieval mysteries in this way, it also bears more than a passing resemblance to farce in its exploration of disgust. The moral world that *Hamlet* seeks to inhabit seems to be distinct from the "real" world of Elsinore and of England, and in its mobilization of the themes of the platea it illustrates how the morality play and farce can function as two sides of a single coin. The disgust that medieval farce regulates cannot be contained in *Hamlet*, something that T. S. Eliot noticed when he remarked that Hamlet's "disgust is occasioned by his mother, but his mother is not an adequate equivalent for it; his disgust envelops and exceeds her" (1920: 92). The viciousness with which Hamlet articulates this disgust, toward Gertrude and especially toward Ophelia in the "get thee to a nunnery" scene, suggests an emotional practice beyond literary rhetoric.

MOBILIZING AND REGULATING EMOTIONS

Affective piety, pathopoeia, and Hamlet's aggressive articulations of disgust are oriented toward the mobilization of emotions, but theater itself often serves to regulate, as well as mobilize, emotions. Early modern drama often resonates with Aristotle's understanding, in the *Poetics* (5th century BCE), of theater's potential to purge or purify pity and fear, leading to catharsis. Analysis of the emotional effects of early modern tragedies tends to employ Aristotle's catharsis as fundamentally a theory about theater's potential to provide this emotional regulation through the experience of pity and fear, though without much consensus about the end result. Catharsis applies very well to *Hamlet*, but not especially well to medieval drama or to a great deal of early modern drama that is not cathartically tragic in nature. In a Christian context, where death is only an intermediate step toward salvation, catharsis can be imagined to have been replaced with affective piety.

Drama is strongly connected to Horace's notion in *Ars Poetica* (1st century BCE) that the point of theater is to profit and please its audience (ll. 333–46; see Hardison and Golden 1995: 17–18 for a translation of this passage and 72–4 for an analysis). While the notion of an intellectual or moral benefit (which is how the "profit" is usually interpreted, and sometimes translated) is most obviously true for plays in the religious tradition, it also applies to farces, though the balance between profit and pleasure shifts toward the latter; if profit can include lessons in how to regulate emotions of disgust and shame, then farce includes much profit alongside the pleasures of its humor. France's *sociétés joyeuses*, one source of medieval French comedy, are perhaps the strongest example of a theater-making culture focused on mobilizing pleasure above all else. As something akin to the Freemasons of fun, or sanctioned fools without masters, these *sociétés* are an appealing future site for emotions research, alongside the amateur satirists *les Basochiens* and other amateur theatrical groups creating some of the earliest secular drama.

In the *Republic*, Plato argues that the feelings generated by theater are indistinguishable from those generated by real life, that it "feeds and waters" feelings associated with sex and anger or "buffooneries" that would otherwise wither (see Jowett [1871] 2010: 122). Plato's complaint is about theater's potential to mobilize emotions, and this mobilization potentially occurs each time a play is performed, years, decades, even centuries after its creation. Performing early vernacular plays circulates their emotions anew; when a modern spectator laughs at a medieval fart joke, a link is forged to the emotional communities that made it. As Mikhail Bakhtin observed in *Rabelais and His World*, understanding the laughter of the past is key to understanding the culture of the past (1984: 6); weeping, too, is a key to the past, though what a culture finds lamentable is perhaps less particular than what it finds hilarious, given the persistence of classical and early modern tragedy in the contemporary repertoire. Contemporary performance can be a powerful introduction to historical emotions, but a somewhat problematic one. Though not particularly focused on the history of emotions, recent feminist scholarship, especially Kim Solga's influential study *Violence Against Women in Early Modern Drama* (2009), has amply demonstrated that performing certain emotions transhistorically—in Solga's case, the emotions associated with rape and domestic violence—can have unintended ethical consequences, particularly when psychological realism is a dominant performance technique. Building on this strand of feminist scholarship in light of emotions scholarship, it seems clear that performance can create a misleading sense of proximity between historical and contemporary emotions. The evolutionary psychologist Paul Ekman (2003), in his book popularizing his theory of universal human emotions, repeatedly returns to the idea of an actor making faces to which spectators cannot help but respond emotionally on a primal level. This is a naïve view of the actor's art: numerous contemporary acting approaches eschew psychological or (to coin a term) biological realism and may be better equipped to capture historical emotional practices or to foreground emotions particular to certain cultures and contexts.

While there is insufficient evidence to produce a complete and authentic "original practices" performance of a play from this period (with the possible and tantalizing exception of the *Lucerne Passion Play*, thanks to the documentary diligence of Monsieur Cysat) and no way of transforming the spectators into medieval or early modern people, approaching these plays as performances in the making, however approximate our ability to render that performance must be, remains a powerful way to appreciate the emotional practices captured in their texts. While they may not be authoritative in an academic way, performances by committed groups such as the Poculi Ludique Societas in Toronto, or with a modern riff such as the epic *York Millennium Mystery Plays* in 2000 or the National Theatre's *Everyman* in 2015, or the enduring tragedy of *Hamlet*, can be emotionally thrilling reminders that this early theater retains its emotional power to profit and please audiences even now.

CHAPTER FIVE

The Visual Arts

PATRICIA SIMONS AND CHARLES ZIKA[1]

The challenge of rendering emotions visible was central to the artistic theory and practice of what is broadly known as the Renaissance. From the time of Giotto in the early fourteenth century, Jan van Eyck and Hans Memling in the fifteenth, through to the High Renaissance of Raphael and Michelangelo, Albrecht Dürer, and Hans Holbein, and then on to the early Counter-Reformation ventures of El Greco, the Carracci, and Caravaggio at the end of the sixteenth century, artists strengthened the impact of their imagery by emphasizing certain emotions, especially those centered on loss and love.

In some geographical areas such as Italy, naturalism and figurative expression were tempered by classicizing idealization, and in the last decades of the sixteenth century by a return to naturalistic effects after the contrived elegance of Mannerism. In other areas, including Catholic Spain and northern Europe, emotions such as grief and suffering were less restrained, amplified primarily in the religious context. Art historians are beginning to take account of the relationship between art and emotions, both at the level of representation and the register of reception, analyzing what was seen and how it was read, which emotions were depicted and which were evoked.

The modern sense of the word "emotion" and its equivalent in various European vernaculars was only slowly emerging, and usually referred to the extreme end of the scale, as something ungovernable and violent (Simons 2017a: 36–9). *Affetti*, on the other hand, were more acceptable and could fit within the parameters of decorum. The Latin *affectus* meant impulse, intention, inclination, and mood, and this sense of emotion gained favor during the sixteenth century, coming to fruition in art theory of the seventeenth century. To be recognizable, communicative, and effective, imagery followed certain gestural, compositional, and iconographic conventions. Mary swooned under the Cross, for example, and Susanna resisted and tried to flee from the Elders, while Diana and her nymphs recoiled and panicked when interrupted in their bath by intrusive Actaeon.

The individual, personal feelings of artists were of little interest to patrons and viewers, beyond political fealty, social respectability, and religious faith. Art was not expected to reveal the artist's personality, but was assessed in relation to skill, social reputation and honor, and professional pride. Over the course of the sixteenth century, however, artistic temperament became more important for the visual effects an artist could produce—such as Raphael's grace or Michelangelo's intensity (*terribilità*)—rather than providing insight into an artist's individual feelings.

TYPES OF EMOTION

Many authors classified and analyzed a variety of specific emotions. In 1584, the blind former painter Gian Paolo Lomazzo classified around 100 emotions (*passioni*) under the general heading of movements (*moti*) and he described a host of relevant bodily and facial features ([1584] 1974: 113–53; 306–49). In actuality, emotional complexity and nuance were difficult to render effectively, and Renaissance artists concentrated on picturing extreme passions like anguish and anger, laughter and lasciviousness.

Responses to works of art were often highly passionate too, physical in manifestation. Still deeply troubled a year after his young son's death, in 1407 the Florentine wool merchant Giovanni Morelli began an elaborate and ultimately consoling ritual of nightly prayer that involved weeping and kissing an image of the Crucifixion with Mary and St. John (Trexler 1980: 176–80). In 1524 in a village near Danzig, the schoolmaster and a group of peasants, enraged at crop failures, removed a gilded crucifix used in weather processions from the church, and castigated the Christ figure for not providing them with grain, despite all the devotion they had lavished on it, and they flogged it with whips until exhausted (Scribner 1998: 93). Revilement and humiliation were cast against men executed *in absentia* by means of visual images that inflicted on them pain and shame (Edgerton 1985; Berhmann 2016). Usually covered now by restoration, scratches and graffiti once defaced devils and evil characters, marks of visceral attempts to disempower and overcome, while other images were worn by pious kissing and rubbing.[2]

Stoic self-control could nevertheless accompany emotional responses, which were often gendered because of masculinity's association with restraint in contrast to feminine lack of control. The very implacability of certain male figures was itself affective, as in the proud victory over Medusa in Benvenuto Cellini's bronze *Perseus,* unveiled in the town hall piazza of Florence in 1554, for example, or the dignity and power of office conveyed in the genre of state portraiture.

Attacks on religious images at the time of the Reformation were primarily based on their power of sexual arousal or the conviction that they were diabolical tricks that made the faithful believe they could assist in salvation. Ulrich Zwingli and Martin Bucer admitted that some images of female saints incited voluptuousness; while Andreas Karlstadt feared for the power that images had over him and other Christians (Scribner 2001: 129–33; Scribner 1998: 109–17; Koerner 2004: 98–105). But as part of the Catholic Church's attempt to reform art, two important publications of the 1580s clarified its effects, adding precision and detail rather than entirely novel ideas. One was Lomazzo's *Trattato,* the other Cardinal Gabriele Paleotti's guide to proper painting, which first appeared in Italian in 1582, then in Latin in 1594 (Lomazzo [1584] 1974; Paleotti 2012). Sacred paintings, according to the Cardinal, should aim at "illuminating the intellect . . . and arousing devotion and heartfelt contrition"; painters were "mute theologians" who, like orators, had to "delight, teach, and move" (Paleotti 2012: 251, 309).

Lomazzo ([1584] 1974: 105; 1598: 73–4) followed the conventional line that viewers usually identify with the depicted mood or subject: they would be stirred to fury when beholding a lively battle scene or would be "afflicted" with "a fellow-feeling" (that is, empathy would be aroused); a male viewer would be moved "to desire a beautifull young woman for his wife, when he seeth her painted naked"; viewers would be "stirred with disdaine and wrath, at the sight of shameful dishonest actions." Lomazzo ([1584] 1974: 106–8) described imitative responses at length, but we must remember that those were in actuality far from literal; images of death, for instance, motivated grief and suffering but not the viewer's death. The illusionistic and emotive power of art engendered strong responses, but most viewers understood the difference between representation and reality.

At least three basic types of response were provoked. The first was empathy, as though one were part of the image—especially incited by self-conscious techniques of contemplation that prompted the devotee to imagine familiar faces and places in the religious narrative (Simons 2015: 305–29, esp. 322–3). The second was sympathy, in which one felt compassion, fear, fury, and other emotions on behalf of depicted figures like the suffering Christ or the battling Hercules. The third encouraged viewers to scorn and censure figures within the image, such as demons, traitors, and other evil characters. The very rise in analyses of emotions indicates a growing intellectual awareness of how the psyche or soul and its body interacted.

BODIES AND EMOTIONS: THEORIES OF EMOTION AND VISUAL CULTURE

Ideas about individual temperaments and humoral complexions, which were illustrated in numerous scientific treatises, also imbued works of art (Klibansky et al. 1964). This historical context needs to be our guide in outlining the relationship of emotions and the visual arts, rather than the recent claims of neuroscience, which tend to see bodies, brains, cognition, and emotion as transhistorical phenomena, instead of being deeply rooted in culture and history.[3] Most famously, Albrecht Dürer's allegorical engraving *Melencolia I* of 1514 (Figure 5.1) depicted the condition of an excess of black bile that led to depression but also thoughtful creativity (Panofsky 1955: 156–71). Furthermore, mental functions

FIGURE 5.1: Albrecht Dürer, *Melencolia I*, 1514, engraving, 23.9 × 18.7 cm (image), 24.1 × 18.7 cm (sheet). National Gallery of Victoria, Melbourne Felton Bequest, 1956 (3486-4).

or "faculties" like imagination, fantasy, reasoning, memory, and "common sense" occurred in the brain's ventricles or cells, as demonstrated in many texts and in the drawings of artists like Leonardo da Vinci (Clarke and Dewhurst 1972: 10–48; Camille 2000: 197–223). Cognition and knowledge depended heavily on the five senses, predominantly sight, which granted compelling efficacy to imagery for its power to impart truth, incite belief, and arouse emotions like desire.

It was axiomatic to artists such as Leonardo that the eye was the window of the soul, a truism with regard to the physical effects of external objects on the sensitive soul, rather than a merely conventional, pious metaphor (1956: 18, 23, 30). Like a seal stamped on soft wax, the soul received images (*species*) that reproduced the material world, akin to the way a portrait resembled the sitter, and the effects were corporeal. If a pregnant woman saw the image of a black man or of a beautiful boy like the infant Christ, for instance, her imagination could influence the skin color or gender of her fetus (Park 1988: 471–2, 1998: 256–64). Painted passions or *affetti* could arouse viewers by "imprinting" on their soul (Dolce 1557: 156; also 23, 301). The ancient philosopher Aristotle, whose ideas were dominant well into the Renaissance, used the analogy of impressed wax when discussing both the active role of male semen in formation of the embryo and the processes of perception and memory (1942: 113, 293; 1957: 137, 295). Manuel Chrysoloras (d. 1415), the influential early teacher of Greek in Italy, applied this to life-like art, which reproduced an image in the soul's imagination "like well-moulded wax," impressing passions such as "laughter or pleasure, anger or sorrow" (Baxandall 1971: 82).

Passionate responses were evoked in the heart and intellectual ones in the brain, each elements of the soul. The core notion of efficacious resemblance informed the art theory of the humanist and amateur artist Leon Battista Alberti, and others, as well as the practice of Renaissance artists like the early Netherlandish painter Rogier van der Weyden or the Florentine Domenico Ghirlandaio, which focused on artistic naturalism. When writing about painting around 1435, Alberti often alluded to the power or force of sight (1972: 39, 55, 61 nos. 5, 19, 25), stressing that painting's goal was "to represent things seen" and to imitate Nature (1972: 67, 69, 73 nos. 30, 32, 35). Furthermore, "painting possesses a truly divine power" that makes "the absent present" and "the faces of the dead go on living." Alberti cited an example from the *Life of Alexander* (74.6) by the ancient Greek author Plutarch, in which one of Alexander the Great's generals "trembled all over" at the sight of his commander's portrait, because "he recognized the majesty of his king" (Alberti 1972: 61 no. 25).

The physical reaction of fear and awe, as though the simulacrum was alive, is akin to other responses invoked through the influence of artistic imagery. Art's communicative and emotive effect was enhanced by vivid naturalism, including perspective, modeling in relief, and the use of recognizable faces and settings. An attractive narrative would "hold the eye of the learned and unlearned spectator for a long while with a certain sense of pleasure and emotion" (Alberti 1972: 79 no. 40). Those positive, powerful impressions generated and heightened religiosity and orthodoxy in particular: "painting has contributed considerably to the piety which binds us to the gods, and to filling our minds (*animos*) with sound religious beliefs" (Alberti 1972: 61 no. 25). The essential connection between naturalism and emotion was even clearer to the Naples-based humanist Bartolomeo Fazio, who in 1456 insisted on the representation of "interior feelings and emotions, so that the picture may seem to be alive and sentient and somehow move and have action" and be "enlivened by a certain vigour." Almost itself a moving being, the work of art explicitly evoked responses like horror, fear, amusement, veneration, and grief, with special praise meted out to Rogier van der Weyden's weeping figures (Baxandall 1971: 103–9, 163–8).

THE VISUAL ARTS

FIGURE 5.2: Rogier van der Weyden, *Deposition*, c. 1436, oil on wood, 204.5 × 261.5 cm. Museo del Prado, Madrid (P02835). Image courtesy of Getty Images.

BODIES AND EMOTIONS: VISUALIZATION OF EMOTIONS THROUGH BODY LANGUAGE

Modern study of the meaning of gestures in medieval and Renaissance art began late, with the publication of various studies by Moshe Barasch (1976), though the issue of corporeal motions and emotions was central to the period's art theory and practice.[4] The link between emotion and motion was primarily sustained in visual representation by means of body language and facial expression.[5] Alberti (1972: 81 no. 41) offered extensive guidance on the best kind of narrative painting or *istoria*, which

> will move spectators when the men painted in the picture outwardly demonstrate their own feelings as clearly as possible. Nature provides ... that we mourn with the mourners, laugh with those who laugh, and grieve with the grief-stricken. Yet these feelings (*motus animi*) are known from movements of the body (*motibus corporis*). We see how the melancholy ... lack all vitality of feeling and action, and remain sluggish, their limbs unsteady and drained of colour [Figure 5.1]. In those who mourn, the brow is weighed down, the neck bent, and every part of their body droops as though weary and past care. But in those who are angry, their passions aflame with ire, face and eyes become swollen and red, and the movements of all their limbs are violent and agitated

according to the fury of their wrath. Yet when we are happy and gay, our movements are free and pleasing in their inflexions.[6]

The notion of visual sympathy was drawn from Horace's recommendation of around 19 BCE that poetry should be "tender and affecting," because people smile on those who smile and sympathize with those who weep (*Ars poetica*, 101–3). Alberti (1972: 83 no. 43) substantially expanded the point, supplying examples of the visible signs of melancholic, mournful, angry, and joyful bodies, later mentioning "fear, desire and so on."

Lomazzo and others also cited Horace, but the repertoire of emotions continued to expand (Baxandall 1971: 104, 164; Lomazzo 1974: 95). The second of seven books in Lomazzo's *Trattato* was devoted to *moti*, "the most important and most necessary" element of painting (1974: 97–8). Artists had to understand *passioni* and *gesti* (actions) that were distinctly human, concentrating on *moto*, which he defined as "a certain expression and extrinsic demonstration in the body of those things that are experienced internally in the soul." Nevertheless, Alberti had already laid what was the fundamental groundwork for several centuries, one much reiterated by Leonardo (1956: 19, 104, 108–9, 149–53).

Alberti acknowledged the artistic challenge of catching the fleeting, mutating nuance of emotions. He noted that "it is extremely difficult to vary the movements of the body in accordance with the almost infinite movements [of the heart]" (1972: 81, no. 42). But much of the body language adopted by artists was codified. Alberti and others drew on the theory of ancient rhetoric, aided by surviving Roman reliefs and statuary, as well as the contemporary practice of preachers. As Cicero put it, "by action the body talks."[7] Rhetorical gestures were a conscious public address, of communicative value rather than personal expression. In ancient Rome, the *adlocutio*, for instance—the raised, outstretched hand—signified a general's speech to his soldiers, and it was reiterated in examples like Titian's *Alfonso d'Avalos addressing his troops*, painted around 1540 (Prado).

One of the most widespread adaptations of classical expression was what has been termed the Hippolytus gesture, arms outflung behind or up in an extreme movement of mourning, often implicitly associated with an open-mouthed cry of grief (Barasch 1976: 23, 69–72, 109, 121). It takes a prominent position and acts as a crucial bridge between the contained, bearded male observers and expressive female mourners when performed by the young, smooth-faced St. John in Giotto's fresco, *The Lamentation over the Dead Christ*, one of the scenes in Padua's Arena Chapel painted around 1305 (Figure 5.3). Integrated as it is with the descending outcrop behind, John's V-shaped gesture becomes central to the entire composition but is also thereby anchored by dignified restraint. Giotto was usually an artist of gravitas, and an overall balance between despair and formality is also secured by the heavily clad, monumental, and often faceless female mourners.

Emotion is largely carried by the ten disconsolate, fluttering angels overhead, who exacerbate the grief below. Whereas several angels had mourned at Crucifixions before, Giotto adds an unprecedented number and endows them with a variety of conventional gestures of mourning (Barasch 1976: 93, 100). The lowest at far left scratches its face in despair, three stretch wide their arms or lift hands in horror, one wipes its weeping eyes, three clutch tight their hands (one holding them up to its cheek, as does the Virgin Mary below), one pushes up and throws back its head in desolation, and at lower right another pulls its hair in anguish. Set against blue sky, their emotions are clear, distinct, varied, and communicative. Understandably, Giotto was described in the mid-sixteenth century as the first modern artist to depict *affetti* (Varchi 1549: 114).

FIGURE 5.3: Giotto, *Lamentation*, c. 1305, fresco, 200 × 185 cm. Arena Chapel, Padua. Image courtesy of Getty Images.

Intensity of gestural language also marks the wailing figures surrounding Christ's dead body in Niccolò dell'Arca's three-dimensional painted terracotta installation in Bologna produced around 1485–90 (Campanini 2001) (Figure 5.4).[8] In the case of this and similar life-size groupings that are placed close to the viewer and not far above their eye-level, devotees are immersed in a scenario of heightened naturalism while also experiencing aesthetic amazement. As in Giotto's fresco, an older, bearded male figure is decorously static at one edge, kneeling at the head of Christ now that his job is done, his hammer and pincers having helped remove the inert body from the Cross. He may be the wealthy donor of Christ's tomb, Joseph of Arimathea, but the tools suggest he is Nicodemus. Often thought to have been a sculptor, Nicodemus acts as Niccolò's representative (and the figure could be a self-portrait), looking steadily out at his audience to ensure that it is properly pious.

Two open-mouthed, swaying women follow, one faltering and unsteady on her feet, the older one being Mary, tightly pressing her hands together and standing next to dumbstruck John, another constrained male character. The last two figures are howling and excessively active, one with raised arms and stretched fingers trying to shield herself from the horrifying

FIGURE 5.4: Niccolò dell'Arca, *Pietà*, c. 1485–90, painted terracotta. Santa Maria della Vita, Bologna. © 2017. Photo Scala, Florence.

sight, the other lunging forward, trailed by agitated, flying draperies. This is Mary Magdalene, who had earlier tenderly washed Christ's feet with her tears and dried them with her hair, kissing and anointing them (Luke 7:38, 46), but now they are lifeless and her loss is beyond bearing. What might be termed emotive realism is created by contortion and exaggeration, from taut necks and wide mouths to massive yet impossibly flying draperies.

Not all gestural accentuation focused on grief. Alberti recommended a quiet but demonstrative gesture of pointing, for instance, that "tells the spectators what is going on" (1972: 83, no. 42). This technique was inherited from preaching and pastoral instruction, as much as from classical culture, as is clear in the *Crucifixion* from the Isenheim altarpiece of the German painter, Matthias Grünewald, commissioned for a hospital specializing in incurable disease (Hayum 1989) (Figure 5.5). On the right, the anachronistic figure of St. John the Baptist stands above the sacrificial Lamb that symbolizes the spilling of Christ's blood, here flowing from its chest into the Eucharistic chalice. The Baptist points emphatically to the flayed, crucified, and agonized body of Christ and highlights the inscription in red, "He must increase, but I must decrease" (John 3:30). The immediacy of the first person speech possibly stimulated clerics to point as well, expounding to patients Christ's sharing in their suffering. Other elements of the altarpiece also mitigate their distress, including protector saints and a radiant, wondrous *Resurrection*. The altarpiece simultaneously incites emotional engagement with horrific ordeal and assurance of salvation.

On the other side of the Cross, tear-stained Mary wrings her hands and swoons into young John's arms while the Magdalene kneels, arms raised and fingers stretched in a gesture of beseeching prayer. Against the dark backdrop, Christ's fingers twist and writhe at the end of his impaled hands and moans issue from the dry lips of a bloody mouth. He is finally being put to rest in the predella below, gently supported by John while weeping

THE VISUAL ARTS 93

FIGURE 5.5: Mathias Grünewald, *Crucifixion, with Lamentation*, oil and tempera on limewood; central panels of the closed state of *The Isenheim Altarpiece*, by Mathias Grünewald (painted panels) and Niclaus of Hagenau (wooden sculpture of the open state), 1512–16, 376 × 668 cm. Musée d'Unterlinden, Colmar. Image courtesy of Getty Images.

Mary looks on and the long-haired, red-eyed Magdalene continues to pray and wail. Although the intensity of creative vision is remarkable, the altarpiece's gestures and conventional symbols are recognizable and thus effectively emotive.

Much body language was far less violent and extreme, especially if physical and emotional pain were not the issue. Melancholic people were renowned in medical terms for being slothful, just as Alberti observed and Dürer depicted (Figure 5.1), though the inaction is supplemented by the gesture of one hand to the cheek or head indicating deep thought and meditation as much as sadness, as it does too with dell'Arca's John (Figure 5.4).[9] Many figures like standing saints are dignified and stoic, offering models of decorous behavior and encouraging internal contemplation that can be deeply emotional. Body language was plausible and followed rules of decorum and appropriateness according to such factors as gender, age and status, advised by Alberti (1972: 85, no. 44) and Leonardo (1956: 62, 105–6, 147–8, 151); it was often conventional but rarely invariable.

BODIES AND EMOTIONS: VISUALIZATION OF EMOTIONS BY FACIAL EXPRESSION

As Alberti (1972: 81, no. 41) had noted, as did others like the sixteenth-century Venetian writer Lodovico Dolce (1557: 97), and as was clear in the physiognomic writings of classical authors revived and expanded by the Neapolitan polymath Giovanni della Porta (1586), the face and its features—mouth, brow, and especially the eyes—were some of the most important instruments for communicating feeling. Sorrow, grief, compassion, and pain were emotions frequently etched on the face in this period, and the shedding of tears appeared frequently and in novel ways in art works, as an expression of new emphases in religious devotional practice. Artists used crying to depict grief or sorrow, either through physiognomy (the widening of mouths, the narrowing and reddening of eyes, the prominence of wrinkles in the corners of the eye), as we see in the mid-thirteenth-century sculptures of the Foolish Virgins in the Magdeburg Cathedral, or by gestures such as the wiping away of tears (Figures 5.2 and 5.3) or the covering of the face (the angel in Giotto, Figure 5.3). Indeed, in the alabaster sculptures of grieving monks completed in 1470 by the Spanish sculptor Jean de La Huerta and the French sculptor Antoine Le Moiturier for the tomb of John the Fearless, Duke of Burgundy, and his wife Margaret of Bavaria, the monks' faces are completely covered, while one also wipes away tears with his hood.

Tears appear as streaks running down the faces of weeping mothers in Giotto's *Massacre of the Innocents* in the early fourteenth-century Arena Chapel. From the early fifteenth century, this new means of conveying grief on the face took the form of individual painted tears. In the *Entombment* triptych of c. 1415 by the Flemish painter Robert Campin (Courtauld Gallery, London), painted tears appear on the faces of those attending the dead body of Christ (including angels) in scenes of the deposition from the Cross, lamentation over Christ's body, and his entombment (Barasch 1991: 85–99; Thürlemann 2011: 56–61). Using oil paint rather than tempera or fresco, Campin and Rogier van der Weyden initiated this technique of painting tears as transparent viscous bodies that roll down the grieving face. In *The Descent from the Cross* (Figure 5.2) tears stream down the faces of the collapsed Virgin and the two attending women on the left and of the richly dressed man on the right, while the red-eyed St. John on the left and Mary Magdalene on the far right also show tears. The display and movement of these tears do not simply act as signs of intense inner grief, but are models for the compassion viewers ought to feel in response to Christ's death and his mother's sorrow in viewing her son's agony.

This invitation to imitative and sympathetic suffering is one of the key elements within late medieval religious culture, evident in sermons, devotional literature, and religious imagery, and continuing well beyond the Reformation in Catholic devotion. The ability to feel compassion and empathy for others was considered to be an essentially Christian quality, and for that reason witches were believed not to be able to cry, or at least not to cry genuine tears (Zika 2017: 48–52).

GRIEF, LOSS, PAIN, DESPAIR AND FEAR

The grief and compassion of the Virgin and the suffering of Christ were registered not only in narratives of crucifixion, deposition, and lamentation, but also in individual images of the Virgin with Christ. A striking example is the *Mother of Sorrows*, a panel painting created by the Master of the Stötteritz Altarpiece in c. 1470 (Cummer Museum of Art & Gardens, Jacksonville, Florida). The Virgin's tears flowing down her cheeks and her severely reddened eyes immediately draw the viewer into an empathetic identification with her sorrow. As David Areford (2014: 43–55) has shown, the cascading folds of the Virgin's veil that she grasps between the fingers of her right hand are a vehicle for touching, which hovers between the wiping of her tears and caring for Christ's body, while her other hand makes a gesture of invitation and intercession to her devotees. Similar images of the Mother of Sorrows were common, sometimes as pendants to those of the suffering Christ (as in the work of the Early Netherlandish painter Dieric Bouts), other times cradling Christ's body in a lamentation known as the *pietà* in Italian and *Vesperbild* in German. Especially in Northern Europe and Spain, the sorrowing mother comes to be depicted with up to seven swords piercing her heart, as she reaches out to viewers to share her grief and compassion for her son's pain (Schuler 1992; Falkenburg 1995; Areford 2014: 13–39).

Such images, and in particular that of Christ as The Man of Sorrows or Image of Pity (*Imago Pietatis*), began to appear from the thirteenth century and were widespread by the end of the fourteenth (Schiller 1971–2: 197–224; Barasch 1995: 33–40; Parshall and Schoch 2005: 238–50). They multiplied in the fifteenth century as the new technology of print-making facilitated individual devotion and a more intimate relationship between devotee and image. The Man of Sorrow images depict the figure of Christ in a variety of ways—as an emaciated and bloody full-length figure displaying his wounds, or as a bust or holy face that looks directly out at the viewer, eyes transfixed and narrowed, brow upraised, a face filled with agony, in some instances also weeping, the transparent tears flowing from the eyes, to be clearly distinguished from the visible dark drops of blood (Figure 5.6).

The lacerated body, the bleeding wounds, the tortured face, the pleading and sometimes piercing eyes, the weeping mourners and the instruments of violence, all confront the viewer and communicate the ongoing suffering of Christ. But the outward gaze of Christ as well as the hands that beckon to the viewer, sometimes supported by the attendant mourners, testify to the devotee's implication in such misery, and consequently the need to recognize and empathize with it and practice repentance for the sins that caused it in the past and continue to do so in the present. Some manuscript illuminations and prints (both in printed books or as independent works pasted into books and manuscripts) were completely covered in red to represent the profusion of Christ's blood. Such techniques, as well as images of Christ's bleeding wounds, were powerful graphic instruments meant to elicit a complex series of emotional responses to Christ's redemptive suffering as the horrifying consequence of human sin (Areford 2010: 45–54; 77–80, for use of red; 228–67, for Christ's side wound).

A different kind of pain, combined with fear, loss, and even despair, becomes a regular feature of the bodily gestures and facial expressions of the damned in depictions of *The Last Judgment* and *Hell* from at least the late thirteenth century. Some gestures are similar to those found in mourners, such as the throwing up of arms, covering of the face, the wailing of open mouths, and the wringing of hands. But here the gestures are more vehement if not entirely new, accompanied by figures that bite their hands, tear at their faces and their hair, their teeth clearly visible in their open mouths so as to draw notice to their screams (or perhaps the biblical reference to the gnashing of teeth), their eyes fixed and protruding in expressions of shock and despair. We see such dissonant and fierce gesticulation, for example, in *The Last Judgment* of the Pisan painter Francesco Traini, frescoed in the cemetery, or Camposanto, of Pisa (c. 1333–6), as well as depictions by a range of fifteenth-century artists such as the Flemish painter Hans Memling and the Cologne artist Stefan Lochner, and then famously in Michelangelo's Sistine rendition unveiled in 1541 (Barasch 1976: 1–20).

Violent self-laceration—the tearing of cheeks and hair—as an expression of indescribable dismay conveys the emotions of the mothers of slaughtered children in some depictions of

FIGURE 5.6: German (Ulm), *Man of Sorrows*, c. 1465/70, hand-colored woodcut (mounted to detached cover of a lost book), 39.7 × 26.2 cm (image), 40.5 × 26.9 cm (sheet). The Art Institute of Chicago, Waller Fund; gifts of Mrs. Tiffany Blake, Thomas E. Donnelley, Emil Eitel, Carolyn Morse Ely, Alfred E. Hamill, Frank B. Hubachek, Monarch Leather, and Mrs. Potter Palmer, 1947.731. ©2017. The Art Institute of Chicago/Art Resource, NY/Scala, Florence.

the *Massacre of the Innocents* (Barasch 1976: 64–8, 80–2, Figures 34, 43a–c, for early Italian examples). In the earlier representations, emphasis is also given to the joined hands of the panic-stricken mothers as they plead for their children to be shown mercy. But from the later fifteenth century, in the fresco of c. 1486–90 by Domenico Ghirlandaio in the Tornabuoni chapel, which depicts a crowded scene of extreme violence and frenetic movement, pleading gives way to resistance as one of the women checks a soldier making off with her child by desperately, forcefully pulling his hair. Lucas Cranach's painting in Dresden of c. 1515 registers repulsion by having a member of Herod's entourage cover his eyes in horror. The overwhelming, large painting of 1590 by the Dutch Mannerist painter Cornelis van Haarlem (Rijksmuseum) adds to a visceral sense of the event's extreme corporeal violence by depicting the soldiers as naked—possibly even suggesting the similarity of their action to sexual rage, by locating between a soldier's bare buttocks the head of a woman pinned to the ground by the soldier's knee as he slits her child's throat. But the artist also depicts the violent revenge of the women in response to the slaughter and terror around them, as four of them beat and gouge out the eyes of a soldier they have brought to the ground.

Grieving and fear were not restricted to religious contexts alone. In the late 1470s the Italian painter and sculptor Verrocchio and his workshop carved a tomb relief (now in the Bargello of Florence) showing a woman dying in childbirth, the midwives wailing and tearing their hair, while the men of the household sadly receive the stillborn child. Mourning was also evoked more subtly in examples such as yearning Venus unsuccessfully trying to restrain Adonis from the hunt (often painted by Titian and his assistants) and then lamenting his subsequent death, joining the elegiac with the pastoral mood popular during the sixteenth century.

OTHER VISUAL MEANS OF REPRESENTING AND STIRRING EMOTIONS

Color, lighting, composition, setting, and implied sound were further instruments by which artists aroused emotion. Alberti (1972: 93 no. 48) wrote of the grace or dignity that could result from the selection of color, noting that "white lends gaiety." Lomazzo (1974: 177) went further, pointing out that black, earth, lead, and dark colors were literally heavy pigments and, when stamped on the mind through sight, gave rise to such moods as sadness, thoughtfulness, and melancholy. The autumnal tones of Titian's *Death of Actaeon* in the National Gallery of London fits Lomazzo's theory, for the colors suit the melancholy narrative, in which the hunter turns into a tawny stag and falls back onto the earth where he will spill blood and merge with brown soil while his dogs attack.

Green, sapphire blue, deep red, and straw-like gold instead engendered pleasure and happiness, and so Lomazzo went on. But there was no standard system of expressive colors, as is evident in Lomazzo's opinion (1974: 177) that white "generates a certain simple attention that is more melancholic than otherwise," a stark contrast to Alberti's fifteenth-century palette. Red commonly represented blood, as described above, or featured on clothing in Grünewald's scene (Figure 5.5), deepening apprehension of Christ's suffering and sacrifice. By extension, red also referred to the shedding of blood through violent acts as well as the destructive nature of fire, and was therefore frequently used in apocalyptic imagery in pamphlet literature to refer to the divine punishment and devastation of the Last Days (Zika 2014: 49–50).

Context was crucial, not only in terms of harmony between colors, but also in relation to their meaning and effect. Green might tinge the sallow flesh of the howling figure of jealousy or despair on the left of Bronzino's London *Allegory*, and acidic green with yellow brings to the fore a deceptively reptilian hybrid on the right (Figure 5.7); but as a richer hue it characterized hope, embodied in the sprigs shooting from the nearly dead tree in Giotto's *Lamentation* (Figure 5.3). Grünewald's bleak nighttime backdrop deepens the painting's somberness, whereas in the case of Botticelli's *Standing Venus* in the Gemäldegalerie, Berlin, undifferentiated black behind the figure enhances the glow of her flesh and its volumetric relief so that the alluring body appears enticingly palpable, an effect thereafter exploited in Cranach's vertical paintings of scantily clad female figures.

As Dolce's *Dialogue* (2000: 97–9) observed, the imagination is also activated by implied sound, the second most effective sense that made an impression on the soul. There is the keening of dell'Arca's mourners, the moaning of Grünewald's Christ and the

FIGURE 5.7: Agnolo Bronzino, *An Allegory with Venus and Cupid*, c. 1545, oil on wood, 146.1 × 116.2 cm. National Gallery, London (NG651). Image courtesy of Getty Images.

shriek of Bronzino's despairing figure. Images of musicians, singers, and dancers conjure sound in the viewer's soul too, of course, some placed on the front panels or lids of actual instruments like virginals and harpsichords. It was commonplace to call painting mute poetry and to praise a represented figure for being so lifelike it all but spoke. Those references to the near-presence of sound went further on occasion. In 1578, the humanist and engraver Dirck Volckertsz Coornhert praised an engraving of Pieter Bruegel the Elder's painted *Death of the Virgin*, saying he had never seen such skill: "Seen? What am I saying? My ears heard, so it seemed, the doleful words, the sighs, the weeping, the chorus of misery" (Campbell 2014: 45, 57, n. 29; Baxandall 1971: 70, 147 for Filippo Villani on Giotto). The rhetorical exercise in ekphrasis pretends to be caught up in aural verism but nevertheless points to one mode of emotional reception.

Composition and setting were also important. Due to the seeming projection of highly lit Christ forward of the picture plane in Grünewald's altarpiece, the bright blood oozing from under his toenails and the soles of his feet appears ready to flow into the real chalice resting on the altar table below. The emotional impact of passionate body language and striking palette is thus intensified by composition and interaction with the viewer's actual space.

Other pictorial devices for augmenting a work's influence on the soul included lively movement: of hair and draperies (Figures 5.3–5.4), as well as of plants, trees, birds, waves, and flames (Lomazzo 1974: 153–63). The rise of pastoral landscape during this period established a new secular means of encouraging pleasurable moods. Paintings like the *Concert Champêtre* in the Louvre (c. 1509) developed from the theme of the Garden of Love, with music, dalliance, and other enjoyable activities set in expansive gardens, verdant fields, or uncultivated forests. The south German painter and printmaker Albrecht Altdorfer and those associated with the so-called Danube School used landscape to convey quite different emotional states. The sharp vertical lines of the forest and white highlights on reddish brown paper in the 1509 drawing of *Christ on the Mount of Olives* (Figure 5.8), create an eerie forest setting, in which Christ seeks comfort from an angel perched on a

FIGURE 5.8: Albrecht Altdorfer, *Christ on the Mount of Olives*, 1509, pen and white heightening on red-brown grounded paper, 21 × 15.7 cm. Staatliche Museen zu Berlin, Kupferstichkabinett. ©bpk/Kupferstichkabinett, SMB/Jörg P. Anders, No: 00048735.

distant vertical cliff, and helps convey his utter isolation and fear as to what is about to befall him (Haug and Messling 2014: 128–9). In Altdorfer's drawing on deep blue paper of the mythological story of the death of Thisbe's lover, Pyramus, the dark forest rising steeply above the insect-like figure of the dead lover prostrate on the forest floor conveys the total distraction that led Pyramus to take his own life (Haug and Messling 2014: 130–1; Wood 1993: 80–8, Figures 42–3).

While Mannerists particularly explored extreme, intellectualized artifice during the sixteenth century (Figure 5.7), it should not be forgotten that what we might think of as aesthetic effects like illusionism and inventiveness were regarded as emotive and powerful in their own right. This could involve material effects, as in the case of Altdorfer's chiaroscuro techniques in his drawings, or the stunning visual intensity and costly preciousness of ground lapus lazuli used for the Virgin's robe. No matter the subject, inventiveness, and material effects stimulated personal pleasure and empathy, sociable conversation, and attentive engagement, sweeping the imagination of viewers into other worlds, taking them out of themselves yet simultaneously heightening their sense of being present in the moment, provoking empathetic response to grief or pain as well as admiration for powerfully illusionistic naturalism—the very core of effective, moving art.

EMOTIONS AS VICES AND SIN—ANGER, ENVY, LUST

A number of the emotions that we generally recognize as such today—anger, envy, lust—were understood historically as vices. The list of the seven capital vices or cardinal sins, standardized by Pope Gregory I in the late sixth century, provided a theological and moralizing filter through which good and evil might be evaluated, of monumental significance at the time of the Last Judgment for whether an individual would spend eternity in heaven or hell. Visual images of such subjects were used didactically to moderate social behavior and to remind viewers of its consequences. So life was often depicted as an armed combat between the virtues and vices. In late fourteenth- and fifteenth-century wall paintings, manuscript illuminations, woodcuts, and tapestries, vices were allegorized either as animals or riders of animals—anger as a woman riding a boar, envy as a monk riding a dog, or lust as a woman riding a goat, for instance—together with other attributes.[10] These intellectual, symbolic personifications that varied across regions and time tended not to show the actual emotion, but aimed at repressing rather than arousing that feeling in viewers.

In the sixteenth century, as the Old Testament began to play a stronger role in providing *exempla* for contemporary Christian life, the personified vices were sometimes linked to biblical stories. The print series engraved by the Dutch engraver and publisher Crispin de Passe, after the Flemish painter Martin de Vos, for instance, was comprised of a female figure with various attributes, but with two biblical scenes in the background. The emaciated figure of Envy devouring her heart was accompanied by the biblical story of Joseph thrown into a pit by his brothers because of their jealousy (Genesis 37), and the jealousy of Herod's wife Herodias, which had her request the head of John the Baptist on a plate (Mark 6) (British Museum Prints and Drawings, D, 6.69). This marked a combination of the older allegorical approach, and a new attempt to resist these emotions by linking them to narratives that demonstrate their fateful consequences.

For wealthy art patrons or collectors, the carved statuettes of the *Deadly Sins* created by the Würzburg sculptor Peter Dell the Elder (1540s, Germanisches Nationalmuseum, Nuremberg) provided a personal warning about sinful emotion (Smith 1994: 310–12,

Figures 273–4). No more than twenty-three centimeters in height, the exquisitely carved pearwood figures represented an ensemble made for self-promotional display and enjoyment of their fine aesthetic qualities. But they also functioned as moralizing warnings. The figures of Gluttony with her protruding belly, Anger with her hateful stare and dagger, and Lust with her seductive smile as she pulls up her dress to reveal her upper thigh testify to the close associations between these emotions and sin that viewers in many post-Reformation European societies were being taught to feel.

PICTURING AND PROVOKING JOY, AMUSEMENT AND LAUGHTER

Paul Barolsky (1978) pioneered the study of Renaissance visual humor, and was followed by many insightful case studies, including examinations of particular artists, visual puns, or themes like Folly; but no new overview, and little explicit attention, has been paid to these emotions since. However, emotional responses to amusing images were acknowledged by Alberti and tackled in 1582 by Paleotti (2012: 239–45). While jokes and urbanities were considered inappropriate for sacred images, they were allowed for relaxation, refreshment, and diversion in the profane realm, as long as they were not immodest or obscene. *Ridicole* images, that is, those to be laughed at or scorned, rouse "the heart in an instant to merriment" and laughter was a "motion of the mind" (*moto dell'animo*), though "different things provoke laughter." Paleotti noted the centrality of novelty to humor, and other contemporary theories similarly built on ancient authorities like Aristotle to emphasize the amusing aspects of incongruity and the unexpected (Simons 2011a: 63, 86–8, 94–7; Simons 2017b). Following the ancient philosopher Cicero (1967: 373, 2.58.235), the sudden and uncontrollable eruption of laughter was considered especially enjoyable (Paleotti 2012: 244–5).

Incongruity is fundamental to satire, and since the calls for widespread religious reform occurred at a time when the new technologies of print were becoming more pervasive, satire played a significant role in Reformation propaganda and political critique more generally. Single-leaf woodcuts or prints illustrating broadsheets or pamphlets were used to arouse support among viewers by offering amusement and simultaneously derision and hate through the ridiculing and demonizing of enemies as antichrist, the devil's excrement, ravenous wolves, or fools (Scribner 1994). Some prints were created to provoke this mixture of derision and humor through personal manipulation: round vovelles (and also small medals) could be rotated or the flaps of trick woodcuts turned back to reveal the realities below the appearance—as in a surviving vovelle (Figure 5.9) that depicts priests as fools and devils (Andersson 1985: 51–7).

So-called low life such as peasants, prostitutes, and fools were easy subjects for satire, caricatured in Leonardo's drawings to amuse the Milanese court, for example, or exaggerated in northern European images of "unequal lovers," such as in *Ill-Matched Lovers* of c. 1520–5 by the Flemish founder of the Antwerp School, Quentin Matsys (National Gallery of Art, Washington D.C.). One of Leonardo's pen and ink drawings of grotesque heads, *A Man Tricked by Gypsies*, of c. 1493, has a man's purse stolen behind his back while he is distracted, a theme found elsewhere, including in six known versions of Hieronymus Bosch's *The Conjuror*, which is reinvented by Caravaggio's *Cardsharps* of c. 1595 (Kimbell Art Museum, Fort Worth) (Clayton 2002: 96–9). In addition to moralizing superiority and pleasure at the pictorial exaggeration, viewers can also enjoy

FIGURE 5.9: Hans Rudolf Manuel Deutsch, *The Changing Faces of the Catholic Church*, trick woodcut, 1556. Left, View 1: *A Prelate as a Fool with a Goiter.* Right, View 8: *A Prelate as the Devil*, Graphische Sammlung Albertina, Vienna, Inv. DG2002/209.

the satisfaction that such images let them in on the joke, seeing and knowing what the depicted dupe cannot.

Dancing was central to a number of satirical woodcuts, such as those by the southern German painter and printmaker Sebald Beham in the 1530s, which focused on the excessive and vulgar behavior of peasants at annual village church festivals (Stewart 1993). Called *kermis* in Flanders and the Netherlands, this annual festival was the subject of numerous prints and paintings. In an engraving after a Bruegel painting by the Flemish printmaker Pieter van der Heyden (Figure 5.10), the movement of the dancers, the thrusting codpieces of the males together with the bagpipes, the kissing couples, the drinking, and raucous guests in the background approaching the bride at the table receiving gifts—all testify to the earthy pleasure of the wedding. Not nearly as satirical and moralistic as many contemporary images of the subject, the text appended below nevertheless suggests that the bride is no longer dancing because she is already pregnant.

Much religious art of the fifteenth and sixteenth centuries was joyful, filled with baby cherubs and smiling, dancing, and music-playing angels. Festive occasions like marriage and birth often gave rise to celebratory imagery, such as busts of laughing boys (one of which, Guido Mazzoni's painted terracotta in the British Royal Collection, may be of young Henry VIII). The famous, supposedly enigmatic smile in Leonardo's *Mona Lisa* could be no more than a witty pun on her husband's last name (Giacondo, Italian for jocund, light-hearted), something indeed to invite viewers to smile about (Barolsky 1991: 62–4). Whether related to wedding poetry (epithalamia) or not, Bronzino's *Allegory* focuses on the embrace and kiss between Venus and Cupid, celebrated by a grinning boy with bells around one ankle merrily rushing in to scatter petals over the amorous couple (Figure 5.7). Other characters frequently performing jovial activities include carousers during Carnival and dancing peasants. Jesters and fools peer out at viewers. Boys laughed at the now-lost panel by the early Quattrocento Italian painter Pisanello (the nickname of Antonio di Puccio Pisano), which depicted a priest distorting his face with his fingers, according to Fazio, who observed that it was "done so agreeably as to arouse good

FIGURE 5.10: Pieter van der Heyden, engraving after Pieter Bruegel the Elder, *The Peasant Wedding Dance*, after 1570, 38 × 43.3 cm. Metropolitan Museum of Art, New York, Harris Brisbane Dick Fund (33.52.29).

humour in those who look at it"—a rare surviving comment about an amused response to a particular work (Baxandall 1971: 107, 166).

Paleotti noted that laughter is sometimes provoked by viciousness. Scorn may be part of the narrative, as in the case of drunken Noah ridiculed by his son Ham, or Christ mocked by spitting, jeering, deformed figures, as in Bosch's panel dated around 1510–16 housed in the Museum voor Schone Kunsten, Ghent. The point in such cases is to provoke viewers to mock the mockers, and sympathize with their target. Wit, in the joint sense of both ingenuity and humor, was at the heart of much visual play, evoking wonder alongside amusement. "Serious jokes" catered to viewers' sense of inside knowledge and of learning about the jokes of nature, strikingly so in the case of the composite heads of the Italian painter Giuseppe Arcimboldo, craftily comprised of a range of objects like fruits, flowers or fish (Kaufmann 2010).

AMOROUS IMAGERY AND ITS RECEPTION

Humor was often a crucial element of erotica, heightening the sense of delight. Fazio, for instance, described a now-lost painting that he attributed to van der Weyden in which a bathing woman is shown with two youths "secretly peering in at her through a chink, remarkable for their grins," appreciation that is thereby openly licensed for viewers (Baxandall 1971: 108, 167). Vital to the enjoyment of the story of adulterous Mars and Venus is that when they were ensnared in Vulcan's marvelously crafted net, the gods laughed at the sight, one of them feeling envy at their sexual pleasure (Ovid, *Metamorphoses*, 4: 187–9). Some of Maerten van Heemskerck's laughing gods in his panel of the scene (c. 1540, Kunsthistorisches Museum, Vienna) even show their teeth, in a dental gesture that more often indicated vulgarity. Composite heads made up of teeming phalli, including one on a maiolica dish (1536, Ashmolean Museum), provoke laughter for their combination of daring, cleverness, and humor.

Erotic art of the period is examined in several exceptionally well-illustrated analyses, but viewers' emotional responses have rarely left textual traces (Camille 1998; Turner 2017).[11] They are usually either assumed or underplayed in scholarship, which has a bias for the disembodied or polite. But in the period, disgust was commonly voiced against imagery deemed immodest or obscene, including homosexuality, comments suggesting its popularity. Particularly influential were the so-called *I modi* series of engravings of various sexual positions (*modi*) designed by Giulio Romano and Marcantonio Raimondi in Rome around 1524–5 (Talvacchia 1999). Soon banned, the images were reissued in woodcut form and disseminated throughout Europe, resulting in other lucrative series like Jacopo Caraglio's much-copied *Loves of the Gods* (c. 1527) and the "*Lascivie*" by Agostino Carracci (c. 1585–95). Writing in the 1580s, the minor French nobleman Pierre Brantôme (1947: 26–31, 321–2; Simons 2011b: 116–19) reported that many women in Paris eagerly purchased versions of *I modi* to spice up their married life or perused colored drawings of sexual activities, and he repeated the story of one woman dashing off to have sex with her male lover after seeing a painting of bathing female beauties. Whether or not the particulars were true, gossip of this kind was considered plausible.

Virtuous love was a common theme for artists, legitimizing love outside marriage, and the intense spiritual longing of nuns for their Christ dolls or images of an adult Christ. Allegorical love between Christ and the Church was pictured in *Virgin and Child* imagery, which expressed affective bonding. Dieric Bouts's panel of 1460–75 (Fine Arts Museums, San Francisco) is a fine example of mother and child posed cheek to cheek, their lips almost touching, their eyes locked in a mutual, intimate gaze. Such facial interactions are reiterated in the secular kiss of Cupid with his mother Venus in Bronzino's *Allegory* (Figure 5.7), except for the unusual, lascivious sight of the female figure's tongue. The squeezing of her nipple, the jutting of Cupid's ivory buttocks, the nudity, and luxuriously intense palette further contribute to the air of frank sensuality.

At times, it was said that viewers fell in love with works of art, as Dolce (2000: 183) wrote of Parmigianino's oeuvre, for instance, a trope that goes back to the ancient tale of Pygmalion desiring and wooing his own statue of a naked woman, as well as Alberti's more recent idea (1972: 62, no. 26) that Narcissus was the inventor of painting. Pictorial seduction constituted Leonardo's key argument for painting's superiority over poetry. Only by sight could one comprehend the "beauty of created objects, especially those that arouse love" (Leonardo 1956: 7). He told the story of King Matthias of Hungary preferring to see and hold a portrait of his beloved rather than hearing a poem about her. He added that lovers kissed and spoke to such pictures, and gave the example of a man who asked that signs of divinity ("rapresentatione de tal deità") be removed from the picture of a holy subject so that he could "kiss the picture without scruples" (Leonardo 1956: 15–16, 19–22, 29).[12] A related cultural notion, based on optical theory and

Petrarch's poetry, was love at first sight—that one is struck by arrows or darts from the eyes of one's beloved. Cupid's flaming arrow in Botticelli's *Primavera* (c. 1482, Uffizi), a large panel hung high, is angled so that when released it would strike desire into viewers below at the point where they admire the sensually dancing, nearly naked Three Graces.

The power of images to arouse sexual desire is illustrated by Giorgio Vasari's report in 1550 that Dominicans removed Fra Bartolomeo's now-lost panel of a naked *St. Sebastian* (1514–15) from public view because they learned through the confessional that female viewers "had sinned due to the gracefulness and lascivious imitation of life" wrought by the artist. Relocation to an area where only friars could see it created a new problem, however, and the disturbed friars sold it in 1529 (Cox-Rearick 1974). Leonardo's unpublished writings also noted that some images of "lust and sensuality ... excited beholders to the same excesses" (1956: 22). More often, corporeal response was referred to by way of the ancient tale of Praxiteles' naked *Aphrodite* on the island of Knidos that caused one man to masturbate and leave a "stain" on the marble, a story retold by Lucian in which the act took place at the statue's rear as though it represented a boy. The undercurrent of homoeroticism doubtless made the story even more titillating, and it was frequently cited as an example of the degree to which art moved viewers (Pliny: 36.20–2; Lucian: 11–18; Turner 2017).

Sight was certainly eroticized, especially in the Italian peninsula, by the French "School of Fontainebleau," Bartolomeus Spranger and the Prague School, German artists Hans Baldung and Lucas Cranach, and a cluster of artists in Haarlem like Hendrick Goltzius and Cornelis Cornelisz. van Haarlem. Depending on the context and circumstances, viewers included rulers, courtiers, lawyers, merchants, servants, courtesans, and single or married men and women. Voyeurism was most often displaced onto satyrs, half-human, half-animal creatures who performed revelation while maintaining the impression that the viewer is both privileged and better than the lusty animal.

Five paintings by Titian and his assistants dated to 1555–65 add a contemporary male figure to the popular scenario of a reclining female nude, positioning him as a courting wooer. Two canvases in the Prado and one in Berlin's Gemäldegalerie show musicians at the foot of Venus's couch, each fingering an organ (Figure 5.11), and in two others (Metropolitan Museum of Art, New York; Fitzwilliam Museum, Cambridge) the lover plays the lute.[13] These activities and instruments all had amusing, double-entendre connotations. In every case, the musician gazes at the pale, plentiful flesh of the reclining nude rather than at her face: the youngest, beardless organist in particular lowers his eyes in the direction of her genitals. Some scholars relate the images to what is said to be a Neoplatonic debate about whether beauty was best perceived by seeing or hearing. They can also be analyzed by reference to the tripartite Neoplatonic scheme of allegorical, sensual and bestial love, different reactions to images being feasible depending on audience and context. These canvases are commercial replicas rather than profound originals, sensual rather than philosophical, emotive more than intellectual. What is undeniable is that suggested sound works here as an affective element, not only issuing from the male musician but also evoked by tinkling satyr fountains occupying the backdrop of the two Madrid examples and in the music of a rustic bagpipe accompanying frolicking dancers in the New York case.

Such complex images could arouse different sensual and emotional reactions on different occasions and in varying contexts. People did not simply identify with fictional characters similar to themselves. Male viewers did not straightforwardly become Venus in their fantasies, but they enjoyed her languid relaxation or sexual fervor as well as their

FIGURE 5.11: Titian, *Venus, Cupid and an Organist*, c. 1555, oil on canvas, 150.2 × 218.2 cm. Museo del Prado, Madrid (P00421). Image courtesy of Getty Images.

visual access to her. The allegorical tenor of Bronzino's painting (Figure 5.7) draws viewers back again and again, and evokes no clear single emotional response. And that is the point, the capacity of the image to entice and to keep engendering courtly conversations on the nature of sensual love.

CONCLUSION

Growing awareness of emotions and their visual representation mark the period known as the Renaissance. Intellectual investigations and personal examinations of emotions went hand in hand with widespread ideas about their corporeal basis and visual impact. The mind, body, and "soul" were considered inseparable. Artists and theorists explored how to expand the repertoire of communicative, emotive visual culture, focusing on body language and facial expression, but also manipulating composition, color, and other tools. The overall context of any detail remained crucial, requiring viewers to bring their pictorial knowledge to bear on the reading of nuance and variety. Emotional responses to art were complemented by self-consciousness about visual skill and bodily sensation.

CHAPTER SIX

Literature

SARAH MCNAMER

Literary texts from the period 1300–1600 offer an especially rich trove for the study of emotions in the past. The European vernaculars came into their own as literary languages during these centuries, and the period is marked by generic inventiveness, by the development of vernacular manuscript traditions, by the spread of literacy and the emergence of print culture, by new conceptions of authorship and a wider range of authorial voices, and by the proliferation of varied textual and emotional communities. Scholarship that attends closely to what literature from this period might tell us about how emotions were understood, imagined, experienced, and practiced in history has been very energetic in recent years. Because literary texts often offer fine-grained descriptions of emotion, much of this scholarship has sought to analyze how certain emotions are represented in particular genres (lyric, romance, affective meditations, books of consolation) or in the work of particular authors, including this period's most prominent canonical figures—Dante, Juan Ruiz, Machaut, Chaucer, Christine de Pizan, Rabelais, Teresa de Avila, Shakespeare, and so on. Another strand of scholarship has asked not only how emotions are represented in literature, but how such representations are ideologically inflected, serving to promote certain power structures and social configurations even as they seem to concern the most intimate, apolitical aspects of the self. A further development adds an additional layer of complexity, asking questions having to do with the "how" as much as the "what" of emotion. How, in other words, did literary texts participate in the making of emotion in history? This question has required methodological innovation and experimentation, but it is also one that is manifestly invited by the strong conventions of *imitatio* and performative reading that mark the use of literature in the late Middle Ages and continue to proliferate in varied domains (the schoolroom, the salon, the prayer closet) through much of the Renaissance.

These strands of scholarship have often been vexed in productive ways by a fundamental question: as verbal art, inflected—by definition—by artifice (formal shaping, verbal play, counterfactual narratives, imaginative worlds, scripts for performance), what can literature really tell us about *history*, including the history of emotion? To put it another way: if the history of emotion as a field is energized, in large part, by the desire to understand a fundamental question, *how did people feel in the past?*, then the artifice at the heart of literature would seem, to some, to compromise its value as historical source. To situate literature under the rubric of "the cultural history of emotion" rather than "the history of emotion" has been one way of handling—some might say delicately sidestepping—this. One broad disciplinary question that requires further investigation, then, is invited by the very title of this series, *A Cultural History of the Emotions*. Some scholarship on the place or function of literature in the history of emotion has questioned the distinction between "cultural history" and "history," suggesting either directly or through its methods that the artifice of literature is in fact part and parcel of the history of emotions *tout court* in this period, rather than a separate entity we might define as "cultural" (e.g., Jaeger 1999; McNamer 2007, 2015; Newman 2016); but this remains food for thought.

What follows, then, is an overview of the state of play in the field that is by no means comprehensive in its coverage, for it clearly would be impossible even to list, let alone describe, the abundant scholarship on literature and emotion in the late Middle Ages and early Renaissance throughout Europe. Important work on major writers and relevant subjects—Boccaccio on consolation, or Diego de San Pedro on love, or Montaigne on melancholy, or Wyatt on loss, for instance—has of necessity been given short shrift or none in these pages (but see Barolini 2015; Munjic 2008; Ferrari 2014; Braden 2004). What I have highlighted here is a sampling of representative work that situates itself directly or implicitly within the confluence of scholarly currents that have taken shape as "the history of emotion" since the turn of the millennium. It would be a mistake, however, to set to one side studies that do not explicitly align themselves with the history of emotion, for most work on emotion in literature from this period does not claim affiliation with the history of emotions as such. Such studies possess indispensable value for those working in this field; our "soundings" of the scholarship will therefore include this category of work. Many of these studies, with their precise delineations of the language and contours of feeling in literary texts, emerged from the twentieth-century tradition of philologically informed close readings and from the rich work on subjectivity and desire inspired by Foucauldian, feminist, and cultural-studies approaches of the late twentieth century.

Studies of literature and the history of emotion have tended to address the subject feeling by feeling—love, grief, anger, compassion, and so on; yet some of the most important conversations have begun to focus more on the "how" of feeling during this period, or the "why" of this period's affective logics and ideologies, than the "what" of particular emotions. The overview that follows, then, will not be consistent in its categories: we will move from certain emotions to methodological issues to particular genres to promising new approaches and so on. This inconsistency itself illustrates the state of play in the field, where fundamental categories of analysis are shifting and provisional—very much "at play." This is an exciting domain of study for that very reason.

Let's begin, then, with the most capacious, important and impossible of subjects, the subject of so much of the literature composed and circulating in the fourteenth through the sixteenth centuries.

LOVE

"Romantic love" or *fin'amor* is said to have emerged as a distinct cultural construct in the centuries just preceding our period here; questions concerning the ways that the troubadour lyric, recastings of the *Song of Songs*, and early vernacular romance participated in the making of this emotion thus lie outside our purview (but see especially Reddy 2012). Yet these lyrics, romances, and related genres had afterlives, and this has been an interesting site of scholarly exploration.

That resonant formulation in the early Italian lyric—"Al cor gentil repara sempre amore" (Love always repairs to the noble heart)—encapsulates one of the fundamental ideas present in this tradition: the idea that love is "ennobling" (Jaeger 1999). Articulated in lyrics composed just prior to the period under consideration here, by Guinizzelli, Cavalcanti, Dante, and other poets of the Tuscan *dolce stil novo* (c. 1265–1305), the concept of romantic love as a "noble" emotion has invited explorations of the multiple meanings of that term as an ethical quality, a marker of elevated social rank, and an aspect of an affective aesthetic. Specific permutations of *gentil* love in the Italian lyric tradition, particularly as this tradition influenced Dante's *Commedia*, have received ample attention from literary scholars, primarily in critical studies that do not locate themselves explicitly in the field of the history of emotion, yet contain much of value to those interested in the interplay of literary and affective histories (e.g., Holmes 2008; Barolini 2014). Gregory Stone's (2015) recent work on Averroist theories of emotion, particularly as embedded in that difficult poem by Dante's *primo amico* Cavalcanti, "Donna mi prega," is likely to prompt a fresh look at the Italian lyric tradition and at Dante's articulations of love in the *Commedia*.

There is potential for taking the issue of the historical redeployment of literary tropes further, by tracing with greater specificity the ways in which urban Tuscan communes adapted affective structures inherited from aristocratic courts or by exploring how forms of feeling articulated in early Arabic literature continued to circulate in the Iberian peninsula through the sixteenth century (Menocal 1987, 1994). One example of the value of such work for the history of emotions is Valerie Wilhite's literary microhistory, "The Urban Consistori and the Reconceptualization of the Court's Love Lyric" (2005). Engaging here with the concept of emotional communities (Rosenwein 2006), Wilhite focuses on a particular community in Catalonia, tracing the appropriation of troubadour motifs by the *Consistori de la subregaya companhia del Gai Saber* in the fourteenth and fifteenth centuries. The *joc florals* or "floral games" of this literary society transformed the emotions embedded in the troubadour lyric into something quite removed from its original ethos, Wilhite argues: a displacement of emotional utterance or display by what Wilhite calls a self-reflexive emphasis on craftsmanship or "materiality," materiality that includes great concern for the presentation of lyrics in expensively illuminated manuscripts (2005: 214). Wilhite argues that this change "comes from the social structure and the values of those dominating and willfully, forcefully, shaping this structure"—values founded on a commitment to religious orthodoxy (2005: 210). The "social shape of the troubadour's terrain," as Wilhite puts it—and with it, "the focal position of the emotion in lyric"—could not last in a community where "orthodoxy, bureaucracy, and written law" dominated (209).

Petrarch is of course the great poet of love in this period, the *Rime sparse* standing as the most complex and influential exploration of love in the fourteenth century and resounding in rich and varied ways in every major linguistic tradition in Europe through the sixteenth. Influential though he was, Petrarch has not yet been absorbed into the history of emotion in a direct and sustained way; studies of the *Rime sparse* or *Canzoniere* have been framed in other terms (e.g., Sturm-Maddox 1992; Braden 1999; Holmes 2000). Yet the potential latent in bringing questions informed by history of emotions research, with its interest in the imbrication of literature and life, can be glimpsed through the case of Louise Labé. As Deborah Lesko Baker observes in her introduction to Labé's complete poetry and prose, Labe's spirited, accomplished and revisionist elegies and sonnets transform both the Petrarchan tradition itself and engage with the celebrated works of her immediate forebears and contemporaries, Marot, Du Bellay, and Ronsard (Baker 2006: 8). Labé's poems have seemed to many readers to be rooted in felt experience—in "history," that is; as Baker observes, they evince an "achingly erotic" quality in which "so many readers have been impelled to hear the thinly veiled confession of a strikingly unconventional life," even as critics recognize that the artistry of these poems is beyond dispute: they are far from artless (Baker 2006: 1; see also Baker 1996).

The interplay between artifice and history, between literary forms and felt experience, remains a compelling subject that could benefit from more extensive work on that most intriguing of pronouns, "I." Given the prominence of the first-person singular in the medieval and Renaissance love lyric, Reddy's concept of emotives would appear to be a particularly fitting tool to deploy in further research on the nexus between literature and the history of emotions in this period. Studies of the "I" of the medieval and Renaissance love lyric have tended to focus on subjectivity or the development of poetic self-consciousness, rather than the affective functions of the lyric "I" in the history of emotion as such (e.g., Holmes 2000; Spearing 2005; Dubrow 2008). Perhaps it is a rather short step for studies of subjectivity or poetic self-consciousness to be brought into productive conversation with the history of emotion as such. My consideration of "the impassioned 'I' in history," while not treating the love lyric itself, suggests how future historicist work on the first-person singular in lyrical modes (prose and poetry) might proceed (McNamer 2010: 67–73).

Heterosexual romantic love was not the only form of intimate love in this period, of course; varieties of same-sex desire have been a keen subject of interest for literary scholars (e.g., Maggi 2005), as have permutations of a closely related affective structure, friendship. In an intriguing essay described as "an attempt at emotional excavation" (Irish 2015: 412), Bradley Irish takes up the matter of friendship, in particular the revival of the Ciceronian ideal of friendship as exemplified in the Latin correspondence between Sir Philip Sidney and Hubert Languet, his friend and mentor. Letters were often considered an art in the early modern period, and this trove is indeed artful. As Irish observes, critical commentary on these letters has emphasized their debt to humanist traditions of the *ars epistolica*, as well as the *ludus literarius* of the Renaissance schoolroom; and their "explicit emotional content—flush with professions of devotion and love—owes largely to the Ciceronian paradigm of *amicitia perfecta*," perfect friendship. "The Sidney/Languet correspondence bears the stamp of this humanist rhetorical machine," Irish writes, "and its affective tenor is turned accordingly . . . But this is not the entire story" (2015: 413). The story Irish excavates demonstrates that these letters deploy Ciceronian tropes and ideals, but are, at the same time, beset by complex tensions: "in their affective complexity these letters recall not only the conventions of classical friendship literature, but also the emotional fireworks of a sonnet sequence, primed with bitter ambivalence, latent aggression, and frustrated erotics" (413). Irish offers a nuanced interpretation of affect and what he calls "counter-affect" in the letters; the latter term, Irish's invention, may prove to be a useful concept to others working in the field. In addition to tracing "the erotic component of Sidney and Languet's relationship," Irish explores the "flip side: the mutually competing frustrations and resentments that fester in the correspondence, emerging both from Languet's overbearing affection and from Sidney's refusal to reciprocate it" (419). Methodologically, Irish's study contributes to the debate about the relationship between "literature" (in this case, letters replete with Ciceronian rhetoric and Petrarchan affective tropes) and "life" in the early modern period by asserting that while we cannot take the sentiments expressed in Renaissance letters to be straightforward barings of the soul, it would be equally remiss to dismiss them as mere rhetoric or convention: given that the letters were "not mere compositional exercises," and that "they really did circulate in the world," it would be a mistake to conclude that their affective dimensions "can be attributed *merely* to the rhetorical conventions of humanist epistolary theory, or that conventionality itself must somehow evacuate emotional sincerity" (413).

ANGER

Most studies of anger in medieval and Renaissance literary texts have tended to focus on its pragmatic functions and their contingent social contexts. The definition of anger in Aristotle's *Rhetoric*—as a painful emotion accompanied by a desire for revenge for a perceived slight (Kennedy 1991: 2.2, 1378a, 124)—has often been cited as a baseline from which to gauge various articulations of this emotion in medieval and Renaissance literature. The extent to which the *Rhetoric* circulated and influenced vernacular writers, especially in the earlier part of the period under consideration here, remains a compelling subject for investigation (Copeland 2014). Literary studies seeking to contribute to the history of anger have tended to offer detailed descriptions of their texts while highlighting the Aristotelian conception of the emotion's practical function in a given social context. One result of these descriptive studies has been to illuminate an aspect of anger's historicity in relation to valence or appraisal, both key terms in emotion studies more generally: that is, that anger—so often understood as a "negative emotion" in modern cultural contexts— was often understood as a positive emotion. Its status as a sin, indeed one of the Seven

FIGURE 6.1: Giotto, Wrath, c. 1305, fresco, 120 x 55 cm. Arena Chapel, Padua. Image courtesy of Wikimedia Commons.

Deadly Sins (depicted with special vividness by Giotto), could be tempered or mitigated by context, as in the case of the "righteous anger" displayed by saints.

There have been some interesting departures from this method, which attends closely to how primary texts themselves articulate anger. One of these engages critical theory—theory that is not only post-medieval, but postmodern—in an effort to understand anger in Dante's *Commedia*. On the face of it, this approach would seem to be ahistorical, and vulnerable to the charge of anachronism. But as Jeremy Tambling argues, critical theory has the potential to expose to view some of the affective complexities embedded in Dante's great poem—complexities that are of *historical* interest; moreover, one could equally describe as "anachronistic" the belief that there is a "determinate knowledge of how the fourteenth century felt, as if the medieval had not been created as such by Romantic or post-Romantic readings" (1997: 402). In "Dante and the modern subject: Overcoming anger in the *Purgatorio*," Tambling excavates allusions to "the modern" in the *Purgatorio*, affording a glimpse of how anger was perceived, even within the medieval period, to have a past as well as a future, with something at stake for the self in choosing to feel in one or the other of these temporal modes. A conceptualization of emotional alterities, in other words, is embedded in the poem. "The link between modernity and anger in the text becomes a teasing one which I want to pursue: it seems that anger becomes a trope of modernity" (Tambling 1997: 402). Anger in the *Purgatorio*, as Tambling sees it, is "not a single emotion, but double" (406). Tambling draws out this doubleness, exposing anger's complex relationship to gentleness, to erotic desire, to melancholy, and to accedia, drawing on an array of theorists of affect and subjectivity—Freud, Kristeva, Lyotard, Nietzsche, and Benjamin—to illuminate very specific features of Dante's poetry. In doing so, he contends that "in anger there is a mutilation or halving of being" (413) that Dante appears to associate with the modern—and, in the end, to disavow. This complex argument and its methods are more risky and controversial than much of the scholarship on literature that seeks to understand emotion in historical terms, but Tambling's use of critical theory as a tool in this endeavor merits renewed attention.

AFFECT THEORY

While the question of how to make productive use of critical theory has been a recurrent concern in literary studies that seek to contribute to the history of emotion, the more salient issue during the past decade has been the question of how—or whether—the history of emotion can incorporate insights and methods from the loosely affiliated body of work that has come to be called affect theory, which draws on certain poststructuralist modes of thought in combination with cultural theory, theories of perception and sensation, and developments in affective neuroscience. *The Affect Theory Reader* has been particularly influential in literary studies (Gregg and Seigworth 2010). The usefulness and limitations of affect theory for the history of emotion, and more particularly for the study of medieval and Renaissance literature, is a subject of continuing debate and probing questions. Stephanie Trigg, for instance, published an article in 2014 that expressed hesitation concerning the use of affect theory—which can appear to be ahistorical—for medieval literary studies that seek to historicize emotion; yet her more recent essay, this one focusing on early modern texts and contexts, seeks to illuminate its potential usefulness (Trigg 2017). The ongoing work of Glenn Burger and Holly Crocker (Crocker 2007; Burger 2017), including their forthcoming edited volume *Medieval Affect, Feeling, and Emotion*, is rich in astute insights regarding the premises and value of "the history of emotions" and "affect theory" as rubrics under which to situate work in medieval and early modern literary studies. In its provocative suggestion that neither rubric is sufficient on its own for evaluating the historicity of affective states in medieval literary texts and their contexts, their forthcoming "Introduction" to that volume is likely to influence the field in ways that cannot yet be predicted.

In one sense, however, "affect" (usually understood as that which lies beneath the threshold of conscious awareness and the will) as distinct from "emotion" (conscious states—often willed, cultivated, and practiced—marked by valence or appraisal) has been a compelling subject of study since 2005 under a different rubric: that of historical phenomenology. The work of Bruce R. Smith is especially noteworthy here. Smith's essay "Hearing Green" (2004) prefigures the richer, more ample treatment of this intriguing subject in *The Key of Green: Passion and Perception in Renaissance Culture* (2009). Drawing on early modern and contemporary theories of the sensory and affective effects of the color green, as well as copious evidence from material culture, Smith demonstrates that green was strongly associated with a quality of longing and desire, a quality that one could hear as well as see. Smith thus excavates a way of perceiving that did not separate sight from sound; indeed one of the major insights of this study is that a phenomenon that we moderns might consider a rarity with its own label, synesthesia, was not a rare curiosity in the Renaissance. Sensory experience did not necessarily align with what is often considered to be a biological given: that there are five distinct senses. Color, in short, had auditory resonance.

Sense perceptions themselves, Smith argues, are cultural constructs—and infused with affective valence. To hear green, in the Renaissance, was "to hear passionately, to hear longingly" (2005: 150). Smith's method rests in part on investigating the history of the word: "In early modern Scots *green* was recognized as a verb. *To green* was 'to desire earnestly, to long *after, for*' (OED, 'green,' v2)" (2005: 150). In this alone, Smith enriches a standard method in history of emotions research, the precise definition of culturally specific emotion vocabularies, by extending lexical inquiry to verbs, adverbs, and

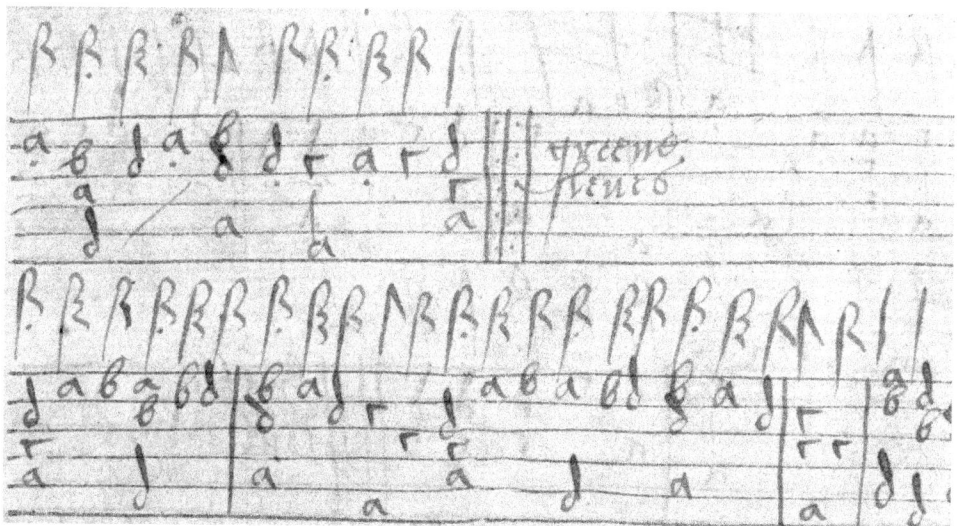

FIGURE 6.2: Lute tablature, "Greensleeves." The Board of Trinity College, Dublin, MS 408, p. 104.

adjectives—lexical forms that have received far less attention than nouns as historians and anthropologists have sought to illuminate the cultural variability of emotion (Wierzbicka 1999; Rosenwein 2002). Smith brings his innovative methods and rich analysis of early modern material culture to bear on an analysis of a wide array of literary texts of the English Renaissance, including poems by James I of Scotland, the popular ballad "Greensleeves," Marlowe's *Hero and Leander*, Marvell's "The Garden," and Spenser's *Faerie Queene*.

Significantly, Smith sees these works as key sources for understanding the cultural construction of emotion, in the sense that they participated in that construction; they are not simply epiphenomenal reflections of forms of theorizing conducted and completed elsewhere, in the scientific or philosophical literature of the time. This itself gestures toward another key issue in the scholarship on literature and the history of emotion at present: the question of how literature serves, or might serve, as source for the history of emotion.

LITERATURE AS SOURCE FOR THE HISTORY OF EMOTION

The question of literature's status or usefulness as a source for the study of the history of emotion is broad and complex. Its reach extends well beyond the temporal and geographical limits of this essay and volume, and a survey of the question would include attention to work in cognitive science and history as well as literature (e.g., Oatley 1999; Reddy 2001; Hogan 2002). Yet this question merits some attention here. A dominant approach in medieval and Renaissance literary studies has been to locate authoritative or influential ideas about emotion in a given historical and cultural context (ideas from theology, philosophy, faculty psychology, astrology, Galenic medicine, and so on) and to examine their impact or uptake in a particular literary text or genre. Work in this vein deploys the term "representation" frequently. The way literature represents an emotion has been of keen interest to literary scholars, and close analysis of how given texts engage in the replication or, alternatively, the creative recasting of a culture's dominant "emotion scripts"—a concept adopted from anthropology, sociology and cross-cultural linguistics (Wierzbicka 1999)—has been a very fruitful enterprise. Some of the most interesting work on literary representations of shame and grief in the medieval and early modern periods, for example, testifies to the value of this approach.

Let's take a look at a few samples of the work in this vein, then, before returning to the broader question at hand. Where shame is concerned, representations of *vergüenza* in Spanish literature have garnered significant attention, in part for the challenges they present to translation; indeed the question of the translatability of shame/*vergüenza* has continued to preoccupy theorists of emotion, in ways that repay attention from literary scholars (Hurtado de Mendoza et al. 2010). In the Italian context, *Due Dialogi della Vergogna*, a sixteenth-century analysis of shame in the form of two dramatic dialogues, has been recognized as a rare and detailed source for the study of this emotion (Gundersheimer 1994: 34). Relationships between shame and other emotions or social constructs—guilt (McTaggart 2012), honor (Trigg 2012), and gender (Flannery 2011)—have produced lively conversations, conversations that show no signs of abating, given shame's status as an emotion so manifestly intertwined with culturally variable ideologies and forms of social control. Attention to grief has been equally energetic. In this case, readings of literary texts have been informed by research on religious beliefs, ritual practices, and material culture, as well as the shifting configurations of friendship and family structures over the course of the period 1300–1600 (Vaught and Bruckner 2003; Sánchez y Sánchez 2010; Rider and Friedman 2011).

Nuanced analyses such as these have been very valuable at showing how certain ideas and ideologies play out in literary texts—and how the emergence of new literary forms, such as the essay, provided cultural space for reflection on affective states (Ferrari 2014). Another strand of scholarship has explicitly engaged with a perceived limitation of these studies, however. This strand has sought to move beyond the model of "representation" to ask how literary texts served to generate affective selves or emotional communities, or how they served to reinforce or contest dominant emotion scripts or affective ideologies or practices of feeling. In short, they ask how literary texts functioned not only to replicate, reflect, or represent ideas about emotion in culture, but how they participated in the making of emotions in history.

In many instances this shift has been enacted in subtle ways, as literary scholars have taken one of the precepts of cultural studies—that there is always at some level a dynamic interplay between the literature and the ideologies at work in history—one step further. To return to the subject of grief, for instance: several recent studies on the death of children have asked not only how certain literary texts represent parental grief, and what kinds of discourses they may be drawing on in such depictions, but how such texts serve to redefine and reevaluate childhood itself or the parent-child bond in the ways they offer or withhold consolation. This body of work participates in a much larger conversation in the history of emotions, a conversation that began many decades ago: whether or how premodern parents mourned the deaths of infants and young children (Hanawalt 2002; Barclay and Reynolds 2016).

In a recent collection of essays dedicated to understanding emotions surrounding the death of children, Andrew Lynch (2016) engages with the interplay between history and literature by taking up a particular genre, that of Christian boy martyr legends in later

FIGURE 6.3: Cologne, Reliquary bust of a young martyr, artist unknown, c. 1310–25, polychromed wood, 27.4 × 23.4 × 11.6 cm. Yale Gallery of Art 1985.42.1.

medieval England. The notion of the "happy" boy martyr provides a striking example of the historicity of emotion, one that the radiant face of a reliquary bust from early fourteenth-century Cologne captures at a glance, especially when we ask the simple question it invites: *why is this boy smiling?*

Legends of boy martyrs present their subjects as *felix* or *beatus*, themselves keywords with rich histories. But Lynch argues that vernacular legends, in particular, do more than reinforce faith. They create a space for grief, and they can also be recognized as "highly emotional narratives that engaged the hopes and fears of medieval people for male children, especially the emotions of mothers" (Lynch 2016: 25). As such, Lynch contends, they served extra-devotional functions: "by breaking down normal medieval judgments about the failings of youth, they also invite their readers to take the emotional life of boyhood seriously and to celebrate it" (25). Lynch calls attention to a conflict at the heart of many of these legends: "how do the elements of naïveté and pathos in the narrative of child death fit with the voluntarist and triumphal rhetoric of martyrdom and with a martyr's *imitatio Christi?*" (26). In doing so, Lynch suggests that the genre as a whole had the potential to challenge one of the dominant beliefs about power relations in the later Middle Ages: "Christ-likeness validated these young victims as conscious and willing agents, hence real martyrs. Without taking away all their boyishness of nature, their status as martyrs credited them, in the most important context, with an emotional alignment that challenged notions of adult superiority" (30). Lynch develops this thought through an extended consideration of the "politics of emotion" in the *South English Legendary* (composed in the thirteenth century, but popular through the fourteenth and fifteenth centuries) before turning to Chaucer's depiction of parental grief in the *Summoner's Tale* and the *Prioress's Tale*. Chaucer raises broad, searching questions in these tales, including questions having to do with genre and its consolations or lack thereof: the recourse to "hagiographic cliché" in the *Summoner's Tale* silences the mother's feelings, thus prompting critical assessment concerning "who has the best right, and who has the cultural power and the approved language, to speak the meaning of a child's death" (38).

The poetics of grief and consolation in the Middle English *Pearl*, described by Barbara Hanawalt as "the most famous and eloquent lament of the death of a daughter from the medieval period" (2002: 454), has been analyzed in a way that yokes the "literariness" of the poem—in particular, its sonic effects—to its performance and historical function (McNamer 2015). This approach participates in a current of scholarship that situates literary texts in contexts of practice, performance and *imitatio*—and thus helps to illuminate mechanisms for the making of emotion in history.

PERFORMING EMOTION

An understanding of the performative dimensions of literary texts and of emotion itself lies behind this strand of scholarship, which gives literature a more visible, constitutive role in the making of emotion in history. Certain genres were overtly designed to "change the heart." Devotional literature of the period is certainly in this category: affective meditations in prose and verse were explicitly designed for the cultivation of intimate love and compassion for Christ. As Anthony Bale (2010) has shown, these explicit designs were accompanied by other affective effects: Passion meditations and related narratives and images also generated forms of anti-Jewish sentiment constitutive of Christian feelings of community and love, as well as a complex cluster of emotions Bale terms "feeling persecuted." I have also traced the performative functions of Latin and vernacular affective meditations (McNamer 2010), calling attention to the ways they literally served to script compassion as a gendered emotion in the later Middle Ages—in ways more direct than the term imported by historians from anthropology, "emotion scripts," would suggest. My characterization of affective meditations as "intimate scripts in the history of emotion" (McNamer 2010: 1–21) has been taken up as a model for thinking about how other forms literature, too, were conceived of and used for the active cultivation of emotion in the later Middle Ages.

There are intriguing, contingent variations on affective meditations on the Passion, both before and after the reformations and counter-reformations of the era. In England, Lollard writings both swerve from and in some ways imitate the affectivity of traditional Passion meditations, fostering a mode of feeling that Fiona Somerset (2014) has called "feeling like saints." In Germany, sixteenth-century sermons redeploy structures of feeling embedded in the rhetoric of late-medieval devotional texts (Karant-Nunn 2010). In the Iberian peninsula, as Cynthia Robinson has shown, the motif of the "transformation of hearts" took on a distinctive cast in Castilian devotional culture of the fifteenth century: efforts to imagine Christ's afflictions with narrative realism, as imagined in and through the pseudo-Bonaventuran *Meditations on the Life of Christ*, were displaced in Castile by texts such as Eiximinis's meditations, in which architectural rather than bodily images become dominant, particularly metaphors of spaces within the heart. Robinson hypothesizes that this distinctive Iberian strand in devotional literature can be traced to the confluence of three major confessional traditions in the Iberian peninsula in the era prior to 1492: "the particularities of Eiximenis's meditations are due at least in part to a cultural climate in which members of three confessional communities lived side by side, but conversions and reversions were frequent and beliefs and confessional expression were profoundly affected by constant contact with other religious communities" (Robinson 2013: 164). In sixteenth-century Spain, as Elena Carrera (2007) has observed, religious and devotional writings become both a site for theorizing emotion and for scripting and enacting it. Drawing technological innovation into her discussion of emotion—for the printing press became a vehicle for the widespread dissemination of devotional texts in this period—Carrera illuminates a rich vein of mutually informing theory and practice in the writings of Ignatius of Loyola, Francisco de Osuna, Bernardino de Laredo, and Teresa of Avila. Carrera illuminates the centrality of "motions": "inner movements... which the individual learnt to perceive, interpret, stimulate, display, repress, or internalize in a methodical way" in the practice of affective prayer (2007: 236).

The overt training of feeling through devotional scripts is not the only site where performance, performativity, and concepts of practice have been deployed to open up new perspectives on the affective dimensions of literary texts. Far from it: practice theory, in its varied dimensions, is rapidly gaining recognition as the most productive framework for thinking about the role of literary texts in the history of emotion in this period. The recent collection *Emotions and War* exemplifies this shift. In this volume, the contributors seek to analyze the interplay between literature and history, in keeping with a fundamental claim: "Literary production and the historical experience of war interact powerfully in the creation of the emotional and cognitive resources with which lives are lived, beyond traditional notions of war literature as pre- or post-experiential 'propaganda' or 'reportage'" (Downes et al. 2015: 3). Most of these essays draw in some way on Monique Scheer's recent articulation of the usefulness of Pierre Bourdieu's theory of practice for the history of emotions; for, as the editors observe, "war inculcates a new *habitus* of emotional practice—and disrupts former practices—through the extraordinary demands that it makes of the body and mind, yet the particular nature of the *habitus* remains directly related to the social circumstances and cultural modes—and one might add, the technologies—within which it is learned and practised as an 'experience'" (3–4). In framing this collection of essays within the terms that Scheer has articulated, the editors highlight the imbrication of literature within history: "Following the logic of Scheer's view, writing is not simply *about* the historical and bodily emotional experience of war, but *of* it" (4). The studies here thus engage directly with key concepts and methods from the history of emotion as articulated by *historians*: emotion lexicons, emotional communities, and emotional regimes (Reddy 2001, 2012; Rosenwein 2006, 2015). Yet they also seek to yoke these concepts to what is distinctively literary; they attend to ways that particular genres and forms produce a distinctive "feel" of war or battle or peace. As a whole, then, this collection offers an array of essays that are valuable not only for their thematic matter, emotion, and war, but for the methods they employ. Stephanie Downes's essay on the French and English lyrics of Charles d'Orleans, for example, is a model of sophisticated literary-historical scholarship that deploys the tools of the history of emotion while engaging in fine close-readings of a genre, amatory lyric verse, that is often abstracted from history (Downes 2015).

Concepts of performance have also informed recent work on the conduct book. In some ways, the conduct book has presented a special challenge to literary scholars because it so overtly instructs its readers in the art and politics of performing emotion; how, then, can the genre be approached with a new degree of sophistication? Where the late-medieval bourgeois household is concerned, Glenn Burger (2017b) draws on affect theory to illuminate protocols of feeling in a range of English and continental texts; his astute attention to the somatic dimensions of affective conduct is particularly innovative (see also Saunders 2009). Where the upper echelons of power are concerned, Machiavelli's *The Prince* was preceded by a long lineage of advice manuals in the mirrors for princes genre, including those of Christine de Pisan, who advises royalty how to cultivate, manage, and display emotion. As Sharon Mitchell (2011) observes, there are intriguing gender differences at play in Christine's writings, not only between the kinds of emotions men and women are expected to display, but in the nexus between feeling and display itself. Who, in short, should feign emotions, and to what ends? Princesses, more than princes, according to Mitchell's nuanced reading. As Mitchell notes, Christine's *Livre du Corps de Policie* advises princes to seek counsel and show restraint; but it stops short of advising princes to fake emotion. The same is not true in the *Livre de Trois Vertus*. There, Christine advises both princesses and their chaperones to engage in what she calls "virtuous hypocrisies"—elucidated by Mitchell as "displays of charity, loyalty, and affection toward people for whom one may feel open hostility, not solely for self-benefit, but for the stability of the realm and the edification of observers who will be moved to imitate and promote these qualities" (2011: 86). One of the most intriguing aspects of Christine's *Livre des Trois Vertus* is its suggestion that "virtuous hypocrisies" should not remain hypocrisies forever: the gap between outward display and inner feeling should be closed. Like the Menagier de Paris or the Chevalier de la Tour Landry, Christine ultimately expects inner virtue to correspond to outward display. Yet Mitchell highlights an intriguing aspect of Christine's advice here, namely Christine's suggestion that chaperones can and should be instrumental in helping to close this gap. How? Not only by encouraging princesses to act the part until they feel the emotion, but by modeling emotional displays for the princess to imitate. As Mitchell notes, the notion that one learns to feel by participating in mimetic rituals was not unique to the plights of princesses: Susan Crane

FIGURE 6.4: Lancelot and Guinevere's first kiss, *Lancelot-Graal*, Northeastern France, 1310–15, New York, Pierpont Morgan Library MS M. 805.6, fol. 67r.

describes such performative rituals as a widespread feature of court culture in France and England during the Hundred Years' War (Crane 2002). Yet the role proposed for chaperones in Christine's book is unusual. Among other things, this passage opens up questions about servants and go-betweens in the history of emotion.

The most celebrated go-between in the history of emotion, of course, is a book: the "Galeotto" of Dante's *Inferno*, Canto V. The mediated nature of desire in Dante's rendering of the story of Paolo and Francesca has received insightful treatment in recent years; Freccero's brief reading of how love happens "by the book" in Dante's great poem is particularly suggestive (Freccero 2009). As one of a large cast of characters populating Arthurian literature, Galehaut and his kind have been the subject of recent studies of medieval reading practices and the history of emotion. Three essay collections focusing on Arthurian material, *The Arthur of the North* (Kalinke 2011), *Arthur of the North* (Bandlein 2015), and *Emotions in Medieval Arthurian Literature* (Brandsma et al. 2015), offer important interventions in this vein. Many of the primary texts discussed in these volumes predate the period under consideration in this chapter; yet romances and sagas composed in the twelfth and thirteenth centuries continued to circulate in the fourteenth and beyond. Reception and adaptation for different audiences and emotional communities and the translation of "language-specific emotional systems" (Larrington 2015: 74) is a major concern in these collections. The editors of *Emotions in Medieval Arthurian Literature* underscore the uptake of literary texts in varied settings as one of the most productive angles for literary specialists to explore, observing that literary texts not only "represent" but "also evoke and play upon emotion in the audiences which heard these texts performed or read" (Brandsma et al. 2015: 3).

Attention to the adaptation, translation, reception, and uptake of Arthurian material in Scandinavia has produced some particularly intriguing results—including observations on the stoic *non*performance of emotions. Frank Brandsma and Carolyne Larrington have observed certain patterns in the recasting of Arthurian material for the emotional cultures of the North: in short, Scandinavian literatures tend to play it cool, minimizing the emotional display, dialogue, and rhetoric of their sources (Brandsma 2015; Larrington 2015). Joyful and sorrowful scenes alike are toned down or eliminated—so much so that Brandsma raises a blunt question: "Where are the emotions?" (2015: 102). Brandsma's wry style underscores a more serious point, that the unemotional style of certain literary texts can itself be a very interesting window into the history of emotion. Indeed Brandsma exposes even greater complexity here by drawing on modern neurological research, specifically on hypotheses concerning mirror neurons and their function; Brandsma suggests that we can identify "mirrored emotions" in "mirror characters, who are explicitly demonstrating, and thus appealing to, a certain emotion. By analysing what is witnessed and by whom, and which reactions are displayed by the witness, we may gain insight into the intended emotional impact of the text on the listeners, and even chart the sequence of projected emotions as the tale progresses" (2015: 101).

Brandsma's concern with identifying mechanisms for the replication of emotions in and through medieval literature gestures toward a subject that has been taken up, from a very different angle, by Lynn Enterline in one of the most sophisticated studies of the performance of emotion to date: *Shakespeare's Schoolroom: Rhetoric, Discipline, Emotion* (2012). Drawing on psychoanalytic theory, Bourdieu's concepts of practice and *habitus*, and a rich archive of materials related to the early modern grammar school (educational treatises, rhetorical and grammatical manuals, popular plays and skits, and set texts from the classical tradition), Enterline presents a complex argument regarding "how the all-male grammar schools affected the emotional registers of early modern masculinity" (2012: 9). Enterline offers a compelling analysis of practices of discipline and *imitatio* in the early modern grammar school. One of her overarching aims is to illuminate how early training of this kind informed the work of Shakespeare, Spenser, Milton, and other early modern writers. But in doing so, she also illuminates another fascinating aspect of the nexus between literature and the history of emotion, namely, the circulation, adaptation, and performance of classical Latin texts in the early modern period. Enterline observes, for instance, that boys were required to translate, imitate, and perform Ovid's renditions of women's voices; what did it mean, then, for a schoolboy to have such robust training in temporarily "becoming" the grieving Niobe, the vengeful Hecuba or the abandoned Ariadne? Enterline suggests that such practices of emotional impersonation, particularly the imitation of Ovid, help to explain Shakespeare's nuanced characterizations of women; but more than this, these practices served to form the psyches of men such as Shakespeare, participating in a form of Renaissance self-fashioning only partly conscious. This book, then, is a deep and nuanced history of emotion, in that it seeks to reveal "connections between humanist rhetorical training and early modern experiences of subjectivity, sexuality, gender, and the inner life of personal feeling" (Enterline 2012: 11). It also asserts, indirectly more than directly, the value of psychoanalytic theory to the historicist enterprise. In doing so, it raises a question that has not yet received direct and sustained attention in recent work on methods in the history of emotion, namely, the usefulness and validity of drawing on psychoanalytic theory. If, as some of the finest theorists and practitioners in the history of emotion have maintained, recent work in neuroscience and cognitive psychology is both relevant and productive, potentially providing useful analytical tools for historicist projects (e.g., Reddy 2001; Stevenson 2010), should not approaches informed by psychoanalysis be welcomed into the historicist fold as well? Enterline's book itself stands as eloquent testimony that it can and should, as do other recent contributions (e.g., Rosenfeld 2011), but this—like many intriguingly unresolved issues at the intersection of literature, history, and emotion—remains a matter for debate.

CONCLUSION

One striking feature of scholarship on literature and the history of emotion in Europe, 1300–1600, is the diversity of approaches to the subject. The multiplicity of voices and methods surveyed here has a very concrete formal analogue: the thematically oriented essay collection has been the dominant form of publication in this field. At present, there is no tone-setting, single-authored book on the particular challenges of taking up literature as a primary guide to understanding the history of emotion; the field lacks a sustained treatment which might offer methodological direction in the way that Reddy's *Navigation of Feeling* or Rosenwein's *Emotional Communities* have done. Perhaps it is in the nature of literature, or literary study as it is currently practiced, that a more comprehensive effort to theorize emotion historically via literary texts from this period has not been attempted; or perhaps it is time for literary specialists to take up the challenge of evaluating and designing theories and methods that are more capacious in scope, now that the way has been paved by so many insightful and experimental forays into literature as a source for the history of feeling.

CHAPTER SEVEN

In Private

The Individual and the Domestic Community

JEREMY GOLDBERG AND STEPHANIE TARBIN

In a much-cited passage from William Langland's later fourteenth-century English religious allegory *Piers Plowman*, the narrator, Dame Study, laments how the lords and ladies "leve the chief halle" and instead "eten by hymselve / in a pryvee parlour . . . Or in a chambre with a chymenee [chimney]" (Langland 1978: 103, Passus X, ll. 98–100). Langland's text alerts us to the fact that attitudes to and practices of privacy, domesticity, and community were not stable in the past, and it also alludes to certain expectations about emotional comportment within noble households. The passage is part of a critique of pride and covetousness, and particularly the lack of charity shown to the poor by the great, who owe their wealth and position to God. Great lords should stay home and liberally look after their dependents, rather than be "[h]omliche at othere mennes houses, and hatien hir owene" (Langland 1978: 103, Passus X, l. 95). The disordered emotions of lords and ladies set the tenor for the household: "Elenge is the halle, ech day in the wike, / Ther the lord ne the lady liketh noght to sitte" (Langland 1978: 103, Passus X, ll. 96–7). The hall and its company will be troubled in the absence of the lord and lady, whose withdrawal expresses a dislike for their own household and privileges selfish desires. Their presence in the hall is necessary for practicing the charitable love that secures household harmony and contentment. The passage shows the emotional dimension of social relationships and, notably, values disciplined performances of charity in shared household spaces above the free expression of individual desire in private rooms.

This chapter explores emotional norms and practices within the "private" realm of the domestic community. It begins by examining concepts of privacy and models of solitude and community, before turning to the household as an emotional community. We will pay particular attention to the cultural meanings of two widely found objects that were symbolic of household life and that have strong emotional resonances, namely the bed and the table. Examining the social relationships that centered on beds and tables helps to illuminate how domestic spaces were constituted as more or less "private" and the emotional practices associated with those spaces (Barclay 2017a: 22). As Tara Hamling has recently observed, "[o]bjects were good for thinking and feeling with" and the household was "the principal site for daily experience and interactions with possessions" (2017: 135). It is also worth noting here that, along with the feelings and affects categorized as "emotions" in modern terms, the medieval conceptual domain encompassed moral conditions and behavioral states such as modesty and chastity. We will finally, and more briefly, explore the gender dimensions of these objects and spaces. Cultural associations of women with the domestic or the private, and emotions in this domain, as opposed to men with the public or the world beyond the home, require examination.

Privacy, like any other concept, needs to be historicized. Lexicography can provide clues. For example, the vernaculars of later medieval England, namely English and the more aristocratic French of England, both have terms that resonate with modern usage. "*In prive*" (Middle English), sometimes used as the antithesis of "openly" or "*apert*," maps onto "in secret" or "in confidence" in current usage (*Middle English Dictionary*: privē, 1.a). Thus the Wycliffe Bible renders Matthew 6:18 as "that thou be not seen fastynge to men, but to thi fadir that is in hidlis [in secret], and thi fadir that seeth in priuey." Similarly when the official French record of the English Parliament talks of a confidential conversation with the king it uses the adverb "*particulerment*" (*Anglo-Norman Dictionary*: "particulerment," adv.). Such usages are found from the last part of the fourteenth century. "In private," used to suggest a more secluded space or restricted company, appears to postdate our period, though we may notice Shakespeare's lines in *Romeo and Juliet*, "Away from light steales home my heauie sonne, / And priuate in his Chamber pennes himselfe" (*Oxford English Dictionary*: "private," adj., 1, II, 9–11). French as spoken in France also came to attribute resonances of the hidden, the secret, and the clandestine to *privé*, *privance*, and *priveté* (Duby 1987: 6).

The emotional associations of privacy in this period are complex and are often associated with secrecy or seclusion. In literature, private feelings and actions were commonly portrayed as challenging, even endangering, communal values and social order. Adulterous lovers and malevolent plotters required privacy to act upon illicit desires. Yet such literary representations also recognize the private domain, or the secluded space, as the appropriate venue for expressing personal feelings and intimate relationships (Goodall 1992; Gibson 2001). In practice, solitude or the capacity to retreat from the company of others was generally regarded with suspicion and was probably neither desirable nor a matter of choice within pre-modern culture. An exception was those devoted to particular religious austerity, such as members of the Carthusian order, which unusually saw a significant expansion of its foundations in the later Middle Ages. Carthusian monks, unlike other religious orders, occupied separate dwellings, each with a small garden arranged around a cloister. They were provided with meals through a hatch, and only joined other members for the daily offices of matins and vespers in the monastic church (Wickerstrom 2000: 244–7). Such living arrangements meant that Carthusian monks were freed from daily social interactions to develop an intensely personal relationship with the divine. Solitude, in this instance, fostered emotional intimacy between monk and God.

Late medieval Catholicism provided models for those few laity who wished to lead a solitary life of devotion such as anchorites, anchoresses, and hermits, but by offering spiritual guidance and receiving alms even they expected regular contact with the communities in which they were located. Later medieval anchorholds, often attached to parish churches, were an essentially north-west European urban phenomenon (Mulder-Bakker 2005: 12–13). The Beguinages of the Low Countries and the Rhineland, as well as the *pinzochere* of Italian towns, provided quasi-conventual communities of devout laywomen with a high degree of social, economic, and spiritual solidarity (Pappi 1992; Simons 2001; Frazier 2005). In such semi-secluded yet socially embedded environments, devout women achieved mystical unions with Christ, expressed in highly charged emotional language and physical imagery. They were increasingly subject to regulation by bishops suspicious of women's devotional movements, which did not fall under a formal (and male) rule (Simons 2001; Deane 2016).

Medieval religious lives were more commonly organized around collective models and experiences. Monastic life required monks and nuns to withdraw from worldly attachments in order to serve God, but their self-discipline and self-denial were supported by shared commitments to obedience, poverty, chastity, and stability. In practice, religious orders enjoyed highly communal lives. Meals were regularly shared and there was interaction with the lay community in terms of lay servants employed and even visits beyond the monastic precinct. Similarly, a collegiate model of communal living with a common hall was increasingly adopted for all ranks of the secular clergy (Bertram 2008). At York, the chantry priests of the cathedral were required to reside in St William's College from the early 1460s. This model was also adopted by university colleges. Community was here equated not merely with commensality, but with hierarchy and discipline. Individual desires were subordinated to the harmonious coexistence of the group.

The adoption of collective and communal models was a characteristic of pre-modern societies generally. Voluntary religious associations aimed to nurture charitable love, drawing on notions of brotherhood and sisterhood to express the strong bonds between members. Craft guilds, whose roots may sometimes have been in devotional confraternities, characterized most towns of any size. Elite males formed their own collectivities, such as the aristocratic *Stuben* found in the German lands, the crossbow guilds of northern Europe, or the youthful Venetian *Compagnie della Calza* (Braustein 1987: 577; Crombie 2011; Brown 2004: 20–1, 141). Such groups served to assert and reinforce gender and status identities and hierarchies. Thus, to be a member of a *Calza* company one had to be young, male, and patrician. In England at the end of the Middle Ages we find guilds of maidens and sometimes guilds of bachelors (Beattie 2007: 119–21). Nonetheless, such expressions of social distinction coexisted with emotional ideals of harmony, peace, and amity within similar status groups.

The family provided an important model for emotional ideals of love, authority, and obedience in social groups. Notions of kinship also implied affective attachments and obligations, while serving to join together people who recognized ties of blood and of marriage, as well as spiritual kinship and fictive bonds. The most basic, most ubiquitous, and most important communal identity, however, was that of the household, the co-resident community usually comprising in western parts of Europe close kin and, particularly in urban contexts in north-western Europe, also live-in servants and apprentices. Pre-modern Europe was a "household society" comprised of communities bound variously by ties of marriage, blood, or, in the case of apprentices and servants, employment (O'Day 2007: 3–5). Households may also be conceptualized as "emotional communities," linked by affective experiences produced within daily domestic life as well as influenced by cultural norms of emotional expression.

The social ties between household members themselves created obligations that were essentially reciprocal and emotional—of parents to nurture and protect children, of husbands to provide for their wives, and of masters to train their apprentices and provide for their servants, but conversely of wives to be obedient to husbands, children to be obedient and dutiful to parents, and servants to be obedient to their employers. The duty of obedience required subordinates to cultivate reverence and fear towards authority, and for householders to exercise that authority prudently and calmly. These are values that were repeatedly spelt out in conduct literature such as the *Ménagier de Paris*, in which *inter alia* the story of Patient Griselda was presented as a model of wifely obedience, or, from towards the other end of our period, Giovanni Bruto's *La Institutione di una Fanciulla*, an ideologically conservative text whose popularity is suggested by translations into French and later English (Scaglione 1991: 423). They might also be reinforced by physical force or even by law. Husbands could strike their wives for disobedience: in a matrimonial case from 1396, John Semer, a former servant in the house, explained that his master Thomas Nesfeld, moved by righteous anger at her "rebellion," struck his wife "with his fist in order to chastise her" when she had allegedly told him to his face that "she wished to go where she would against the will of the same Thomas her husband" (Goldberg 1995: 142). Yet repeated warnings of advice literature to householders not to chastise subordinates in the heat of anger, but to temper discipline with mercy, indicates that the expression of righteous anger was a difficult ideal to achieve in practice (Tarbin 2015).

The relationships within the household may have been reciprocal, but in terms of power dynamics it was a hierarchical community defined in relation to a head, corresponding to the Latin term *pater familias* and the German *Hausvater*. The 1427 Tuscan *catasto*, for example, lists under personal exemptions household members by name, age, and relationship to the designated taxpayer. Wives invariably follow immediately after their husbands and children are listed either in descending age order or by gender and age order, males preceding females (Klapisch-Zuber 1985: 54). Similar observations may be made, for example, of the later fourteenth-century English poll tax returns or of the 1506 enumeration for Ypres, both of which also include servants as household dependents (Pirenne 1903: 15; Goldberg 2004: 16–19). Wives were understood to be dependent on and subordinate to their husbands. Thus the 1379 English poll tax assessments followed common law conventions and treated husband and wife as one person for tax purposes; numerous 1379 returns consequently fail to mention wives altogether. Though we may be seeing common bureaucratic conventions here, they nevertheless signal underlying cultural understandings of the household that apply despite considerable cultural differences across time and space. Moreover, commonly shared assumptions about power relations within the household had implications for the emotional expectations and experiences of its members. The pre-eminence of male heads of households indicates their importance in setting the emotional tenor of the domestic community. Yet the identification of wives with husbands not only gave them a share of authority over servants and children but also, as we shall see, created the possibility that wives might influence husbands through the intimacy of the marriage bed.

The hierarchical and reciprocal relationships of the domestic community provide a general template for analyzing emotional norms and experiences in the variety of living arrangements prevailing across Europe, over time, and according to social rank. The households associated with magnates might be especially large at times, such as that of the early sixteenth-century Duke of Buckingham, who had 145 household staff on the payroll, or that of the Earl of Northumberland, with 166 (Given-Wilson 1987: 89). In practice such very large households were atypical and English households below the level of the aristocracy appear to have been nuclear from the later fourteenth century, though it is possible that stem-families prevailed c. 1300 (Goldberg 2004: 13–20). Nonetheless, servants were integral to the household community at all social levels but the very poorest. Indeed, service was seen as a useful vehicle for socializing young people of both sexes and providing them with skills and training. This was especially true of artisanal and mercantile households in north-western Europe after the Black Death as seen, for example, in numbers of English towns in 1377, at Reims in 1422, Ypres in 1506, or Coventry in 1523 (Goldberg 1992: 160–1). The presence of servants within households may have helped to temper the strongly hierarchical dynamic of the domestic community through the formation of emotional bonds and alliances between servants, children, and even wives (Maddern 2008; Tarbin 2008; Barclay 2017b: 246). The bond between servant and employer, though bound by contract, could also become close and affectionate, mirroring the idealized parent–child relationships that advice writers held up as a model for employers and servants (Goldberg 1999; Gordon 2009).

The propensity of some cultural regions to take in adolescent servants was related to larger cultural differences. The pattern of householding so well documented by the Tuscan tax record, known as the *catasto*, of 1427 was one broadly characterized by the stem-family, with its emphasis on preserving family resources from one generation to the next and its reliance on family labor. Here one son was permitted to marry and bring his spouse into the natal home, but other children were required to leave on marriage, though in practice numbers of sons tended to remain into early adulthood (Herlihy and Klapisch-Zuber 1985; Klapisch-Zuber 1985: 23–35). A young wife would thus find herself subject not only to the authority of her invariably somewhat older husband and his father, but also that of her mother-in-law. She would have also to negotiate her place alongside brothers-in-law who may have been older than her. She was never considered a full member of the family. If widowed she had the right to return to her natal family, but she would have to leave any children she had behind. Such "abandonment" was evidently a cause of resentment on the part of male family members—one man wrote in 1417 that Niccolaio Niccolini's widow departed leaving "her children on the straw with nothing"— and to the children left behind. It was no doubt also a source of distress to the widow, though her sentiments seem not to be so readily recorded. Moreover, the family into which she had married had no formal obligation to her save to return the dowry with which she was first married, though even this obligation caused resentment (Klapisch-Zuber 1985: 117–31). For male members of the family, however, the family model served to create tight bonds.

Whereas in England and elsewhere in north-western Europe sending children into service was commonplace throughout society, it was anathema in southern Europe where it implied a failure of patriarchal supervision and responsibility. Thus the Venetian author of the so-called *Italian Relation*, an account of England written c. 1500, famously remarked of "the want of affection in the English . . . manifested towards their children," citing how "they put them out, both males and females, to hard service in the houses of other people" (Sneyd 1847: 24). It seems that the Venetian writer construed the exercise of authority—keeping children at home under paternal supervision—as an expression of parental love. Yet his report of the English justification of service, "that their children might learn better manners," implies a different view of how parental affection might be expressed: children were thought to be best prepared for independent living by learning crafts or householding skills under the supervision of others. Affection lay in the willingness to let offspring fly the nest. There is a suggestion, too, that a degree of emotional distance helped in the teaching and acquisition of appropriate behavior and emotional comportment. Despite the different values attached to service in different parts of Europe, and the cultural variations in household composition and dynamics, there were still commonalities in emotional norms and expectations. These include the importance for heads of households of instilling social and emotional norms into the next generation, as an essential part of exercising authority.

Men, though they never entirely monopolized headship of households since widows too might so act, were most conspicuous in this capacity. Unlike widows, however, men usually headed a household with the support of a spouse. The union of husband and wife was indeed an important dimension of the cultural understanding of the household, an ideological position that was perhaps reinforced with the advent of Reformed teaching (see Roper 1991; Grace 2015). The ties between husband and wife provided a foundation, and a pattern, for those that bound the household as a whole, where reciprocal obligations of mutual aid and affection coexisted with hierarchical relationships of authority and obedience. Husband and wife shared bed and dining table: the legal separation that was occasionally permitted to a married woman or man under Catholic canon law by reason of adultery or cruelty was a separation *a mensa et thoro*—from board and bed. Both are symbolic of the shared intimacies of family life and helped define the household as a community that ate together and slept under the same roof.

At all social levels, it was customary for beds and sleeping spaces to be shared. Travelers regularly shared beds at inns, even with strangers (Sarti 2002: 121–2; Woolgar 2006: 35). Children invariably shared beds. When in 1366 the ten- or eleven-year-old Alice de Rouclif, an heiress to a minor gentry family, came to live at the home of Anabilla, the sister of the man to whom she was contracted in marriage, she shared a bed with one of Anabilla's daughters who is described as her companion in bed (Goldberg 1995: 62). The young Anna Sforza shared her bed with a black slave girl (Sarti 2002: 143). Jean Gerson urged the use of single beds, but if beds had to be shared suggested that brothers sleep with brothers and sisters with sisters "as is the custom in Flanders." In fact the children of a family might regularly share a single bed. At the Hôtel-Dieu in Paris "little children" sometimes slept eight to ten or even twelve together in bed (Contamine 1987: 497–8). The scholars of Winchester College were likewise expected to share a bed until they reached the age of fourteen, when they were to follow the monastic model of sleeping singly in the common dormitory (Woolgar 2006: 35). The poorest households lacked physical beds altogether and a whole family, such as that of Jeannot D'Esparvans, d. 1361, of Sancey in eastern France, may have bedded together on straw (Ladurie 1987; Sarti 2006: 46).

Lena Orlin suggests that the shared bed provided a space for informal social monitoring in the context of post-Reformation cultural anxieties around conformity (Orlin 2007: 226). But the shared bed was also what people were socialized to expect from infancy. It offered warmth and companionship. The bed was thus not a private space people aspired to, but rather a social space. Only religious and those vowed to celibacy—conditions that were of course anathema to Reformed ideology—were actually expected to sleep alone lest carnal desire should distract them from prayer. As places of rest, warmth, and companionship, shared beds could represent emotional comfort and security. Still, the presence of other people, particularly strangers, in shared sleeping spaces might well be disturbing, signaling a site of tension and vulnerability within the emotional community of the household.

Privacy of the body was almost unknown in shared beds and sleeping spaces. Irrespective of age, gender, or even social rank, it was customary for people to sleep unclothed. Only religious orders were required by their rule to don night attire and preserve strict modesty. The nightwear we find associated with the elite such as the black satin nightgown Henry VIII purchased for Anne Boleyn is, however, conventionally understood as intended for use prior to retiring to bed or upon first rising. Like her subjects, the queen probably retired naked to bed (Worsley 2011: 85). Christine de Pizan notes of the nuns of Poissy, who slept in their habits, that they possessed "no nightgowns or lingerie," which might suggest a different custom, at least in respect of women at the French court (Contamine 1987: 493). The corollary is that family members must have often have been visible to one another unclothed. Even the act of relieving oneself may potentially have been visible to other household members. The use of chamber pots during the night was probably fairly ubiquitous. In Renaissance Italy the latrine or *destro* was often an unenclosed niche connected to the waste pipes near the kitchen. Privies located in yards, again sometimes shared by neighboring properties, are also commonly found, but peasants may often have made use of bushes and fields (Hanawalt 1986: 41; Schofield and Vince 2003: 82–3). In such close conditions, the ideals of modesty and shamefastness, urged particularly upon women, must have been difficult, if not impossible, to achieve in practice, particularly among the lower social orders.

Yet there are signs that privacy of the body was becoming increasingly valued, particularly among urban elites in the later Middle Ages. In sixteenth-century Italian society, the better-off came to have privies associated with bed chambers, and more effort was made to shield the space if only to contain unwanted odors (Cavallo 2006: 183). More private arrangements are also found in a bourgeois context in northern Europe: for example, a shared toilet with glazed window located on a second-floor gallery linking chambers in adjacent houses and opening onto a cesspit below, is noted in an agreement made between adjacent householders at Rouen in 1433 (Contamine 1987: 484). Concern to discourage people from relieving themselves in public was an especially urban phenomenon: urinating in the street was actually outlawed in Bologna (Nicholas 1997: 332–3; Hoffman 2014: 23). In early fifteenth-century London a public "longhouse" comprising sixty-four stalls for men and women alike was built over the Thames (Rexroth 2007: 262). The adoption of nightclothes also indicates a concern to shield the body from view, allowing the wearer to demonstrate modesty and affluence, and perhaps to enjoy greater warmth and comfort. Depositions in late medieval matrimonial cases from the Court of York suggest that it became unusual for witnesses to report seeing couples naked in bed together from the earlier part of the fifteenth century, though this was true of urban society some decades earlier than it was of rural society (Goldberg 2006: 114). This picture relates primarily to what persons who were not regular household members might witness, not to the visibility of household members to one another. It nonetheless implies a greater sense of privacy around the body, if naked bodies were only visible to those belonging to the household.

Sexual intimacy, which was both permissible for and expected of married couples when they retired to bed, must often have been witnessed or at least audible to family members sharing the same room. Such was the case, for example, when as a child Joan de Rolleston overheard the sounds of a couple having sex in the next bed that was reported in an English matrimonial case from 1366 (Goldberg 2008c: 106–7). Illicit sex between unmarried couples was probably largely conducted outdoors, though an irate master in early fifteenth-century York suspected his apprentice of having had sex with one of his women servants when he discovered them in suspicious circumstances in a hay-strewn upstairs room (Goldberg 1995: 110). In aristocratic and bourgeois society beds equipped with curtains would have permitted couples some privacy from the gaze of others, even if the drapes served only partially to muffle sound. Such beds are widely documented in testaments and probate inventories across Europe. In 1460, for example, Perrette la Havée, a bourgeoise of Paris, possessed a substantial bed, presumably shared with her husband, which was equipped with headboard, canopy, and curtains (Contamine 1987: 494). English late medieval bourgeois households likewise invested substantially in the provision of beds and bedding, including bed curtains (Goldberg 2008c). Well-to-do households were also most likely to provide a separate chamber for a married couple so allowing additional privacy. Aristocratic households undermined such practices by having servants sleep on pallets or trundle beds in the chamber or perhaps in the wardrobe (or garderobe) so as to be able provide service to their employers during the night (Contamine 1987: 498; Cooper 1999: 296). As witnesses to the sexual lives and bodily functions of their employers, servants themselves may also have welcomed the greater separation allowed by curtained beds and separate rooms.

For couples, sexual intimacy was not synonymous with emotional closeness, although there may have been some expectation by the later Middle Ages that the two would be linked in marriage. Marital sex enjoyed social approbation and took place in comparative comfort. But the Christian conviction that lust was sinful meant that licit marital sexuality was subject to conditions and limitations in official teachings. Canonists writing about marital affection (*maritalis affectio*) tended to leave the sexual element of marriage aside to focus on the companionate, respectful, and deferential aspects of the spousal relationship (McCarthy 2004: 94–5). Some theologians, such as Thomas Aquinas and Jean Gerson, allowed that sexual pleasure within marriage could be an important part of conjugal love (Brown 1987: 231, 237). An expectation that emotional closeness should develop from sharing a marital bed is suggested, somewhat ironically, by the example of Margery Kempe. After a long struggle to get her husband's consent to live chastely, she had a vision in which she shared her bed with Jesus, who asked to lie with her and be "homely" with her (Staley 1996: ch. 36; Morgan 2017: 49–51). The "homely" relationship here is modeled on an ideal marriage, where sharing a bed leads to familiarity, companionship, and emotional closeness.

Kempe's desire to live chastely with her husband, and her reluctant nursing during his illness, signals other emotional responses, including revulsion and disgust, to the physical intimacies of marriage. Sarah Salih reminds us that the marriage bed was a site of power, where the prescribed equality of spouses in rendering the "marriage debt" was undermined by the emphasis on wives' subjection to husbands. Salih suggests that women nonetheless might find pleasure and satisfaction in understanding themselves as obedient and virtuous wives despite the carnal "unpleasures" of the marriage bed (Salih 2011).

Bed companions were able to talk frankly and confidentially to one another. The curtained bed provided a rare space for husband and wife to converse privately and hence the one legitimate place for wives to voice criticism of their husbands (Slone 2008: 92–3; Morgan 2017: 77–94). The young wife of the Ménagier of Paris asked him to admonish her for mistakes in their chamber rather than in front or strangers or members of the household (Rose and Greco 2009: 49). Discreet criticism showed respect for the authority of wives, as well as husbands, over the household, fostering trust and companionship. A sense of fellowship may also have been a result of siblings or servants sharing beds, particularly where they were permitted their own chamber. Beds and sleeping chambers seem to have been particularly important as a place to talk about troubles and express strong feelings. When sharing beds with servants, children told them of their unhappiness about arranged marriages and experiences of sexual assault (Tarbin 2015: 122–3; Dolan 2016: 97). Anticipating her future remarriage, the Ménagier warned his wife not to complain publicly if she had an abusive husband, telling her, "Rather, go into your chamber and weep quietly in a low voice and complain to God. That is what wise ladies do" (Rose and Greco 2009: 149).

The most intimate conversations were between the individual and their God. That the bed and the chamber might function as devotional spaces is suggested, for example, by the notices of hangings painted with devotional scenes within chambers. The inventory of

FIGURE 7.1: The Virgin sits in a comfortably appointed chamber which features an image of St Christopher on paper pinned above the fireplace. Maître de Flémalle (Robert Campin?), *Annunciation*, c. 1415–25, Inv. 3937, Royal Museum of Fine Arts, Belgium. Image courtesy of Wikimedia Commons.

John Cadesby, a mason of Beverley, dating to the 1430s, includes among the possessions of his chamber a cloth painted with St. George, another painted with the Virgin and a coverlet decorated with St. Catherine's wheels (Stell 2006: 558). Alabaster sculptures, pipeclay figurines, and print images of devotional subjects also provided less expensive ways to furnish chambers with devotional imagery (Hamling 2010: 30–1). The 1494 inventory of Robert Waryn, a shopkeeper of Lynn, Norfolk, included three "tables of ymagery of allabaster" valued at two shillings in the parlor and an alabaster head of St. John valued at twelve pence in an upper chamber (Foister 1981: 281).

We have seen already how Margery Kempe imagined herself literally in bed with Christ. The Ménagier de Paris provided his young wife with prayers to recite in bed at midnight and in the morning on waking (Rose and Greco 2009: 55–7). There was some continuity in practice over the period, irrespective of changed devotional affiliation. Thus the earlier fourteenth-century mystic Richard Rolle wrote of his bed as a place for prayer and meditation. More than two centuries later the Puritan minister Richard Greenham practiced meditation in his bed and the bed was commonly understood as an appropriate place for prayer. As Alec Ryrie observes, however, such prayer was often audible to bed companions or others in the chamber (Ryrie 2013: 112, 160–1; Morgan 2017: 49–55). The example of the Ménagier de Paris suggests that intimate relationships with the divine were not necessarily exclusively individual and personal.

The employment of the bed and the chamber as devotional spaces may be related to their likely function as a place for the use of devotional books and for devotional reading. Although it has been argued that silent reading became commonplace in the early modern era, numbers of scholars have remarked that reading was a social activity and have suggested the more well-to-do household as the venue for collective reading. This has been described using evidence from heresy trials relating to the use of heretical texts, notably the Lollard reading groups documented, for example, in Coventry, Norwich, and London from the fifteenth to early sixteenth centuries. Margery Baxter, for example, tried to invite Joan Clyfland of Norwich to come to her room and "hear her husband read the law of Christ to them, which law was written in a book which the said husband was wont to read to Margery at night" (Goldberg 1995: 293; Copeland 2001: 8–10).

Much the same might be said of later Protestant reading practice, which no doubt also paralleled practice in Catholic households (Riddy 1993: 104–27; Cambers 2011: 54–71). The advent of printing, of course, made the dissemination of texts much greater; its implications for a shared reading culture are, for instance, the subject of a classic essay on sixteenth-century French society by Natalie Davis who describes reading groups even within rural society (Davis 1987: 189–226, 326–36). The more privileged might have the opportunity to engage in private devotional reading, a practice that seems to have been particularly attractive to high-status women, both Catholic and Protestant. Such private reading may have offered women an interior space of their own which facilitated intimacy with their God (Morgan 2017: 59–60). Separate bedchambers may have given material substance to this imagined space. At the end of the sixteenth century the young Elizabeth Cary bribed the household servants to supply her with candles so she could devour books, "so was she bent to reading" Calvinist theology in bed at night even though her mother had forbidden it (Cambers 2011: 56–7). However, it was the privacy afforded by separate chambers within a well-to-do household that facilitated Elizabeth's secret reading.

It is apparent from probate evidence and from visual sources that the higher echelons of society might invest significantly in the furnishing of beds and of associated chambers in terms of feather mattresses, sheets, pillows, hangings, bed covers, testers, and curtains. Matching bedspreads, bed curtains and hangings for the chamber represented a visually striking fashion, such as we see for example in the Arnolfini wedding portrait (Contamine 1987: 494–5; Morgan 2017: 24–41, 185–8). One reading is to suggest that bourgeois wives may have influenced expenditure on the chamber so as to create a space befitting its various functions as a place of devotion, of sanctioned marital intimacy, and the venue for birthing and for dying. It was also a place where women might receive and entertain female friends, suggesting it could function as a space of socializing and entertainment more generally (Morgan 2017: 112–23).

Investments in furnishings for beds and bedchambers were emotional as well as financial and social. The adornment of rooms, beds, and fabric hangings with heraldic devices of the aristocracy speaks to pride in lineage and dynastic power. The arms of Philip the Good of Burgundy are clearly visible on the head of the sumptuous bed depicted in the presentation frontispiece of Jean Melot's translation of the *Traité sur l'Oraison Dominicale* (c. 1454–7). Aristocratic women, too, displayed personal emblems on tapestries and fabric furnishings, like Elizabeth of York who, in 1486, had a crimson satin canopy embroidered with her arms and gold crowns in her lying-in chamber at the birth of Prince Arthur. Elizabeth L'Estrange suggests that such use of personal emblems allowed aristocratic women to assert their centrality in the household and their importance in the fulfillment of dynastic hopes (L'Estrange 2008: 87). The wills of urban women show

FIGURE 7.2: Chambers functioned as spaces for entertaining and for displaying emblems of family pride and personal identity, as shown in this miniature of Queen Isabella of Bavaria in her chamber receiving a manuscript from Christine de Pizan. From the poems of Christine de Pizan, c. 1410–15. Harl 4431 fol. 3, British Library, London, UK/© British Library Board. All Rights Reserved/Bridgeman Images.

frequent bequests of beds and furnishings to daughters, friends, and servants. Tracing the material culture of childbirth, Katherine French argues that intergenerational transfers of linen and items related to childbirth invested such objects with memories and "evoked ties of affection, family and neighbourliness." Beds and bedding could give physical expression to a sense of belonging and pride in family identity, as suggested by a London widow's bequest of a bed and furnishings to her daughter to help her to "remember her ancestors" (French 2016: 132).

By the later Middle Ages, separate chambers for sleeping and curtained beds provided some spaces for a semblance of solitude and withdrawal from the domestic community, at least among social elites. Bedfellows and married couples could enjoy opportunities for companionship and intimacy in such relatively private settings. The conventional norms of emotional comportment required the upholding of relationships of authority. Submission might be relaxed, but moral teachings stressed that its maintenance was necessary for good governance. Chambers also provided settings for hospitality and ceremony in life-cycle transitions such as childbirth and death. On these occasions, the furnishings and decorations of chambers, along with associated rites of passage, were as likely to direct participants' thoughts to bonds of kinship, patronage, and Christian community as to individual relationships with God. These were also emotionally charged moments that were marked by ritual. Women gathered by invitation to attend the expectant mother in her darkened and secluded lying-in chamber (Morgan 2017: 191–200). Kin were likewise summoned to attend the dying. These were communal rather than private occasions.

Turning from beds to tables, our focus shifts from problematizing privacy to problematizing commensality. Sharing meals was an important, if quotidian, rite of household life. We have seen, from the example of *Piers Plowman*, that the ideal noble household dined together in amity and charitable love. Dining was also a key function of the bourgeois household, to judge from the array of cooking utensils, pewter, and other vessels for eating, and provision of tables, benches, stools, chairs, and related furnishings and equipment which are to be found in probate inventories from Bruges or York. Even the more modest peasant hearth was equipped for cooking, though provision for dining in any formal sense might be limited (Sarti 2002: 123–4; Goldberg 2008: 124–44; Baatsen et al. 2015: 179–202). In practice, dining customs varied across time and space and often served to reinforce gender, status, and age hierarchies within the household, although knowledge of peasant customs mostly postdates our period. In the late medieval great household it was an occasion for the lord to be seen, but also literally to exercise oversight of his household when he sat on the raised dais at the "high" end of the hall (Woolgar 1999: 147–65; Wells 2004: 67–82). At all social levels, the chair was a high-status item and may have been reserved for the male head of household. In peasant society it was not necessarily the case that all were seated. It may have been more common for women and children to stand whilst the male head of household was seated. This pattern was perhaps more conspicuous in southern Europe where distinctions of gender were sharpest (Sarti 2002: 155–6). Toward the end of our period, high-status Italian homes might include provision for women to dine separately from their husbands (McIver 2013: 167). The subtle display of social distinctions at meals prompted participants to observe appropriate forms of emotional expression, such as children and servants showing reverence and obedience toward householders, or lords displaying benignity and kindness to their subordinates.

The bourgeois household probably permitted most household members, including servants, to sit together at meals. Joan Scharp testified in 1430, for example, that she and a fellow servant sat at table with her master and his wife and that they "eat, drank, and relaxed together" (Goldberg 1995: 241). But conviviality was in tension with the observance of social hierarchies during meals. Advice literature counseled householders to limit servants to simple nourishing food and to discourage excessive socializing. The Ménagier of Paris thought that one dish and a nourishing drink was sufficient for servants, compared with a minimum of three courses with multiple dishes required for entertaining noble and other visitors. There was to be no dallying, lingering, sharing stories, or leaning on elbows during servants' meals and they were to return to work swiftly (Rose and Greco 2009: 222–3, 253–70). Two hundred years later, by which period servants may more commonly have dined apart, Thomas Tusser agreed that while dining "altogether is gay, / Dispatch hath no fellow, make short and away," warning the good housewife to "Giue seruants no dainties, but giue them inough." Tusser advised that servant behavior needed close monitoring at table and that good tableware was to be reserved for "manerly feasts" (Tusser 1570: fols. 32–3). Both writers depict a sense of camaraderie among servants, in contrast to the emotional distance advocated for employers to exercise authority effectively.

A conspicuous feature of bourgeois houses, to judge for example by evidence from probate inventories or from visual depictions in Flemish art, is the degree of investment in the furnishing of the hall with benches, cushions, and hangings (Goldberg 2008: 124–44). Robert Campin's *Mérode Altarpiece* of the later 1420s, for example, mirrors the sorts of hall furnishings found in the (rather more modest) home of the York girdler, Robert Talkan, little over a decade earlier (Stell 2006: 523–4).

FIGURE 7.3: The central panel of the *Mérode Altarpiece* (c. 1427–32) by the Master of Flémalle (Robert Campin?) mirrors the sorts of hall furnishings found in urban homes of merchants and prosperous craftsmen. © The Cloisters Collection (1956), The Metropolitan Museum of Art.

The investment in tableware, furniture, and furnishings associated with dining displayed the wealth, social status, and good manners of the household, suggesting a sense of pride in ownership (Goldberg: 2008: 132–5). Domestic goods and furnishings also demonstrated the "substance" of the household, in terms of economic credit and moral probity. Hence objects and settings associated with dining might also bear religious imagery and relate to devotional sentiments. Tara Hamling, writing of post-Reformation Britain, has shown how religious subjects featured on the wall hangings and alabaster sculptures found in the halls and parlors of the more prosperous. The less affluent used pipe-clay figurines and print devotional images to like effect. In mercantile households, pottery tiles, tableware, and drinking vessels could bear religious inscriptions or images. Sets of "Apostle" spoons were popular among the well-to-do. These were often given as baptismal gifts and then passed down as heirlooms and so were strongly invested in family sentiment. A sixteenth-century example is inscribed with "IHS" on the bowl, and has individual figures of the Apostles and Christ on the hand (Hamling 2010: 30–2). Sets of "Apostle" spoons recalled the Last Supper and Christ's self-sacrificing love of humanity, perhaps reminding users to strive to recreate ideals of charitable love within their household communities and social networks. More generally, religious imagery in shared domestic spaces may have served to promote ideals of social and emotional comportment, and respect and deference towards authority.

Dining at table was not necessarily confined to members of the household. The entertainment of guests was a common feature, of both bourgeois and aristocratic society, and one that was reflected in the furnishing of the hall. For those engaged in trade or commerce, entertaining might be an essential way of nurturing business relationships and building trust within an economy which, before the early modern era, was frequently starved of ready cash and where many transactions depended on credit. We see this, for example, from an early fifteenth-century debt case where a York merchant hosted a female chandler with whom he had business dealings and her husband (Goldberg 1995: 239–43). A well-furnished hall and parlor signaled financial security, but it is possible that a

FIGURE 7.4: Peasant festivities took place inside barns or in the open air, as with this decorous feast depicted in an engraving from the mid-sixteenth century. *The Peasants' Feast or the Twelve Months*, 1546–7, by Sebald Beham. Gift of J. Rockman, 1942 © The Metropolitan Museum of Art.

sense of connection and trust was also fostered by the comforts afforded by cushions and wall hangings and the familiar reassurance of devotional imagery. Peasant halls tended to be more Spartan in their furnishing and it is likely that entertaining guests to dinner was not a usual activity of the peasant household. Here instead entertainment was displaced outside of the home as is represented, for instance, in depictions of peasants by Hans Sebald Beham or Pieter Breughel the Elder (Goldberg 2008: 128–9, 2011: 215). While images of rural festivity, with peasants mingling, dancing, and drinking, commonly suggest how norms of physical and emotional comportment were relaxed during celebrations, yet the arrangement of diners around a table nonetheless conveys a sense of social decorum and proprieties observed.

Mealtime gatherings of household members and guests at table epitomize the highly communal nature of domestic life. In houses that the majority of the population across Europe habited, whether in town or in the countryside, both living space and the provision of separate rooms was limited. Even where we notice large houses allowing for greater provision of separate chambers, such as was particularly true of more well-to-do bourgeois families and also of the aristocracy, these tend to coincide with larger households and the presence of servants. The character of space indoors, where servants and small children were ever present and day-laborers or journeymen were often nearby during working hours, was communal and very likely crowded. In the case of the urban poor, dwelling in a single room, communal living may have been inescapably stressful, in comparison with the greater order and regulation possible in bourgeois houses with separate rooms for eating, sleeping, and working (Riddy 2008: 27–8). Yet, as with bed-sharing, people must have been socialized from infancy to expect close proximity with others and continual monitoring during indoor activities. In the shared space of the hall, in particular, adults were able to oversee children and subordinate household members during the daily round, just as employers were urged by Thomas Tusser to correct the behavior of servants at mealtimes. The authority and good government of bourgeois householders was signaled subtly through the hierarchical organization of space within the hall (Grenville 2008: 113–18). Norms of emotional expression were also clear: young people were to display reverence for authority and enact obedient submission. While the lived practice of household relationships probably fell short of these ideals, schooling young people in emotional restraint and controlled expression was intended to develop the discipline and self-regulation required for the prudent, moderate, and industrious management of households of their own. Certainly, young people were socialized for encounters with authority in the hierarchical society beyond the household, while the ability to show respect, defer, and obey within the household contributed to the realization of a sense of calm and harmonious order.

Langland's lament about lords retiring to "eten by hymselve / in a pryvee parlour" cited at the beginning of this chapter reflects the proliferation of spaces most marked in very high-status housing, but it also prompts us to think that privacy was a driving factor. While the Middle English adjective "privee" here has resonances of hidden or secret as a moral contrast to the hall as the proper place for a lord to dine, we may also infer that withdrawal from communal dining offered householders a reprieve from the demands of vigilant supervision, as well as opportunities to honor chosen guests and to cultivate closeness and trust.

The notorious porosity of pre-modern housing makes it likely that the "privee parlor" might offer only limited privacy for holding secret or confidential discussions. The possibility of supposedly private conversations in town houses being overheard is well documented, for example, in depositions from the Church courts. In later fifteenth-century London, for example, Angela Harew and Stephen Robert made their contract of marriage in a parlor, while Angela's teenage brother Ralph Penne stood outside the door, listening surreptitiously. At seventeen years of age, Ralph was probably too young to witness the contract formally, but his presence outside the door testifies to the kind of informal monitoring that young people might carry out on more senior members of the household (McSheffrey 2006: 127). In this light, fears of servant gossip in advice literature, which stressed the importance of being discreet and measured in dealings with subordinates, seems justified and suggests the vulnerability at the heart of household authority.

Activities that needed to be kept private, from illicit sex to conversations, seem often to have been located outdoors. A 1366 matrimonial case from the ecclesiastical Court of York recorded that one private conversation took place in an orchard and another particularly intimate exchange between a young girl and a visiting abbot, who was probably her grandfather, took place whilst they were out riding (Goldberg 1995: 61–2). When William Roper needed to communicate privately with his father-in-law, Sir Thomas More, after Sir Thomas had been charged with high treason, he did so in a garden out of hearing of other family members (Orlin 2007: 231, 233). Within a bourgeois or aristocratic context the garden may have been especially valued as an essentially private space. In literature, too, the garden often functioned as the setting for private conversation or secluded contemplation. These examples illustrate how gardens, in particular, were valued as spaces for privacy within the domestic community but may also have represented the privacy of the household in relation to outside observers. The queen's garden in royal palaces invariably represented an enclosed space with highly controlled and restricted access, symbolic of the queen's chastity and resonating with the concept of the *hortus conclusus* associated with the Virgin (Howes 1997: 34; Richardson 2003: 140, 144, 148, 163). As emblems of female sexual purity in cultural representations, enclosed gardens carried associations of integrity and seclusion.

The sense of the garden as private and inviolable space goes some way to explain the sense of outrage that is communicated in legal records that document complaints about intrusion by neighbors. In 1362, for example, Roger Newe and his wife prosecuted Richard de Worstede, a London mercer, and his wife for making a number of windows in their house that overlooked their garden such that they could "see all their private business." To add insult, it was further alleged that they also threw refuse into the garden. On this occasion the mayor ordered that the offending windows be blocked up (Chew and Kellaway 1973: 128). Riddy suggests that such cases witness an emerging sense of the "privacy of the home," which was perceived as the appropriate place for carrying out, and concealing, bodily functions from public view in accord with ideals of modesty and shamefastness (Riddy 2008: 32–3). Another reading of urban nuisance cases is that they express an idea of the "privacy of the household" as a space subject to oversight by a householder (and his wife) but closed to the gaze or interference of neighbors and outside authorities. Both perspectives view the household as a locus for regulating bodies and emotions, which asserted the moral probity and good repute of the domestic community to outside observers.

Our final theme concerns the question of how far the home was particularly associated with women and worked to construct a division between the public world beyond the home and a private world within. Paolo da Certaldo, a Florentine merchant writing in the fourteenth century, addressed the guardians of young women, urging them to "keep females in the house," such was the anxiety of men for the virtue of the women over whom they had authority (Certaldo 1945: 105; O'Faolain and Martines 1973: 182). "How the Goodwife Taught her Daughter," an English text of similar date, but which circulated through much of our period, advised young women more directly "wone [stay] at home," though it offered plenty of guidance on behavior outdoors as well (Mustanoja 1948: l. 73, 199). Social practice tends to lack the certainties of normative ideology, but just as Certaldo's Florentine text is more prescriptive than the presumably clerically authored "Goodwife," so it is likely that Mediterranean culture was much more restrictive of women's movement outside the home than was generally true of north-western Europe. However, Barbara Hanawalt has made the case that English peasant women did spend much of their working day "in and around" the home in contrast to peasant males who spent most working hours outdoors (Hanawalt 1986: 145–6). This influential view, modelled on a nineteenth-century bourgeois ideology of separate spheres, has more recently been challenged as too simplistic and dogmatic (Goldberg 1991: 75–81, 2008a: 253–62). Such an ideology is even less applicable to the artisanal home where work and domestic activities both took place under the same roof, though it may well be that there was more distinction between the two over the course of our period (McSheffrey 2006: 121; Goldberg 2011: 228–31).

The notion of the home as an emotional refuge from the demands of the public realm is not apparent in a medieval context. Rather, the household functioned as a venue for enacting benevolent authority and as a training ground in emotional values and practices that were required for the successful negotiation of hierarchical social relationships in the wider world. The proliferation of rooms and the gradual refinement and definition of the use of space that is found over our period, mainly in respect of more well-to-do households, offered some possibilities for privacy. Parlors and gardens, separate bedchambers, and curtained beds afforded householders, in particular, spaces for relationships of trust and intimacy. In such settings, the discipline required to exercise authority could be relaxed but the ideal of emotional control remained paramount within the communal setting of daily household life. For children and servants in the household, and for wives in relation to husbands, there was less at stake in the maintenance of emotional control but the enactment of obedient submission and respect for authority nonetheless appears to have required significant self-containment.

More rooms and more opportunities for privacy did not necessarily equate with greater individualism. The individual's aspiration to have space of her or his own, or to be alone, seems not to have been considered desirable within pre-modern culture. The supposed rise of individualism associated with Reformed religion, the advent of portraiture, the creation of private journals and records, or the fashion for private reading—to cite just some of the indicators that have been used to make the case—appear on closer inspection to have been at best phenomena of a privileged elite, but also a primarily male elite (see Braunstein 1987: 536 ff.; Cooper 1999: 7–13; Sharpe and Zwicker 2003: 10–15). From the perspective of emotions, male householders were perhaps a similarly privileged group, since the exercise of authority entailed legitimate access to emotions, such as righteous anger and pride, which were inappropriate for subordinate household members. Similarly, emerging concepts of privacy around the body reveal less about developing senses of individuality and more about perceptions of the household as the appropriate place for managing bodily functions. For most people, it seems that the possibilities for privacy around the body in the home were limited. In the close quarters of domestic life, daily practices of courtesy and observance of emotional norms provided strategies for negotiating household interactions. For wives, children, and servants who were subject to the authority of household heads—husbands, fathers, or masters—the household did function as an emotional community but, as with all communities, one that demanded that its members conformed to certain values and mores, and that tended to place the needs of the community above those of individual members.

CHAPTER EIGHT

In Public

Collectivities and Polities

JELLE HAEMERS

In 1452, the city of Ghent rose in revolt against the Count of Flanders and Duke of Burgundy, Philip the Good. According to the rebels, the duke had violated the privileges of the town more than once, though Duke Philip contested this allegation. Taking the duke's side, Jacques Du Clercq, a chronicler from Lille, asserted in his *Mémoires* that the rebellion was an irrational outburst of anger from a Flemish mob. He saw the Ghent revolt as a plot of certain "people of lower status and the poor"[1] who—in his words—"had moved and emotioned the people"[2] into fighting against their lord (Du Clercq 1823: 12). The revolt, in his view, was led by malicious citizens who had stirred up or "moved" the people. Du Clercq was not the only one to claim that irrational crowd behavior was responsible for popular insurrection. The discourse that portrayed revolts as emotional outbursts by angry mobs appears in many chronicles that reported on social disturbances in the late medieval and early modern periods. "Emotion" was used as a synonym for agitation in the fifteenth century, while we understand it more as a "feeling" or "sentiment" today. In 1475, for instance, the authorities of the French city of Bourges started an investigation into the origins of a neighborhood disturbance, because they "wanted to know where the emotion originated, and that the king would overrule if they would find a rebellion"[3] (Chevalier 1982: 299). Indeed, writers could use the words "emotion" and "insurgency" interchangeably during this period.

The etymological origin of "emotion" is linked to the collective agitation of medieval crowds. "Emotion" comes from Old French "*esmocion*," as a substantive of "*esmouvoir*," derived from the Latin "*ex-movere*" meaning "move out, remove, or agitate" (von Wartburg 1949: 300; Godefroy 1891: 498–9; Tournier 2004: 121–5). While "emotion" could refer to people's moral conflicts (e.g., when Georges Chastelain described the mental pains of the French king Louis XI in 1475), it was more commonly used to describe tumult, agitation, and mobilization of rebels or warriors (e.g., when chronicler Jean Lemaire wrote about the wars of Troy in 1512) (Chastellain 1863: 224; Lemaire de Belges 1882: 107). Today, we would use the word "commotion" ("*émeute*" in French), a term also known to medieval and early modern authors. They preferred, however, to use emotional terminology for collective "irrationalities," such as group or mob violence and deeds of retribution. It was logical that chroniclers should have a long tradition of dehumanizing criminals and social protesters, since chroniclers themselves were often targets of uprisings. Nevertheless, it is striking that they usually employed an "emotional discourse" for that purpose. The popular revolts brought images to their

FIGURE 8.1: In 1379, two urban functionaries are killed during a violent revolt in Montpellier, in *Chroniques de France, dites de Saint-Denis*, Paris, after 1380. British Library, MS Roy. 20 CVII, f. 212r.

minds that were best expressed in terms of domestic animals gone wild (Deploige 2010: 245; Hanawalt 2011: 52).[4] They described the collective violence of communities with words that referred to instincts, mostly to disapprove of such "irrational" actions. In addition, the iconography of popular unrest spread a similar image: insurgents were depicted as warlike soldiers, outrageous madmen or furious crowds (Challet and Haemers 2016).

HISTORIANS, SOURCES AND EMOTIONS

This chapter does not impose a binary of emotion and rationality, because the two interact. Researchers now posit that emotion itself is a basis for moral and social behavior (Larrington 2001: 252), while some scholars consider emotions as social constructions and products of social interactions.[5] In these studies, emotions emerge as both social shapers and socially shaped entities (Lutz and White 1986: 412). Many scholars have consequently concluded that specific forms of social organization regulate the expression of emotions (Sommers 1998).[6] Not only do humans react emotionally, they also *use* their emotions. For instance, emotions such as fear and anger emerge when changes in the relationship between a group and the world around it threaten the group's interests. Medieval townsmen, such as the Ghent rebels, reacted very emotionally to a precarious situation, but their revolts were never the calamitous eruption of a mad crowd, as we read in the *Mémoires* of Du Clercq. On the contrary, the urban rank and file used emotions as an instrument to achieve political goals, for emotions are among the tools humans use to manage social life in general (Rosenwein 2002: 842).[7] Moreover, as some anthropologists have concluded, emotion can be seen as a strategy for defending a group's preferred type of social organization (Lutz and White 1986: 420). This chapter will show that through the use of emotions people in this period demanded preservation or extension of their rights. Their collective emotions were channeled through theatrical rituals of communication, which warned authorities not to continue the offending policies. Taking that view, this chapter focuses not only on the collective demonstration of emotions such as anger, fear and fury, but also on the rituals that expressed these emotions.

In the past, historians have often taken a pitying tone when they describe emotions. Though nineteenth-century romanticist historians (such as Jules Michelet) dealt with popular emotions in order to reveal the identity and the "real" nature of the people involved, historians did not examine medieval and early modern people's feelings and passions in their own right. Historians considered collective emotions as irrational behavior, or nearly animal-like instincts. In connection with the fifteenth-century revolt in Ghent, mentioned above, Victor Fris, the Ghent city archivist of a century ago, made a striking comment. Musing in one of his works on Ghent history, he quoted the French poet and adventurer François René de Chateaubriand to explain why the artisans of his beloved city rebelled so many times in the period between 1300 and 1600. He wrote: "One is inclined to think 'that they rebelled ceaselessly, just because they cannot be peaceful,' to quote Chateaubriand" (Fris 1913: 115).[8] While considering crowds as moody and inflammable mobs that reacted instinctively to impulses, as Fris did, reveals much about the way in which historians looked at collective popular emotions in the first half of the twentieth century, this attitude has changed as the years have advanced. In this chapter, I briefly survey recent approaches to collective violence, rebellious crowds, and angry men and women who lived in Europe in the late Middle Ages and the sixteenth century. Focus on these political movements of crowds, the "emotions" as they would have called these events themselves, also reveal the usually hidden operations of collectivities in the sources. Chronicles typically said nothing about the emotions of ordinary people, as their interest was in the history of courts, bishops, and kings. Moreover, when chroniclers reported on a mad mob, they refused to interpret fairly the motives behind collective anger, because their task was to justify repression of disturbances and rebellion by the lords or their mighty patrons (Challet and Forrest 2015; Firnhaber-Baker and Schoenaers 2016). Now, however, detailed scrutiny of sources, combined with new interdisciplinary insights, has led historians to evaluate crowds and their emotions on their own merits.

Rather than giving a complete historiographical survey of recent trends in the history of collective emotions, this account concentrates on several noteworthy historical examples

FIGURE 8.2: Eat, drink, and be merry: elite and popular dining culture around 1500, in V. Maximus, *Faits et dits mémorables des romains*, Bruges, c. 1480. Getty Museum, MS 43, f. 50r.

exemplifying new insights from research. Its emphasis on the expression of emotions and the accompanying rituals highlights the significant features of the "emotional style and practices" of collective groups of people, discussing how people manifested the emotions of rage and passion by moving their bodies in parades and using them ritualistically to attain certain goals. As Monique Scheer has stated, people have a "knowing body," one that stores information from past experiences in habituated processes and contributes this knowledge to human activity and consciousness (2012: 201).[9] As a result, the "habitus," as Pierre Bourdieu would call it, the embodied history of people, conditions the utterance of emotions. Even though people's anger can be seen as a biological or impulsive reaction to injustice, social groups have developed skillful behaviors, habits, and traditions to share and employ these emotions and bodily acts of expression. Therefore, in this study of what Rosenwein has called "emotional communities," and others have identified as the "emotional style" of a unique historical community, I examine carefully the connotations of emotions and how these affected people's lives (Rosenwein 2006: 23; Frevert 2011; Gammerl 2012: 161–75). The aim is to add a significant contribution to the social and cultural history of collective emotions by putting them into their social context, as Peter Burke advises us to do (2005: 35), even though it is impossible to write an exhaustive overview of the rich palette of historical emotions expressed by these people.

COLLECTIVE EMOTIONS, RITUALS AND SPACE

If people want to live together, they have to temper the expression of their emotions. To be civilized means to channel passion and repress anger (Rosenwein 1998: 3).[10] Humans have to regulate their emotions to avoid hurting others physically or psychologically. This regulation normalizes human relations. The "calm after the storm" is the logical result of a universal concern for living together and the fear of revenge or retribution. One of the most efficient means to regulate and calm passions is to put them into a ritual. Ritual regulates emotions, as it channels anger into a more acceptable, more social form. For instance, the sight of symbols in an emotionally overwhelming parade full of music and joy could put the hearts and minds of individuals at rest. These parades were built on emotions and kept them vivid. The ritual use of space and the dramatic quality of symbols provoked an emotional response from the participants (Kertzer 1988: 11).[11] Such activities primarily channeled emotions and prevented individuals from harming collective interests by over-reacting. Rebellions ("emotions" in the original sense) reveal the practices and strategies medieval and early modern people had developed to regulate feelings of anger and fear and to use them as a force. Emotions became a handy tool to defend a group's social position, and groups used an emotional language to obtain their political goals.

In times of commotion, insurgents followed a familiar script. François Olivier Touati, Claude Gauvard, and Rodney Hilton have noticed a number of *"traits de rationalité"* at work when people expressed their wrath about injustice (Touati 1990: 12–14; Gauvard 1999: 1208; Hilton 1989: 25–33). Revolts often followed a stereotypical scenario familiar to all the participants. Serge Moscovici called this the "choreography of the masses," a term which approaches the notion of "the repertoire of collective action" of Charles Tilly (Moscovici 1981; Tilly 2006). Just as every population had a specific choreographed way of rebelling, in the example from late medieval Flanders that opened this chapter, the choreographed response was the so-called *"wapening"* ("gathering with weapons"). In Ghent, in 1452, this *wapening* was led by craftsmen who ritualistically gathered in the main square of the city, the Friday Market (Arnade 1994: 497; Haemers 2005). In contrast to characterization of the chronicler Jacques Du Clercq quoted above, the assembled crowd did not behave as a riotous bunch of angry men. They were well-off guildsmen who occupied the market square in an orderly manner to demonstrate their power. Petitions delivered to the authorities made their claims public. The collective emotions of the craftsmen provided the driving force, but these emotions did not become a powerful political instrument until they were expressed collectively in a central public space of the city (Haemers 2016: 50). The marketplace was frequently chosen as backdrop to rebellious gatherings because it functioned as a playing field on which the political communities of city and state claimed, fought for, and negotiated political credibility and public prestige (Boone 2002: 621–40; Masschaele 2002: 383–421). Alternatively, people gathered in front of guild houses, symbolic buildings, or the palace of a governor. These were theaters of power, but also places by which people identified themselves. They used them as loci to express anger. For instance, the Zürich revolt of 1489 against Mayor Hans Waldmann began with a gathering of an enormous angry crowd (a *"Gemeinde"*) of 4,000 people who assembled near the city walls, the symbol of urban liberties. They protested against new laws which the urban council had promulgated to the detriment of older common rights (Jucker 2006: 112). By claiming such a symbolic space, crowds could appropriate it to legitimize the uprising.

One should not forget that places in themselves can evoke emotions. Gathering together in a public space that served as an incarnation of civic identity gave people an emotional interest in the event. Following the idea imbedded in social and cultural geography, that the articulation of emotion is spatially mediated in a manner that is not simply metaphorical, scholars have shown the special meaning topographies have held for the emotional involvement of people in collective action (Rollo-Koster and Holstein 2010: 150).[12] Authorities as well as rebels tried to involve bystanders psychologically by using the connotations of space during acts of retribution. The execution of the popular leader Cola di Rienzo in Rome in 1355 demonstrates that the staging of public events in parts of the city with strong associations to the past speaks eloquently about the powerful meaning of these topographies. Cola's body was dragged from Capitoline Hill (where he was killed) to the church of San Marcello near the palace of his principal enemies, the Colonna family. There his body was subjected to demeaning humiliations. The Capitoline Hill, the center of communal Rome, was the location of the Senate house, where Cola had "sentenced others," as a fourteenth-century chronicler mentioned. Symbolically, Cola was himself sentenced on the hill, and moved in a funeral procession to the property of his enemies. Indeed, the new authorities used the symbolic value of space to heighten the parade's emotional impact in order to convince the witnesses that the execution was just. In allegorical terms, people moved through space on this occasion, but the space also moved people. In a very different context, the English enclosure riots in the fifteenth and sixteenth centuries can also be seen as an occasion in which space aroused emotion. In 1525, for instance, in a furious rage, the commons of Coventry pulled down the gates and hedges that bordered the common lands around the city. In an anxious reaction to the enclosure of these lands and thus the violation of their collective rights, they closed one of the town gates and refused entry to the chamberlains. It was a highly emotional use of spatial elements designed to show that the community disagreed with the governing policies on land. Of course, a political and economic rationale led people to fight for their rights and appropriate customs, but they enacted that struggle in remarkable emotionalized rituals on emblematic spots—just as the opponents of Cola di Rienzo had done in Rome (Liddy 2015: 7).[13]

In general, these gatherings started with an outburst of anger by one or several individuals, who then gathered sympathizers. In 1511, the fury of the inhabitants of Murano (an isle in the Venice Lagoon) over the high taxes which they had to pay to sustain the Venetian wars against France moved them to throw snow at the resigning governor of the island. It is impossible to determine now who started this playful though significant act of disapproval of the governor's policy, but it is clear that the anger was collective. When the governor hastily tried to leave the isle to escape the snowballs, the Muranese sang in chorus "Chase away this hound, who has ruined Murano"[14]. Tensions grew high, and the humiliated governor quickly fled the island on a boat to Venice, where he launched a lawsuit against the leading agitators (Judde de Larivière 2014: 12). In addition to the Venetian Lagoon incident, slogans and shouts accompanied an uprising because rebels often used noise to express anger. "*Al Arma! Al Arma!*," cried the inhabitants of the Languedoc village of Villeveyrac in 1355, when the frightened villagers witnessed the entry of foreign troops into their valley. Likewise, the men and women of Toulouse (1357) and Béziers (1381) shouted "Kill the traitors!" (in the vernacular) when their governors were accused of corruption. In both cities, the selfish behavior of elitist families provided the catalyst for a furious reaction from citizens (Challet 2014: 222). Crying out for retribution, but not actually killing anyone, calmed the anger in these cases, but others

FIGURE 8.3: Peasant armies in fourteenth-century England, Wat Tyler meets John Ball, in J. Froissart, *Chroniques de France et d'Angleterre*, Bruges, 1475–1500. British Library, MS Roy. 18 E I, f. 165v.

used similar shouts as a kind of "emotional violence" toward rulers. Spreading fear among the elite or one's political opponents was an integral part of the offensive reaction of those who were afraid. A more self-defensive move was to shout phrases such as "Long live the king and the community!"[15], as did the inhabitants of the Castilian town of Duenas (near Valladolid) in 1520 during the so-called revolt of the "Comuneros" (Oliva Herrer 2014: 55). With such slogans, rebels warned their rulers that violence might occur, but they had not yet blown up any bridges. The slogans were a forceful cry for attention aimed at the authorities, who were thereby warned to take into account the anger of subordinate townsmen.

WORDS, BELLS AND FLAGS

These cases demonstrate that not only gestures but also verbal utterances were common means of expressing popular emotion. Violence was probably the exception during collective actions of crowds, whereas subversive utterances, though always risky, must have been almost the rule of daily politics in late medieval and early-modern Europe (Dumolyn and Haemers 2012: 86). The origins, forms, and outcomes of these speech acts were determined by the space in which they were performed and the specific balance of power at that moment. There were numerous examples of communities that dishonored their enemies with insults. Judges employed multiple terms to describe such inappropriate behavior. The fourteenth-century jurors of certain English villages used Latin terms, such as "*maledictrices*" and "*objurgatrices*," for women who expressed their anger by scolding. In 1359, for instance, three Bradford (Yorkshire) women were presented as "*communes et notorii objurgatrices*" or "common and notorious scolds" because they had insulted fellow townsmen, while in Battle (Sussex) men were often cited for committing assaults "*in verbis contumelios*" (with insulting or outrageous words), which may have been accompanied by physical violence (Bardsley 2006: 84, 100). Less ordinary, but also attested, were whole communes who committed offences while trying to stir up emotions of shame and dishonor. In 1466, the inhabitants of Dinant (a town in the bishopric of Liège) publicly affronted Charles the Bold, the Duke of Burgundy (ruler of neighboring territories), by hanging a life-sized effigy of him on their city walls after he had tried and failed to conquer the city. Similar Italian practices, precise rituals during which winners delivered insults in front of the walls of a conquered city, unequivocally displayed and confirmed an enemy's defeat in wartime (Lecuppre-Desjardin 2007: 161).[16] The public humiliation inflicted on the adversary by this display was naturally a source of pride for the winner, but also an invitation for revenge. When the offended duke finally succeeded in conquering Dinant shortly afterwards, his reaction, burning the city down, indicated that these kinds of acts would not be tolerated. There will be more about this episode later.

Sounds accompanied words and gestures to express emotions. Bells often gave voice to collective anger, as loud, dominant ringing filled the air with emotional tension. The ringing of bells in uprisings was a European phenomenon.[17] Since the sound of bells stirred up emotion, the authorities continually tried to regulate their use. During the Jacquerie in rural France in the 1350s, for example, authorities legally restricted use of the bells because ringing them unlawfully could spread fear amongst the populace. The "*son de cloche*" or bell-ringing was only permitted when foreign troops approached a village (Firnhaber-Baker 2014: 364). Since bells were used to warn people of imminent danger (the threat of pillaging, fire, etc.), legislation on "illegal ringing" shows how important it was for authorities to prevent their abuse. Another interesting case involving bells occurred during the "afterlife" of the Bruges revolt of 1488 when Maximilian of Habsburg, the son of the Holy Roman Emperor, was imprisoned. In June 1488, a month after Maximilian was released, an anonymous Bruges craftsman caused an enormous commotion in town when he managed to ring the bell of the belfry without the permission of the city council, installed in February by the leaders of the craft guilds after they had taken control of the city. Several armed members of the city guilds who had run to the market square as a result were very angry when they discovered that a craftsman had rung the bells illegally. The city aldermen arrested the man, and after a public trial he was executed in the market square because he had acted "with his bad will in his *own* head" (Haemers 2005: 73). The ringing of the bell was a common right, and nobody had the right to threaten this privilege. While the anonymous craftsman's reasons for ringing the bell are unknown, it is clear that he did not succeed in setting the city on fire. This anecdote supports our argument that a collective emotion could not originate in a single individual's emotion. A collective emotion could only arise when common interests were threatened.

Flags had strong emotional significance for both rulers and ruled. Flags channeled emotional outbursts and united crowds. In 1521, inhabitants of la Feria, the northern city quarter of Seville, protested high grain prices and the failure of the authorities to remedy the situation by invading one of the houses of a *jurado* (a local magistrate). With them, they carried the Green Standard, called the *Pendón Verde*, captured in battle from the Moors in the thirteenth century and normally kept in the parish church of All Saints. Although the seizure of the banner clearly was an attempt to make some sort of statement in the context of political machination, in time it became inextricably associated with the neighborhood's potential for violent disaffection (Knezevic 2014: 175–8). More than an emotional response to a past political act, the display of armed, banner-waving, but still non-violent anger also communicated a quasi-juridical evaluation of the act and the person or persons deemed responsible for it. To display anger publicly about an act was to construe the action as an injury, a wrongful deed that caused harm, an offense against people's honor.[18] Furthermore, every time an insurgent from la Feria in Seville beheld his banner, he was reminded of the reason why he was not at work. He participated in the parade or stood nearby the banner to defend his rights, and he would not temper his emotions until these rights were restored. Ritual flag display also unified possibly diverse meanings and created a vital bond among all participants. It was so emotionally compelling that the message of the gathering and the guiding role of its leaders were beyond debate. In addition, flags sometimes were the first victim of popular fury because they symbolized power. In 1345, "the populace and artisans" ("*populari et artefici*") rose up against Orvieto's oligarchic government of the Seven. The anger exploded when one of the ruling Seven came into the town square with his friends, bearing a flag with his family coat of arms. The artisans attacked the banners, dashing them to the ground. The Siena revolt that toppled the Nine ten years later began with the ritualized ripping apart of flags and ended with the rebels destroying all the Nine's symbols of power—the governmental coats of arms painted on all their houses (Cohn 2006: 182–3).[19] In sum, in Seville, Orvieto, Siena, and elsewhere, powerful symbols were important carriers of emotions.

Music and singing can also be seen as emotionally important, though their use was multifunctional. Chanting ballads as they marched through the streets overwhelmed the participants in a ritual parade. A Roman diarist and eyewitness described his fellow citizens battling the king of Naples in 1407 when they formed their armed assembly. "Illuminated with candles, they waved the banners at the head of each *rione*" (i.e., the inhabitants of certain parishes in Rome). Ready to engage in battle against the king's men, they chanted "death to this traitor, the king, and to all his men" (Cohn 2006: 181). In Venice and the Lagoon, the *popolani* took part in similar festive parades and announced their claims by singing and playing music (Judde de Larivière and Salzberg 2013: 1135).[20] Such noisy and (as in Rome) illuminated spectacles naturally shared much in common with processions and ceremonies that expressed devotional and religious feelings. It is not a coincidence that early Protestants regularly used these highly demonstrative displays to challenge religious and political opponents. The Lyon printing workers, for instance, organized similar processions in 1551. They did not act mindlessly, as their historian Natalie Zemon Davis remarks. A few hundred armed journeymen led other artisans and their wives up the streets, as they sang the Psalms in French interspersed with shouted insults aimed at the noble canon-counts at the cathedral of Saint-Jean (Zemon Davis 1975: 4–5). Their numbers and the activist fellowship of their singing not only helped them face the risk of arrest, but also allayed more profound fears of death and human isolation. After all, it is logical that these deeply religious people would attach great emotional value to (quasi-)religious songs and practices.

In Renaissance Italy, poetry, ballads, and insulting songs were an integral part of the collective actions of citizens. No eruption of political feeling seems to have been complete,

FIGURE 8.4: Fifteenth-century procession in a city in the southern Low Countries, in *Spinola Hours*, Bruges, c. 1510. Getty Museum, MS Ludwig IX, 18, f. 48v.

or deeply enough felt, unless the anger also spilled over into verse or even paintings or "defamatory graffiti" ("*pittura infamante*"). In 1440 Florence for instance, a few insulting lines, identifying an enemy of the Medici by name and tersely summarizing his crimes, described him in a poem as a "serpent-like queer, bent, shamed and false" person. In the ruthless political world of Renaissance Italy, similar verses could stir up murderous passion (Martines 2001: 247). Elsewhere in Europe, collectively shouted insults at governors or clerics also aroused crowds and frightened rulers. In the imperial city of Augsburg, Jakob Herbrot became the object of such ballads in 1552, when he was briefly reinstalled as city mayor and again forced to resign due to religious upheaval. After his resignation, he appealed to the city council to punish those who spread libels mocking him. This shows that the public sphere of early modern towns was full of laughter used as a weapon to undermine the authority of (former) power holders (Kuhn 2007: 87). In English towns, anonymous libels often accompanied peaceful and violent protests and incited adversaries. In 1536 York, for instance, a man confessed to involvement in a bill-posting campaign against one of the city's aldermen. The bill alleged that he had bribed the city council with venison and wine. The mayor and aldermen's anxieties lay in the fear that, from such bills, "murder, varyance, stryf and debate was verey lyke to ensue emongs all the commonaltie of the seyd city." Bills were political ammunition, ready to destroy the carefully crafted public image of urban rulers and thus make them vulnerable to further popular dissent (Liddy 2011: 460).

The purpose of these pamphlets, as written weapons of emotional violence, was to convey a clear message to the authorities. The deployment of fear became a form of rhetoric, a propagation of the message through a complex symbolic performance. However, unlike physical attack, the use of emotional violence indicated that rebels still sought to negotiate with the city government or territorial powers. Traditional literature often neglects a fundamental aspect of emotions, namely, that humans utilize them to gain a certain interaction. Following research that focuses on the communicative aspect of collective action, scholars have put forth the thesis that ritualized emotions perform this communication, arguing that demonstrative acts and emotional behaviors decisively determined medieval public life (Althoff 1998: 74). Emotions telegraphed information. The use of emotions—their "performance"—indicated the possibility of peace to the authorities (Rosenwein 2002: 841). For Gerd Althoff, emotions had social functions and followed social rules (1996: 60–79). Therefore, emotional uprisings contained a well-understood sociopolitical code, with anger as a "social signal" which, paradoxically, helped to keep the peace. A ritualized parade was a symbolic sign to start negotiations over the insurgents' claims. In these negotiations, collective emotions were a useful political tool. Faced with the real danger of a furious and armed crowd in the market square, the city government or other central authority was forced to find a fair solution for the problem.

Petitions made the claims of rebels real. These written requests were "rational" and juridical means of making political complaint and seeking redress of grievances. But evidence shows that the collective emotions (along with the military power, of course) of petitioners put pressure on the authorities to incorporate the petitions into urban bylaws. For instance, in London in 1316 during a wave of insurrections which threatened the country and dynasty, angry citizens forced the authorities to take their demands into account. Starving during one of Europe's worst famines in the medieval and modern era, crowds rose against local authorities (as in Bristol) but also against the king, Edward II. A chronicler recorded that the king was forced to regulate the grain market in the capital "by the clamour of the excited people" (*ad clamorem populi excitatus*), but that clamor had not led to a riot (Cohn 2013: 145). Almost two centuries later, in San Vicente de la Barquera (Castile) in 1496, the Catholic monarchs heard the complaints from the craft guilds after an outburst of indignation had led to the composition of a successful petition. With this document, guild representatives asked for the right of political participation. The petition stated that the offices of town councilors "belonged to a few lineages and did not take the rest of the inhabitants into consideration, even though these were as skilful, prepared, and rich as the others, and, as a result, the craft guild felt deeply offended." King Ferdinand and Queen Johanna accepted these arguments and ordered that the guild's deputy henceforth should attend meetings (Solorzano Telechea 2014: 191). Fear, shame, and offence led people to take up arms against those who could remedy a situation considered unjust.

VIOLENCE, SHAME AND FORGIVENESS

When gatherings, parades, and petitions were unsuccessful, the outburst of emotions could lead to violence. Violence is about the expression of anger, even though contemporary historians are well aware that physical brutality has a certain ambivalence. As Hannah Skoda contends, anger dramatically encapsulates the multiple layers of ambivalence surrounding the reading of violence. It engages the audience through shared sentiment and makes no definite distinction between instrumental and expressive emotion, even when it is physically manifested. Anger is the cipher through which the audience is drawn into the disturbing problem of violence (Skoda 2013: 240). On one hand, violence brings disorder to society but, on the other, it contains the social message that order should be restored, especially when a community uses it. Of course, there were many examples of violence arising from quarrels of hotheads who felt insulted or dishonored, such as after bloodshed in taverns. For instance, Skoda described a huge brawl in 1288 in the parish of Sainte-Geneviève (in Paris) caused by an argument between a pimp and drinker that exploded into a conflict involving many drinking companions. The dispute generated into a joyous and anarchic spectacle of brutality, with no point and no significance, apart from the fun of the fight (Skoda 2013: 112; Tanon 1883: 361). Fights, feuds, and vendettas colored the history of the late medieval and pre-modern era, and many historians wonder about the extent to which this was merely senseless hatred. Scholars are well aware that political power, economic dominance, and social influence were at work when families fought each other. In fifteenth-century Florence, for instance, irrational fear and lust for aggression certainly fed the factional dispute between the Medici and their political rivals, but political supremacy was the primary issue at stake (Crouzet-Pavan 2001: 152; Boquet and Nagy 2015: 326).[21] In periods of economic crisis, fiscal pressure, or religious uncertainty, with the atmosphere vibrating with tension, a violent event could inflame people and cause an explosion of belligerent emotions. The murder of the Duke of Guise in 1588, for example, disturbed individuals and moved the common people in French cities into a spiral of violence that brought no solution to the multiple conflicts in the kingdom (Caroll 2000: 336; Carpi 2008: 256; Broomhall 2013: 19). Emotions of envy and disgust intensified these clashes, fed as they were by pointless sadism.

In most cases, however, anger and violence had a meaning because they communicated a message to the victim of the hostility and to the wider audience as well. Particularly when force was used collectively, the perpetrators of the violence made it clear that they would no longer tolerate certain acts. A striking example involving a Calvinist parade in sixteenth-century Valenciennes shows that violence could be very targeted and restricted during a commotion. In 1562, in a daring rescue of two Calvinists condemned to burn at the stake ready to meet their martyrdom, a psalm-singing crowd erupted as the urban authorities led the prisoners to the execution site. Suddenly, a woman threw a shoe at the magistrates, and the crowd responded by throwing a hail of rocks at the men guarding the execution site. Sensing a riot underway, the aldermen quickly whisked the men back to the prison, while onlookers rushed the barricades and destroyed the stakes and wood piles (Arnade 2008: 72–3). The rescuers had boldly converted the tools of the execution into the means of its prevention. Even though pure religious conviction motivated the Protestants' act, they staged it with emotional words and gestures that forced the authorities to yield. Rather than being blind or outrageous, the violence was merely intended to induce tolerance and forgiveness for dissidents (in this case, religious). Likewise, executions performed by rebels were highly emotional acts; brutal, of course, but not meaningless. In the abovementioned Zürich rebellion of 1489, the decapitation of former Mayor Hans Waldmann by rebels took place with rituals including bell ringing and the public confession of the victim, who asked the audience to sing an "Ave Maria" for him (Jucker 2006: 119). In the rebels' eyes, Waldmann had violated urban law. Therefore, for the rebels, his criminal punishment was necessary to restore public order. Perhaps the spectators became calm after the execution, moved as they were by the spectacle. That was certainly the case in Bruges after the execution of the local public enemy number one, Pieter Lanchals, during the revolt of 1488. As the local sheriff, Lanchals had acted cruelly, violated urban privileges, and spent public money for private purposes, as the rebellious craftsmen explained. The executioners refused to give him a religious burial though from the scaffold Lanchals had implored them to do so. However, after his violent death, the crowd gave in and agreed to an official burial ceremony, because, as a chronicler commented, "their hearts had already started to soften" (Despars 1840: 391).[22]

Of course, crowds did not have a monopoly on violence. Judgments pronounced on rioters by the authorities had similar characteristics to the collective actions of the crowds. Governors of towns, kings, and bishops also used emotions as tools to frighten opponents and punish subjects. For instance, one of the most shameful punishments for mutineers was the humiliating ride through the city in a kind of "procession of shame," accompanied by flags, noise, and sometimes singing. In 1403, a resident of the Hungarian city of Buda named Martin Sclavus endured this fate because he had rebelled against the magistrates. Locked in chains, he was tied to a horse's tail and dragged through the town in a degrading parade (Zupka 2014: 358). Shame was an important means of repression, for it excluded perpetrators of violence from the community and provided a fearsome example for others. Daniel Smail has shown that the weapon of dishonor and shame, often used by authorities, did not necessarily mean that punishment had to be violent. Smail disagrees with the claim of many historians that "old regime sovereignty" was built on rumors of torture and spectacles of punishment that displayed the frightening capacity of rulers to inflict violence on city residents. Studying fourteenth-century Lucca and Marseille, he suggests that debt regulation was far more influential than the repression of interpersonal violence in Mediterranean Europe. "Predation," as Smail calls it, the urban governments' practice of seizing goods for repayment of debt, was a more familiar punishment for criminals in these towns. Having one's property seized was a shameful action. As a result, the considerable investment in the infrastructure for debt-related coercion in Lucca and Marseille is a sign that late medieval urban courts of law were primarily engaged in regulating honor. This interpretation explains why courts routinely transformed violent offenders into debtors. Indebtedness, in this world, was a vector of shame (Smail 2012: 7–34). Indeed, late medieval and early modern justice was not a barbaric and brutal machine, as it is often depicted, crushing its victims without mercy or exception. Emotional embarrassment was also part of repression.

Furthermore, though rites of torture and humiliation are an irrefutable part of European history, remission and grace were perhaps more common. Of course, there were many examples of furious princes instructing their troops to plunder cities to punish the residents for their (alleged) disobedience. In 1482, the French King Louis XI ordered all the inhabitants of Arras to leave the city because they had not supported him in his wars; Emperor Charles V sacked Rome in 1527; and royal troops set fire to the city of Issoire (in the Auvergne) in 1577 during a violent phase of the French wars of religion.[23] However, princes more often expressed anger in words than in deeds. The fury and indignation uttered during speeches or in letters generally came without concrete consequences, though the princes clearly used (faked?) feelings to intimidate opponents and subjects. Sentiments were, therefore, an influential feature of medieval and early

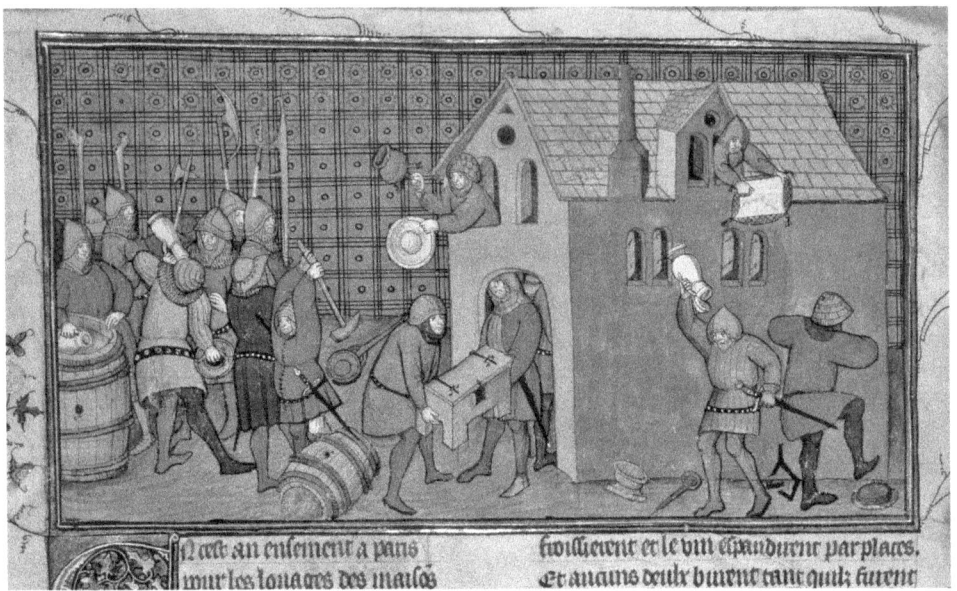

FIGURE 8.5: In 1306, Parisians pillage the house of the royal exchequer, in *Chroniques de France, dites de Saint-Denis*, Paris, after 1380. British Library, MS Roy. 20 CVII, f. 134r.

modern politics (Smagghe 2012).[24] Grace, pity, and forgiveness were also weighty tools princes utilized to exercise power. Particularly important in the context of this essay is that emotions used by rebels could form a mitigating circumstance that led the prince to forgive the rebels. The remission letter of Duke Philip the Good for the riots that took place in the city of Ghent in 1437, which preceded the revolt mentioned at the beginning of this chapter, explicitly stated that the violence was forgiven because it was instigated by emotions. Among other deeds, the Ghentenars had pillaged the house of a former alderman because he had used public money to refurnish it. His fellow citizens clearly would not tolerate this corrupt act, and showed it by taking back what belonged to them by sacking his house. Nevertheless, the riots were not premeditated; as Duke Philip the Good said of them, "fever was running in the blood" (Fris 1901: 204–5).[25] The "heat of the citizens' blood" (*hitten van den bloede*), i.e., their collective emotion, was used as an argument to pardon the citizens for their violent behavior. Yet, as we know, it was not the last episode in the city's history in which the emotions of Ghentenars ran high.

CONCLUDING REMARKS

Fear, anger, passion, pity, and shame have been driving forces in history. This overview of the expression and use of emotions by princes, subjects, and insurgents has undermined the validity of the assumptions of nineteenth-century historians about the role and function of emotions in the European West during the turbulent period between 1300 and 1600. In the politics of collectivities, emotions were real, and they had a function. Princes used them as a means to frighten citizens, urban authorities organized rituals and parades of shame, and popular leaders carefully tried to channel the anger of crowds in order to influence the political decisions of courts and mighty rulers. The many studies cited here show scholarly awareness that the public expressions of emotions were not naïve performances of instinctive behavior, but meaningful acts of communication. People and communities used a sophisticated, intense repertoire of rituals to express their feelings collectively. Although the local characteristics differed from time to time and region to region, there was a general pattern. In public, people used their sentiments to affect the behavior of others. Even though aggressive emotions flared out in the open, blind, outrageous violence was not the goal of collective anger. Communication and interaction remained the main purpose of the expression of emotions, in whatever style they were articulated. There is much research still to be done on this topic. The collective emotions of women, young people, the poor, and urban commoners have hardly been touched. While the discursive strategies of (some) princes have been analyzed in detail, many speech acts, letters, and chronicles of clerics, female rulers, and mighty urban families await scrutiny. Last but not least, scholarship on the relationship between personal emotions and the cultural patterns of collectivities would certainly enable historians to rewrite the history of collective emotions.

NOTES ON CONTRIBUTORS

Susan Broomhall is Professor of History at The University of Western Australia and researches gender, emotions, material culture, cultural contact, and the heritage of the early modern world. She was a Foundation Chief Investigator in the Australian Research Council Centre of Excellence for the History of Emotions, Europe 1100–1800, and now holds an Australian Research Council Future Fellowship, researching emotions in the political activities and correspondence of Catherine de' Medici. She is the editor, most recently, of *Early Modern Emotions: An Introduction* (Routledge, 2016); *Ordering Emotions in Europe, 1100–1800* (Brill, 2015); *Gender and Emotions in Medieval and Early Modern Europe: Destroying Order, Structuring Disorder* (Ashgate, 2015); *Authority, Gender and Emotions in Late Medieval and Early Modern England* (Palgrave, 2015); *Spaces for Feeling: Emotions and Sociabilities in Britain, 1650–1850* (Routledge, 2015); and with Sarah Finn, *Violence and Emotions in Early Modern Europe* (Routledge, 2015).

Denis Collins is a Senior Lecturer in Musicology at The University of Queensland, Australia. His research interests are in counterpoint in late medieval and early modern music. He has been an Associate Investigator with the ARC Centre of Excellence for the History of Emotions (2013–2017) and a Chief Investigator in two three-year ARC Discovery Project grants on the role of canonic techniques in European musical traditions from the fourteenth to seventeenth centuries. He is the author of the article "Counterpoint" in *Oxford Bibliographies Online: Music* and his recent and forthcoming articles are in *Music Analysis*, *BACH*, *Music Theory Online*, *Acta Musicologica* and *Musica Disciplina*.

Jelle Haemers (1980) is senior lecturer at the University of Leuven (KU Leuven, Belgium). He has published on the social history of medieval politics, and the urban history of the Low Countries. He is a member of the Young Academy of Belgium.

Jeremy Goldberg is a cultural and social historian of the English later Middle Ages with particular interests in gender, family, childhood and youth, sexuality, urban drama, and the relationship between people and buildings. His publications include *Women, Work and Life Cycle in a Medieval Economy* (Clarendon Press, 1992), *Medieval Women, c. 1275–1525: Documentary Sources* (Manchester University Press, 1995), *Medieval England: A Social History 1250–1550* (Arnold, 2004), and *Communal Discord, Child Abduction and Rape in the Later Middle Ages* (Palgrave, 2008). He is a member of the Department of History and of the Centre for Medieval Studies of the University of York (UK).

David Lederer is senior lecturer at Maynooth University, Ireland. His publications include, as editor, *German History in Global and Transnational Perspective* (London, 2017); a co-edited special issue of *the Journal of Social History – The Politics of Suicide: Historical Perspectives on Suicidology before Durkheim* (2013); *Religion, Madness and the State in Early Modern Europe: A Bavarian Beacon* (Cambridge University Press, 2006; winner,

Gerald Strauss Prize for best book in Reformation History, 16th Century Society). Over thirty articles range from the history of suicide, emotions, and demonic possession to ghosts, gender, and popular religion. Under the auspices of a Marie Skłodowska-Curie Fellowship from the European Commission, he researched brotherly love at the Australian Research Council Centre of Excellence for the History of Emotions, Europe 1100–1800, in Adelaide and the Wellcome Trust Centre for the History of Emotions at Queen Mary University of London, from 2015 to 2017. He is currently writing a global history of suicide.

Andrew Lynch is a Professor in English and Literary Studies at The University of Western Australia, and Director of the Australian Research Council Centre of Excellence for the History of Emotions, Europe 1100–1800. He has written extensively on emotion in the medieval literature of war and peace and its modern afterlives. His recent publications include *Emotions and War: Medieval to Romantic Literature* (Palgrave Macmillan, 2015), with Stephanie Downes and Katrina O'Loughlin, and *Understanding Emotions in Early Europe* (Brepols, 2015), with Michael Champion. He is co-editor of the journal *Emotions: History, Culture, Society*.

Sarah McNamer is Professor of English and Medieval Studies and Director of the Medieval Studies Program at Georgetown University. Her primary interest is in the interplay between literature and the history of emotion. Her book *Affective Meditation and the Invention of Medieval Compassion* (University of Pennsylvania Press, 2010) received the Book of the Year award from the Conference on Christianity and Literature for 2010. Her critical edition and translation, *Meditations on the Life of Christ: The Short Italian Text*, (University of Notre Dame Press, 2017) won the MLA Aldo and Jeanne Scaglione Publication Award for a Manuscript in Italian Literary Studies for 2017. At present she is writing a book on the *Pearl* poet.

Jennifer Nevile has published widely on early modern dance practices and their relationship with other contemporary artistic practices and intellectual movements. Her research has appeared in her monographs *The Eloquent Body: Dance and Humanist Culture in Fifteenth-Century Italy* (Indiana University Press, 2004) and *Footprints of the Dance: An Early Seventeenth-Century Dance Master's Notebook* (Brill, 2018); in edited collections of essays including *Dance, Spectacle, and the Body Politick, 1250–1750* (Indiana University Press, 2008), *The Cambridge Companion to Ballet* (Cambridge University Press, 2007), *Die Musik in der Kultur der Renaissance: Kontexte, Disziplinen, Diskurse* (Laaber-Verlag 2015), and most recently *Medieval Theatre Performance: Actors, Dancers, Automata and their Audiences* (D.S. Brewer, 2017); as well as journals including *Dance Research, Renaissance Quarterly, Early Music* and *Early Theatre*. She currently holds an honorary research position in the School of the Arts and Media, The University of New South Wales, Australia.

Kathryn Prince is Vice Dean of the Faculty of Arts and Associate Professor of Theatre at the University of Ottawa, as well as the General Editor of *Shakespeare Bulletin*. Her recent books include *Performing Early Modern Drama Today* (Cambridge University Press, 2012), *History, Memory, Performance* (Palgrave Macmillan, 2014), and *Shakespeare and Canada: Remembrance of Ourselves* (University of Ottawa Press, 2016). Her current research focuses on emotions in early modern English drama and on empathy and wonder in early modern intercultural encounters.

Patricia Simons is a Professor in the Department of History of Art at the University of Michigan, Ann Arbor. Her books include *The Sex of Men in Premodern Europe: A Cultural History* (Cambridge University Press, 2011) and *Patronage, Art, and Society in Renaissance Italy* (Clarendon Press, 1987), co-edited with F. W. Kent. She has published in numerous anthologies and peer-review journals, with essays ranging over such subjects as female and male homoeroticism, gender and portraiture, the cultural role of humor, and the visual dynamics of secrecy and of scandal. She is currently working on a book-length analysis of the visual and cultural history of beards in early modern Europe.

Stephanie Tarbin is a Research Assistant with the Australian Research Council Centre of Excellence for the History of Emotions, Europe 1100–1800, based at The University of Western Australia. Her main research interests are gender representations in and the social history of late medieval and early modern England, and her doctoral thesis examined moral regulation in London, c. 1380–1530. She has since worked on fragmented families and childhood, and has published essays on moral regulation, masculinity, women's friendships, and children's experiences. With Susan Broomhall, she is co-editor of *Women, Identities and Communities in Early Modern Europe* (Ashgate, 2008).

Charles Zika is a Professorial Fellow in History and Chief Investigator in the Australian Research Council Centre of Excellence for the History of Emotions, Europe 1100–1800, at The University of Melbourne. His interests lie in the intersection of religion, emotion, visual culture, and print in early modern Europe. Recent books include *Love: Art of Emotion 1400–1800* (National Gallery of Victoria, 2017), co-edited with Angela Hesson and Matthew Martin; *Disaster, Death and the Emotions in the Shadow of the Apocalypse, 1400–1700* (Palgrave Macmillan 2016), co-edited with Jennifer Spinks; *The Appearance of Witchcraft: Print and Visual Culture in Sixteenth-Century Europe* (Routledge, 2007). Recent articles explore the emotional economy of pilgrimage; apocalyptic time, emotion and disaster; anger and dishonor in sixteenth-century broadsheets; and ridicule and cruelty in seventeenth-century witchcraft imagery.

NOTES

Introduction

1. "voz deux enffans dicy se portent fort bien et croissent en grandeur et beaulte et le petit David est fort plaisant. . . . Ledict David se recommande à sa mere, à son frère et sa soer et a ma baisie ce matin pour fere sadicte recommendation," February 2, 1570, Archives générales du royaume à Bruxelles, Conseil des Troubles 96.

Chapter One

1. "Ut Chalybem magnes attrahit, ipsa sequor"; "quam propter vacuo linquor et ipsa thoro"; "Id saltem vereor, ne, dum lentissimus absis, Quod mea sit reduci forma probata minus."
2. Gherardo or Monte di Giovanni di Miniato, Miniature portraits of scientific patron, Filippo Strozzi and son and Alfonso (bottom right) on the first page of *Historia naturale di Caio Plinio Secondo, tradocta di lingua latina in fiorentina per Christophoro Landino*, available from the Bodleian Library, Oxford. Arch. G b.6, fol. 5r: http://digital.bodleian.ox.ac.uk/inquire/Discover/Search/#/?p=c+0,t+,rsrs+0,rsps+10,fa+,so+ox%3Asort%5Easc,scids+,pid+,vi+9f365e11-53c9-48e4-8930-36fa27f7009f (accessed September 5, 2017).
3. "aunque con mucho sentimento suyo, mas vence la necessidad del amor de la paz, al justo dolor."
4. "non seulement rejouïssez vos Vers par aggreables senteurs, ains les en soulagez en la plus-part de leurs maladies."
5. "j'apperceu aussi que les arbres de la circonference de la forest se jettoyent & courboyent ou s'enclinoyent devers le costé des terres, comme si les autres arbres leur estoyent ennemis."
6. "les natures végétatives" "sensibles et les raisonnables."
7. "vilainement meurtri. Penses-tu que la seppe qui est ainsi fendue et esclattee en plusieurs lieux, qu'elle ne se ressente de la fraction, et extorsion qui luy aura esté faicte?"
8. "Wir sind von Mangel an allem gedrückt, womit eben Gott die zügellose Trunksucht straft."

Chapter Two

1. On devotional aspects, see Rubin (2004).
2. For a critique, see Shank (2008).
3. On the anthropological distinction between hypercognized and hypocognized emotions see Levy (1975); contextualized in Plamper (2015: 95f.). The historical applicability of hypercognized emotion is tested in Lederer (2011). Annals historians frequently deploy collective consciousness as developed by Durkheim, though some scholars (Lucien Lévy-Bruhl and, more recently, Bruno Latour) are critical of the concept. Hegel's philosophy of history invokes the Zeitgeist, whereas Schumpeter employed the term "voice" (*Stimme* or *Stimmung*) as social mood.

4. Two recent collections from the cycle on fear in 2007/8 held at Princeton's Davis Centre for Historical Studies include the work of the fellows edited by Laffan and Weiss (2012), and interdisciplinary contributions to a workshop edited by Plamper and Lazier (2012). Bourke (2005), Plamper (2009) and Stearns (2006) are good examples of modern fear studies by leading emotions scholars. Noteworthy early modern studies include Lefebvre (1973), Naphy and Johnson (1997) and Bähr (2013).
5. See also Delumeau (1990), and for an appropriately titled review see Doniger (1990).
6. For a seminal example of the influence of medieval philosophy for Luther's attack on Catholic universalism, see Oberman (1963).
7. Pope Benedict XVI, who resigned in 2013, has been the only other.
8. In 1315, Louis X allowed them to return after extorting an enormous sum from the community and permitted them to repurchase their synagogues.
9. Composed in 1312, it later appeared on the papal index of prohibited books, the Index Librorum Prohibitorum, in 1585.
10. On the role of emotives in an emotional regime, see Reddy (2001: 125f., 314f.). See also Plamper (2015) and Rosenwein (2006).
11. On the role of capitalism and art patronage during the Renaissance, see Goldthwaite (1995, 2009, [1968] 2015).
12. Charged with all the usual crimes (e.g., heresy, sodomy, piracy, incest, schism), he was declared an anti-pope, and his name was retired from the list of official popes until the name was finally rehabilitated in 1958. The second/official John XXIII was responsible for convoking the Second Vatican Council in 1963.
13. A beautifully illustrated early incunabula version of 1466 is available from the Library of Congress Online Collection at: http://lcweb2.loc.gov/cgi-bin/ampage (accessed 17 November 2016).
14. On the concept of spiritual physic, see Lederer (2006).
15. This and most other documentation associated with her life and trial are available in Taylor (2006).
16. On her trial, see Hotchkiss (1999: 49–68).
17. On the illustrations in Molitor, see Kwan (2012). The secondary literature on demonology relevant to emotions history is enormous because of links between both subjects with the history of psychology/psychiatry as well as the centrality of demonology in the moral casuistry of vices as sins. Basic relevant works include: MacDonald (1981), Midelfort (1999), Roper (1994, 2004), Lederer (2006).
18. In Venice, for example, see Ruggiero (1993). More recently, Seitz (2011: 42f.).
19. The debate between Eric Hobsbawm and Hugh Trevor-Roper over the nature of a General Crisis in seventeenth-century Europe began in 1954. Geoffrey Parker, perhaps the most vocal advocate of the theory, has advanced its scope to encompass a *Global Crisis: War, Climate Change and Catastrophe in the Seventeenth Century* (2013).
20. In chapter 108, Brant refers directly to the work of Homer, the subject of Lucien's *True Stories*, the satire upon which the *Ship of Fools* is based; see Lederer (2009).
21. For an excellent new appraisal of Folly from an emotions historian, see Essary (2017).
22. The classic study of the subject remains Scribner (1981).
23. Katharina von Bora, his spouse, constantly referred to him as "Herr Doktor."
24. The literature on the reformation of marriage, sexuality and patriarchy is vast and ever growing. Some prominent examples include Ozment (1985), Wiesner-Hanks (1986), Roper (1991), Watt (1992), Harrington (1995), and, most recently, Grace (2015).

Chapter Three

1. Denis Collins thanks Graeme Boone and Jessie Ann Owens for kindly sharing their unpublished work on emotions with him and for their lively discussions on emotions research during their visits to Australia in 2015. He is also grateful to Jason Stoessel for his helpful comments on an earlier version of this chapter. Support for this research was provided by the Australian Research Council's Centre of Excellence for the History of Emotions in Europe, 1100–1800 (grant number CE110001011).
2. Although the present-day use of the word "emotion" has no equivalent label in medieval language, this word is still useful for enquiries into the richness of mental and physical experiences in the period considered in the present study. I thank Graeme Boone for sharing his thoughts on this matter with me.
3. In this respect, it is salutary to recall Bruce Holsinger's observation that "the study of music and poetic language as interdependent discursive formations in medieval culture can yield a richer and more nuanced account of the period's cultural history than that afforded by the traditional division between musicology and literary criticism" (1997: 191). The situation has generally evolved toward this state in recent decades.
4. See especially Tables 2, 3, and 4 of Palisca's study for comparisons of modal nomenclature between Greeks and Christians. For instance, the Greek Dorian mode became the Christian Phrygian with a consequent mix up of their ethical and affective characteristics. Palisca's study is reproduced with frequent though minor editorial changes in Palisca (2013). For other tabular summaries of the emotional or affective qualities of the modes, see Judd (2002: 375) and Tomlinson (1993: 80–1). The difficulties experienced by medieval and Renaissance musicians in reconciling the traditions of modal affect with musical practice is also discussed in Powers and Wiering (n.d.).
5. See especially Chapter 4 ("Observance of the Mode as a Means of Word Expression"), Chapter 5 ("Examples of Modally Irregular Procedure throughout an Entire Work") and Chapter 6 ("On the Affective Characteristics of Modes").
6. In her discussion of the only poem by Christine de Pizan set to music (by Gilles Binchois), Diane Curtis notes that the lament was a genre that had a long association with women (2001: 268).
7. A related point is made by Graeme Boone (1997: 88) about the chanson *Craindre vous vueil* by the fifteenth-century composer Guillaume Dufay. Boone points out how inflections on the notes E and B demonstrate the composer's exploration of available tonal colors, not simply superficial word-painting. In this way, "the emotive resources of the text" are opened up.
8. Machaut's motets are written mostly for two voices with French texts set over a Latin tenor.
9. Precedents for the rhetorical concept of music may be detected in fourteenth-century treatises by Marchetto of Padua, Heinrich Egar von Kalkar, and Gobelinus Person (I thank Jason Stoessel for drawing these sources to my attention).
10. In a study that complements Fuhrmann's work, Anne Walters Robertson (2015) examines specific compositional strategies in the fifteenth and early sixteenth centuries for settings drawn from the Song of Songs, Passion of Christ, psalms, and what she calls "other emotional texts."
11. Other terms abound in the historical sources, several of which continue to pose problems of interpretation and understanding. For instance, the word "frisque" has generated considerable discussion over its musical connotations. While no definitive meaning has been asserted, Margaret Bent (2004: 107) quotes from the work of Christopher Page (1996: 3–4) to suggest

that it may be "an affective response to the surface sound of music." This matter is also considered in Wegman (2003) and Fallows (1987). A study of terminology from a later period, much of which relates to emotions, is in Haar (1983).

12. An earlier lament was written in the late 1370s on the death of Guillaume de Machaut. Jacqueline Cerquiglini-Toulet (1997: 141–2) considers this lament in the context of what she calls networks of materials and people, including poets and musicians, in fourteenth-century France. Her work in some ways foreshadows the notion of emotional communities in later scholarship.
13. For more on the *Académie de Poésie et de Musique* and the belief that dance could affect the viewers' emotions, see McGowan (2008a).
14. "*Alla conversatione di questa nostra vita sono necessarij honesti piaceri, & le recreationi dell'animo, quanto à quella i dispiaceri, e travagli sono pernitiosi . . . frà le quali hà luogo l'uso del Ballare . . . poi che nelle conversationi, & società humane eccita gli animi alle allegrezze, & quando quelli si trovano oppressi da qualche perturbatione, gli solleva, e ristora, e gli tien lontani da ogni pensiero noioso, e dispiacevole. Ne tal qualità è di poco ornamento; poiche è congionta con la Poesia, & con la Musica, facultà frà l'altre molto degna; & è parte di quella imitatione, che representa gli effetti dell'animo con movimento del corpo*" (translation by Jennifer Nevile).
15. An example of this approach is seen in Monahin (2011: 211–30).
16. "*Non domandar s'aven giubilli i chori / & se le damigielle miran fiso / veggiendosi da lloro far tanti onori. / Pareva quel trepudio il paradiso / di gierarchie angeliche che balla / & era pien ciaschun di gioia & riso.*"
17. "*Io credo che lle dame mangnie & dengnie / il dì faciessero ardere mille fochi / sanza fucile o pietra, zolfo o lengnie. / . . . Chi danza chi sollazza & chi motteggia, / chi è mirato & che fisso altri guarda / & chi è vagheggiato & chi vagheggia.*"
18. "*questi gentilhomini dil Re una moresca da ridere, essendo venuti molti de loro con camise sopra li zupponi e panicelli in testa, scufie de rete nanti il volto e calze da contadini in gamba, et con torze a[ccese] in mani se fecero veder moreschando nanti il Re et Regina*" (translation by Jennifer Nevile).
19. The information in this paragraph on the anti-masque dances from *The Masque of Queens* is taken from Daye (2014: 194–7).
20. This dance is described in *Li nuptiali*, a book written around 1500 by the Roman nobleman Marco Antonio Altieri, in which he discusses the proper conduct of Roman wedding festivities.
21. Skinner is quoting Muratori (1741: 131).
22. The rest of the information in this paragraph about these entries comes from Cano (2005: 125–8).
23. It is described by Domenico (n.d.: 2r) and Cornazano (n.d.: 6r–6v). For an example of the creative juxtaposition of movement and stillness in the *ballo Sobria*, see Nevile (2004: 28–9).
24. "*en dançant un balet gay, inventé tout a propos, ores s'entre-faisants sauter l'une l'autre, ores s'entre-frappans des mains, puis des pieds, tantost se tenans d'une main seulement, puis des deux ensemble, ores elles tournoyoient comme en rouë d'une vitesse presque incroyable, avec une infinité de passages, cadances, & mesures, coup sur coup entre-coupées, qui ne se peuvent representer qu'en les voyant a l'oeil*" (Brach 1576: 195v). For an extensive discussion of this masquerade, see McGowan (2003: 17–23) and Dawkins (1969: 3–15).
25. The common passage is the second section of the dance, and bars 20 to 29 of the chanson.

Chapter Five

1. Patricia Simons and Charles Zika thank Julie Davies for assistance in obtaining the images and permissions for this chapter, and Richard Young for his technical assistance.
2. For Sassetta's *St. Anthony beaten by devils* (Pinacoteca Nazionale, Siena) before restoration, see Carli (1957: Pl. II); for the rubbed image of the pregnant Virgin Mary in a manuscript, see Schmidt (2011: 106, n. 5).
3. For exploration of the relationship between art, history and neuroscience, see Freedberg (2011), and other articles at http://warburg.sas.ac.uk/about/people/david-freedberg (accessed November 29, 2016). For a proponent of the new field of neuroarthistory, see Onians (2008); and for a critique, Cooter (2014).
4. On the historiography, see Steinhoff (2012: 38–41).
5. For the early link, see Simons (2017b); for an overview with earlier bibliography, see Sturgis (2016). For more focused studies, see Baxandall (1972: 56–71); Barasch (1976, 1991, 1995).
6. Karel van Mander, writing *Het schilder-boeck* (*Book on Painting*) in the last decade of the sixteenth century (published Haarlem, 1604), also claimed that emotions are revealed through bodily gestures, but especially through emphasized facial gestures, which he referred to as *leden van den aenghesichte* (physiognomical limbs). See Melion (1991: 66–9); Hoecker (1916: 136 stanza 4).
7. For example, on gestures and voice, including the recommendation for variety that Alberti emphasized, see Cicero (1968: 169–79, at 179 (3.56–9)).
8. The reproduced photograph shows an earlier arrangement; the original spacing is unknown.
9. For other examples of the gesture see Barasch (1976: 31–2, Figure 31, and 73, Figure 38 (with two hands)); Baxandall (1972: 63–4).
10. For an overview, see Evans (1971: 15–27); Male (1986: 285–317).
11. For a psychological rather than historical reading of "Arousal by Image" see Freedberg (1989: 317–44).
12. The holy subject was probably the Virgin Mary or a female saint, but it could conceivably have been a male figure, similar to Bramante's half-length *Christ at the Column* (c. 1490, Brera) or Perugino's close view of *St. Sebastian* (1493–4, Hermitage).
13. The earliest is the Prado canvas with a bearded organist, and thereafter some degree of workshop participation is evident.

Chapter Eight

1. "*Gens de moindre estat d'icelle ville et povres gens*".
2. "*Avoient emeu et esmouvoient le peuple*".
3. "*Veulent savoir la vérité dont cette esmotion provient et que on face en façon que le roy soit maistre se on trouve rebellion.*"
4. See also Emirbayer and Goldberg (2005: 473–4).
5. See also Rosenwein (1998: 247).
6. See also Lutz and Abu-Lughod (1990: 3–10) and Frijda (1998: 11–17).
7. A useful introduction is also (Deploige 2005: 3–24).
8. I put this quotation in its context in Haemers (2005: 63–81).
9. For what follows, see also Nagy and Boquet (2008: 15–51); Roodenburg and Santing (2014: 7–19); Hoegaerts and Van Osselaer (2014: 452–65).
10. See also the conclusion of Elias (1939: 434–54) and Schwerhoff (1998: 561–605).

11. See also Althoff (2002a: 1–17).
12. Rollo-Koster and Holstein refer to Davidson and Milligan (2004: 523).
13. Similar examples in Wood (2013).
14. "*Caccia via questo can, che ha ruinato Muran.*"
15. "*Viva el rey y la Comunidad!*"
16. For Italy, see Taddei (2012: 81–97) and Trexler (1984a: 872–91).
17. See Garrioch (2003: 5–25); Van Uytven (1998: 129–43). Sometimes the artisans used light to express their presence: Lecuppre-Desjardin (1999: 23–43).
18. Compare with White (1998: 140).
19. See also Trexler (1984b: 357–92); Stella (1993); Lantschner (2014: 3–46), about the revolt in which the rebelling Ciompi workers of Florence created a flag in 1381 with "Libertas" on it.
20. See also Salzberg and Rospocher (2012: 9–26).
21. See also Martines (2003); Throop and Hyams (2010).
22. About the execution: Boone (2007: 183–218).
23. These examples are studied in detail in several essays in Gilli and Guilhembet (2012).
24. See also Hecker (2014: 135–56).
25. Philip the Good pardoned the rebels because "*de voorschrevene faiten niet bi vorraden, nemaer in hitten van bloede gheschiet zyn bi ghemeenten*" ("those facts did not happen premeditated but by the heat of the blood of the community").

REFERENCES

Akbari, S. C. and K. Mallette, eds. (2013), *A Sea of Languages: Rethinking the Arabic Role in Medieval Literary History*, Toronto: University of Toronto Press.

Alberti, L. B. (1972), *On Painting and on Sculpture*, ed. and trans. C. Grayson, London: Phaidon.

Allen, V. (2005), "Waxing Red: Shame, the Body and the Soul," in L. Perfetti (ed.), *The Representation of Women's Emotions in Medieval and Early Modern Culture*, 191–210, Gainesville, FL: University Press of Florida.

Anger, J (1589), *Jane Anger Her Protection for Women*. London: Richard Jones and Thomas Orwin.

Althoff, G. (1996), "Empörung, Tränen, Zerknirschung: 'Emotionen' in der Öffentlichen Kommunikation des Mittelalters," *Frühmittelalterlichen Studien*, 16: 60–79.

Althoff, G. (2002a), "Die Kultur der Zeichen und Symbole," *Frühmittelalterliche Studien*, 36: 1–17.

Althoff, G. (2002b), "Ira Regis: Prolegomena to a History of Royal Anger," in B. Rosenwein (ed.), *Anger's Past: The Social Uses of an Emotion in the Middle Ages*, 59–74, Ithaca, NY: Cornell.

Altieri, M. A. ([c. 1500] 1995), *Li nuptiali di Marco Antonio Altieri*, ed. E. Narducci, Rome: Roma nel Rinascimento.

Andersson, C. (1985), "Polemical Prints in Reformation Nuremberg," in J. Chipps Smith (ed.), *New Perspectives on the Art of Renaissance Nuremberg: Five Essays*, 41–62, Austin: Archer M. Huntington Art Gallery, College of Fine Arts, University of Texas at Austin.

Anglo-Norman Dictionary, published electronically at http://www.anglo-norman.net/gate/ (accessed October 13, 2017).

Anon. (c. 1515), *Everyman*, London: Richard Pynson.

Arbeau, T. ([1596] 1972), *Orchésographie*, fac. ed., Geneva: Minkoff.

Arcangeli, A. (2000), *Davide o Salomè? Il dibattito europeo sulla danza nella prima età moderna*, Rome: Viella.

Archambeau, N. (2011), "Healing Options during the Plague: Survivor Stories from a Fourteenth-Century Canonization Inquest," *Bulletin of the History of Medicine*, 85 (4): 531–59.

Areford, D. (2010), *The Viewer and the Printed Image in Late Medieval Europe*, Farnham: Ashgate.

Areford, D. S. (2014), *The Art of Empathy: The Cummer Mother of Sorrows in Northern Renaissance Art and Devotion*, London: Parebo.

Aristotle (1942), *Generation of Animals*, trans. A. L. Peck, Cambridge, MA: Harvard University Press.

Aristotle (1957), *On the Soul*, trans. W. S. Hett, Cambridge, MA: Harvard University Press.

Arnade, P. (1994), "Crowds, Banners and the Market Place: Symbols of Defiance and Defeat During the Ghent War of 1452–1453," *Journal of Medieval and Renaissance Studies*, 24: 471–97.

Arnade, P. (2008), *Beggars, Iconoclasts, and Civic Patriots: The Political Culture of the Dutch Revolt*, Ithaca, NY: Cornell.

Baatsen, I., J. de Groot, and I. Sturtewagen, (2015), "Single Life in Fifteenth-Century Bruges: Living Arrangements and Material Culture at the Fringes of Society," in I. Devos, J. de Groot, and A. Schmidt (eds), *Single Life and the City 1200–1900*, 179–202, Basingstoke: Palgrave.

Bähr, A. (2013), *Furcht und Furchtlosigkeit: Göttliche Gewalt und Selbstkonstitution im 17. Jahrhundert*, Göttingen: V&R unipress GmbH.

Baines, A. (2009), "Fifteenth-Century Instruments in Tinctoris's *De inventione et Usu Musicae*," in T. J. McGee (ed.), *Instruments and Their Music in the Middle Ages*, 53–60, Farnham: Ashgate, 2009. Originally published in *Galpin Society Journal*, 3 (1950): 19–26.

Baker, D. L. (1996), *The Subject of Desire: Petrarchan Poetics and the Female Voice in Louis Labé*, West Lafayette, IN: Purdue University Press.

Baker, D. L. (2006), *Louise Labé: The Complete Poetry and Prose*, ed. with critical editions and prose translations by D. L. Baker and poetry translations by A. Finch, Chicago: University of Chicago Press.

Bakhtin, M. (1984), *Rabelais and His World*, trans. H. Iswolsky, Bloomington, IN: University of Indiana Press.

Bale, A. (2010), *Feeling Persecuted: Christians, Jews and Images of Violence in the Middle Ages*, London: Reaktion Books.

Bale, A., trans. (2015), The Book of Margery Kempe, Oxford: Oxford University Press.

Bandlein, B., S. G. Eriksen, and S. Rikhardsdottir, eds. (2015), *Arthur of the North: Histories, Emotions and Imagination*, special issue of *Scandinavian Studies*, 87 (1).

Barasch, M. (1976), *Gestures of Despair in Medieval and Early Renaissance Art*, New York: New York University Press.

Barasch, M. (1991), *Imago Hominis. Studies in the Language of Art*, Vienna: IRSA.

Barasch, M. (1995), "The Weeping Man of Sorrow," in M. Knapas and M. Ringbom (eds.), *Icon to Cartoon: A Tribute to Sixten Ringbom*, 33–40, Helsinki: Society for Art History in Finland.

Barbu, D. (2015), "'Idolatry' and Religious Diversity: Thinking about the Other in Early Modern Europe," *Asdiwal*, 9: 39–50.

Barclay, K. (2017a), "Space and Place," in S. Broomhall (ed.), *Early Modern Emotions: An Introduction*, 20–3, Abingdon: Routledge.

Barclay, K. (2017b), "Family and Household," in S. Broomhall (ed.), *Early Modern Emotions: An Introduction*, 244–7, Abingdon: Routledge.

Barclay, K. and K. Reynolds (2016), "Introduction: Small Graves: Histories of Childhood, Death and Emotion," in K. Barclay, K. Reynolds, and C. Rawnsley (eds), *Death, Emotion and Childhood in Premodern Europe*, 1–24, London: Routledge.

Bardsley, S. (2006), *Venomous Tongues: Speech and Gender in Late Medieval England*, Philadelphia: University of Pennsylvania Press.

Barolini, T. (2014), *Dante's Lyric Poetry: Poems of Youth and of the "Vita Nuova,"* ed. and with gen. intro. and introductory essays to the lyrics by T. Barolini, with new verse translations by R. Lansing; commentary trans. by A. Frisardi, Toronto: University of Toronto Press.

Barolini, T. (2015), "A Philosophy of Consolation: The Place of the Other in Life's Transactions ('se Dio m'avesse dato fratello o non me lo avesse dato')," in F. Ciabattoni, E. Filosa, and K. Olson (eds.), *Boccaccio 1313–2013*, 89–105, Ravenna: Longo Editore.

Barolsky, P. (1978), *Infinite Jest: Wit and Humour in Italian Renaissance Art*, Columbia, MO: University of Missouri Press.

Barolsky, P. (1991), *Why Mona Lisa Smiles and Other Tales by Vasari*, University Park, PA: Pennsylvania State University Press.

Bauman, J. S. and T. F. Bauman (2002), "Chronos, Kairos, Aion: Failures of Decorum, Right-Timing, and Revenge in Hamlet," in P. Sipiora and J. S. Baumlin (eds.), *Rhetoric and Kairos: Essays in History, Theory, and Practice*, 165–86, Albany, NY: SUNY Press.

Baxandall, M. (1971), *Giotto and the Orators*, Oxford: Clarendon.

Baxandall, M. (1972), *Painting and Experience in Fifteenth Century Italy*, Oxford: Clarendon Press.

Beattie, C. (2007), *Medieval Single Women: The Politics of Social Classification in Late Medieval England*, Oxford: Oxford University Press.

Behringer, W., H. Lehman, and C. Pfister, eds. (2005), *Kulturelle Konsequenzen der kleinen Eiszeit*, Göttingen, Vandenhoeck & Ruprecht Verlag.

Behrmann, C., ed. (2016), *Images of Shame. Infamy, Defamation and the Ethics of Oeconomia*, Berlin: Walter De Gruyter.

Benay, E. E. and L. M. Rafinelli (2015), *Faith, Gender and the Senses in Italian Renaissance and Baroque Art: Interpreting the Noli me tangere and Doubting Thomas*, London: Routledge.

Bent, M. (2004), "The Musical Stanzas in Martin Le Franc's *Le Champion des Dames*," in J. Haines and R. Rosenfeld (eds.), *Music and Medieval Manuscripts, Paleography and Performance: Essays Dedicated to Andrew Hughes*, 91–127, Aldershot: Ashgate.

Bent, M. (2010), "Grammar and Rhetoric in Late Medieval Polyphony: Modern Metaphor or Old Simile?," in M. Carruthers (ed.), *Rhetoric Beyond Words: Delight and Persuasion in the Arts of the Middle Ages*, 52–71, Cambridge: Cambridge University Press.

Berger, C. (2003), "Machaut's Balade *Ploures Dames* (B32) in the Light of Real Modality," in E. E. Leach (ed.), *Machaut's Music: New Interpretations*, 193–204, Woodbridge: Boydell.

Berger, K. (2006), "Concepts and Developments in Music Theory," in J. Haar (ed.), *European Music 1520–1640*, 304–28, Woodbridge: Boydell Press.

Bertram, J. (2008), "The European Context: Collegiate Churches on the Continent," in C. Burgess and M. Heale (eds.), *The Late Medieval English College and Its Context*, 28–43, Woodbridge: York Medieval Press.

Bloom, H. ([1998] 1999), *Shakespeare: The Invention of the Human*, London: Fourth Estate.

Boccadoro, B. (2013), "The Psychotropic Power of Music during the Renaissance," trans. K. G. Jafflin, in T. Cochrane, B. Fantini, and K. R. Scherer (eds.), *The Emotional Power of Music: Multidisciplinary Perspectives on Musical Arousal, Expression, and Social Control*, Oxford: Oxford University Press.

Boone, G. M. (1997), "Tonal Color in Dufay," in J. A. Owens and A. M. Cummings (eds.), *Music in Renaissance Cities and Courts: Essays in Honor of Lewis Lockwood*, 57–99, Warren, MI: Harmonie Park.

Boone, M. (2002), "Urban Space and Political Conflict in Late Medieval Flanders," *The Journal of Interdisciplinary History*, 32: 621–40.

Boone, M. (2007), "La Justice Politique dans les Grandes Villes Flamandes. Etude d'un Cas: la Crise de l'Etat Bourguignon et la Guerre Contre Maximilien d'Autriche (1477–1492)," in Y.-M. Bercé (ed.), *Les Procès Politiques (XIVe–XVIIe siècles)*, 183–218, Rome: Ecole française de Rome.

Boquet, D. and P. Nagy (2015), *Sensible Moyen Age: Une Histoire des Emotions dans l'Occident Médiéval*, Paris: Editions du Seuil.

Bordier, J. (1998), *Le Jeu de la Passion: Le message chrétien et le théatre français*, Paris: Champion.

Bourdieu, P. (1990), *The Logic of Practice*, trans. R. Nice, Stanford, CA: Stanford University Press.

Bourke, J. (2005), *Fear: A Cultural History*, London: Shoemaker Hoard.

Bouwsma, W. J. (1982), "Calvin and the Renaissance Crisis *of Knowing*," *Calvin Theological Journal*, 17 (2): 190–211.

Brach, P. de (1576), *Les Poemes de Pierre de Brach*, Bordeaux: Simon Millanges.

Braden, G. (1999), *Petrarchan Love and the Continental Renaissance*, New Haven, CT: Yale University Press.

Braden, G. (2004), "Wyatt and Petrarch: Italian Fashion at the Court of Henry VIII," in D. S. Cervigni (ed.), *Petrarch and the European Lyric Tradition*, 237–63, special issue of *Annali d'italianistica*, 22.

Brainard, I. (1990), "Pattern, Imagery and Drama in the Choreographic Work of Domenico da Piacenza," in M. Padovan (ed.), *Guglielmo Ebreo da Pesaro e la danza nelle corti italiane del xv secolo*, 85–96, Pisa: Pacini.

Brandsma, F. (2015), "Where are the Emotions in Scandinavian Arthuriana? Or: How Cool Is King Arthur *of the North?*," in B. Bandlein, S. G. Eriksen, and S. Rikhardsdottir (eds.), *Arthur of the North: Histories, Emotions and Imagination*, special issue of *Scandinavian Studies*, 87 (1): 95–106.

Brandsma, F., C. Larrington and C. Saunders, eds. (2015), *Emotions in Arthurian Literature: Body, Mind, Voice*, Woodbridge: D. S. Brewer.

Braunstein, P. (1987), "Towards Intimacy: The Fourteenth and Fifteenth Centuries," in G. Duby (ed.), *A History of Private Life: Revelations of the Medieval* World, 535–630, Cambridge, MA: Harvard University Press.

Brooks, L. M. (1991), "Cosmic Imagery in the Religious Dances of Seville's Golden Age," in *Proceedings of 14th Annual Conference of Society of Dance History Scholars, February 1991*, 82–4, Riverside: SDHS.

Broomhall, S. (2005), *Women and Religion in Sixteenth-Century France*, Basingstoke: Palgrave.

Broomhall, S. (2013), "Reasons and Identities to Remember: Composing Personal Accounts of Religious Violence in Sixteenth-Century France," *French History*, 27: 1–20.

Broomhall, S. (2018, forthcoming), "Cross-Channel Conflict: The Challenges of Growing Up in Minority Huguenot Communities across the Channel," in L. Underwood (ed.), *Childhood, Youth and Religious Minorities*, Basingstoke: Palgrave.

Brown, D. C. (1987), *Pastor and Laity in the Theology of Jean Gerson*, Cambridge: Cambridge University Press.

Brown, H. M. and K. Polk (2001), "Instrumental Music, c. 1300–c. 1520," in R. Strohm and B. J. Blackburn (eds.), *Music as Concept and Practice in the Late Middle Ages*, vol. 3 of *The New Oxford History of Music*, 97–161, Oxford: Oxford University Press.

Brown, P. F. (2004), *Private Lives in Renaissance Venice*, New Haven, CT: Yale University Press.

Bruster, D. and E. Rasmussen (2009), *Everyman and Mankind*, London: Bloomsbury.

Bryant, G. (1984), "The French Heretic Beguine: Marguerite Porete," in K. Wilson (ed.), *Medieval Women Writers*, 20–46, Athens, GA: University of Georgia Press.

Burckhardt, J. ([1860] 1960), *Die Kultur der Renaissance in Italien: Ein Versuch*, Stuttgart: Philipp Reclam.

Burger, G. (2017a), "'Pitee renneth soone in gentil herte': Ugly Feelings and Gendered Conduct in Chaucer's *Legend of Good Women*," *Chaucer Review*, 52: 66–84.

Burger, G. (2017b), *Conduct Becoming: Good Wives and Husbands in the Later Middle Ages*, Philadelphia: University of Pennsylvania Press.

Burke, P. (2005), "Is there a Cultural History of Emotions?," in P. Gouk and H. Hills (eds.), *Representing Emotions: New Connections in the Histories of Art, Music and Medicine*, 35–47, Farnham: Ashgate.

Bynum, C. W. (1987), *Holy Feast and Holy Fast: The Religious Significance of Food for Medieval Women*, Berkeley, CA: University of California Press.

Cambers, A. (2011), *Godly Reading: Print, Manuscript and Puritanism in England, 1580–1720*, Cambridge: Cambridge University Press.

Camille, M. (1998), *The Medieval Art of Love*, New York: Abrams.

Camille, M. (2000), "Before the Gaze: The Internal Senses and Late Medieval Practices of Seeing," in R. Nelson (ed.), *Visuality Before and Beyond the Renaissance*, 197–223, Cambridge: Cambridge University Press.

Campanini, G., ed. (2001), *Il Compianto di Niccolò dell'Arca a Santa Maria della Vita*, Bologna: Editrice Compositori.

Campbell, L. (2014), *The Sixteenth Century Netherlandish Paintings with French Paintings before 1600*, London: National Gallery.

Cano, D. S. (2005), "Dances for the Royal Festivities in Madrid in the Sixteenth and Seventeenth Centuries," *Dance Research*, 23 (2): 123–52.

Carli, E. (1957), *Sassetta e il Maestro dell'Osservanza*, Milan: Aldo Martello.

Carlino, A. (1999), *Books of the Body: Anatomical Ritual and Renaissance Learning*, trans. J. and A. C. Tedeschi, Chicago: University of Chicago Press.

Carlson, M. (2016), *Shattering Hamlet's Mirror: Theatre and Reality*, Ann Arbor, MI: University of Michigan Press.

Caroll, S. (2000), "The Revolt of Paris, 1588: Aristocratic Insurgency and the Mobilization of Popular Support," *French Historical Studies*, 23: 301–37.

Caroso, F. ([1600] 1980), *Nobiltà di Dame*, fac. ed., Bologna: Forni.

Carpi, O. (2008), "Elites Citadines et Sédition en France à l'Epoque des Troubles de Religion," in P. Depreux (ed.), *Révolte et Statut Social de l'Antiquité Tardive aux Temps Modernes*, 255–71, Munich: Oldenbourg.

Carrera, E. (2007), "The Emotions in Sixteenth-century Spanish Spirituality," *The Journal of Religious History*, 31: 235–52.

Carrera, E. (2013), "Anger and the Mind–Body Connection in Medieval and Early Modern Medicine," in E. Carrera (ed.), *Emotions and Health, 1200–1700*, 94–146, Leiden: Brill.

Carsaniga, G. (2004), translation of MS from Florence, Biblioteca Nazionale Magliabechiano VII 1121, fols. 63r–69v, in J. Nevile, *The Eloquent Body: Dance and Humanist Culture in Fifteenth-Century Italy*, 141–57, Bloomington, IN: Indiana University Press.

Castiglioni, A. (1943), "The Attack of Franciscus Puteus on Andreas Vesalius and the defence by Gabriel Cuneus," *Yale Journal of Biological Medicine*, 16 (2): 135–48.

Castonguay, A., J.-F. Kosta-Théfaine, and M. Legault, eds. (2007), *Amour, Passion, Volupté, Tragédie: Le Sentiment Amoureux Dans La Littérature Française Du Moyen Âge Au Xxe Siècle*, Paris: Séguier.

Catherine of Siena (1980), *Catherine of Siena: The Dialogue*, trans. Suzanne Noffke, New York: Paulist Press.

Cavallo, S. (2006), "Health, Beauty and Hygiene," in M. Ajmar-Wollheim and F. Dennis (eds.), *At Home in Renaissance Italy*, 174–187, London: V&A Publications.

Cerquiglini-Toulet, J. (1997), *The Color of Melancholy: The Uses of Books in the Fourteenth Century*, trans. L. G. Cochrane, Baltimore, MD: Johns Hopkins University Press.

Certaldo, P. da (1945), *Il Libro di Buoni Costumi*, ed. A. Schiaffini, Florence: Vonnier.

Challet, V. (2014), "'Mueyron, Mueyron los traidors': Histoire d'un Cri Judiciaire," in F. Chauvaud and P. Prétou (eds.), *Clameur Publique et Émotions Judiciaires: de l'Antiquité à nos Jours*, 221–34, Rennes: PUR.

Challet, V. and I. Forrest (2015), "The Masses," in C. Fletcher, J. P. Genet, and J. Watts (eds.), *Government and Political Life in England and France c. 1300–c. 1500*, 279–315, Cambridge: Cambridge University Press.

Challet, V. and J. Haemers (2016), "La Révolte Médiévale en Image," in *Images & Révoltes dans le Livre et L'estampe (XIVe–milieu du XVIIIe siècle)*, 53–77, Paris: Bibliothèque Mazarine & Editions des Cendres.

Chastellain, G. (1863), "Chronique," in T. Kervyn de Lettenhove (ed.), *Œuvres de Georges Chastellain*, vol. IV, Brussels: Heussner.

Chater, J. (1999), "'Such Sweet Sorrow': The *dialogo di partenza* in the Italian Madrigal," *Early Music*, 27 (4): 577–99.

Chaucer, G. (1988), *The Riverside Chaucer*, ed. L. D. Benson, New York: Oxford University Press.

Chavasse, R. (2008), "Humanist Educational and Emotional Expectations of Teenagers in Late Fifteenth-Century Italy," in S. Broomhall (ed.), *Emotions in the Household, 1200–1900*, 69–84, Basingstoke: Palgrave Macmillan.

Chevalier, B. (1982), *Les Bonnes Villes de France du XIVe au XVIe Siècle*, Paris: Editions Aubier.

Chew, H. M. and W. Kellaway, eds. (1973), *London Assize of Nuisance 1301–1431: A Calendar*, London Record Society Publication, vol. 10. London Record Society.

Christian, William A. (1981), *Apparitions in Late Medieval Spain*, Princeton, NJ: Princeton University Press.

Christianson, J. R. (2000), *On Tycho's Island: Tycho Brahe and His Assistants, 1570–1601*, Cambridge: Cambridge University Press.

Cicero (1968), *De Oratore: Book III*, trans. H. Rackham, Cambridge, MA: Harvard University Press.

Clarke, E. and K. Dewhurst (1972), *An Illustrated History of Brain Function*, Oxford: Sandford.

Clayton, M. (2002), *Leonardo da Vinci: The Divine and the Grotesque*, London: Royal Collection.

Cockcroft, R. (2003), *Rhetorical Affect in Early Modern Writing: Renaissance Passions Reconsidered*, London: Palgrave Macmillan.

Coëffeteau, N. (1620), *Tableau des passions humaines, de leurs causes et de leurs effects*, Paris: S. Cramoisy.

Cohen, E. (2010), *The Modulated Scream: Pain in Late Medieval Culture*, Chicago: University of Chicago Press.

Cohen Hanegbi, N. (2009), "The Matter of Emotions: Priests and Physicians on the Movements of the Soul," *Poetica*, 72: 21–42.

Cohen Hanegbi, N. (2012), "Pain as Emotion: The Role of Emotional Pain in Fifteenth-Century Italian Medicine and Confession," in E. Cohen, L. Toker, M. Consomi, and O. E. Dror (eds.), *Knowledge and Pain*, 63–82, Amsterdam: Rodopi.

Cohen Hanegbi, N. (2016), "A Moving Soul: Emotions in Late Medieval Medicine," *OSIRIS*, 31: 46–66.

Cohen Hanegbi, N. (2017), *Caring for the Living Soul: Emotions, Medicine and Penance in the Late Medieval Mediterranean*, Leiden: Brill.

Cohn Jr, S. K. (2007), "The Black Death and the Burning of Jews," *Past & Present*, 196 (1): 3–36.
Cohn Jr, S. K. (2010), *Cultures of Plague: Medical Thinking at the End of the Renaissance*, Oxford: Oxford University Press.
Cohn, S. (2006), *Lust for Liberty: The Politics of Social Revolt in Medieval Europe, 1200–1425*, Cambridge: Cambridge University Press.
Cohn, S. (2013), *Popular Protest in Late Medieval English Towns*, Cambridge: Cambridge University Press.
Colombetti, G. (2014), *The Feeling Body: Affective Science Meets the Enactive Mind*, Cambridge, MA: MIT Press.
Conley, J. (1969), "The Doctrine of Friendship in Everyman," *Speculum*, 44 (3): 374–82.
Contamine, P. (1987), "Peasant Hearth to Papal Palace: The Fourteenth and Fifteenth Centuries," in G. Duby (ed.), *A History of Private Life: Revelations of the Medieval World*, 425–505, Cambridge, MA: Harvard University Press.
Cook, A. (2010), *Shakespearean Neuroplay: Reinvigorating the Study of Dramatic Texts and Performance through Cognitive Science*, London: Palgrave Macmillan.
Cooper, H. (2004), *The English Romance in Time: Transforming Motifs from Geoffrey of Monmouth to the Death of Shakespeare*, Oxford: Oxford University Press.
Cooper, N. (1999), *Houses of the Gentry 1480–1680*, New Haven, CT: Yale University Press.
Cooter, R. (2014), "Neural Veils and the Will to Historical Critique: Why Historians of Science Need to Take the Neuro-Turn Seriously," *Isis*, 105 (1): 145–54.
Copeland, R. (2001), *Pedagogy, Intellectuals, and Dissent in the Late Middle Ages: Lollardy and Ideas of Learning*, Cambridge: Cambridge University Press.
Copeland, R. (2014), "Pathos and Pastoralism: Aristotle's *Rhetoric* in Medieval England," *Speculum*, 89: 96–127.
Cornazano, A. (n.d.), *Libro dell'arte del danzare*, Rome: Biblioteca Apostolica Vaticana, Codex Capponiano, 203.
Cox-Rearick, J. (1974), "Fra Bartolomeo's St Mark Evangelist and St Sebastian with an Angel," *Mitteilungen des Kunsthistorishen Institutes in Florenz*, 18 (3): 329–54.
Crane, S. (2002), *The Performance of Self: Ritual, Clothing and Identity During the Hundred Years' War*, Philadelphia: University of Pennsylvania Press.
Crisciani, C. (2004) "Éthique des *consilia* et de la consultation: à propos de la cohésion morale de la profession médicale (XIIIe–XIVe siècles)," trans. M. Nicoud, *Médiévales*, 46 (2004): 23–44. Available online: https://medievales.revues.org/989?lang=en#bodyftn67 (accessed September 7, 2017)
Crocker, H. (2007), "Affective Politics in Chaucer's *Reeve's Tale*: 'Cherl' Masculinity After 1381," *Studies in the Age of Chaucer*, 29: 225–58.
Crombie, L. (2011), "Honour, Community and Hierarchy in the Feasts of the Archery and Crossbow Guilds of Bruges, 1445–81," *Journal of Medieval History*, 37 (2011): 102–13.
Crouzet-Pavan, E. (2001), *Enfers et Paradis: L'Italie de Dante et de Giotto*, Paris: Albin Michel.
Cunningham, A. (1997), *The Anatomical Renaissance: The Resurrection of the Anatomical Projects of the Ancients*, London: Routledge.
Curth, L. H. (2016), "Working Animals," in S. Broomhall (ed.), *Early Modern Emotions: An Introduction*, 337–40, London: Routledge.
Curtis, L. (2001), "Christine de Pizan and "Dueil Angoisseux," in T. M. Borgerding (ed.), *Gender, Sexuality, and Early Music*, 265–82, New York: Routledge.
Dante, A. (2002), *Inferno*, trans. Robert and Jean Hollander, New York: Doubleday.
Dante, A. (2002), *Paradiso*, trans. Robert and Jean Hollander, New York: Doubleday.

Daston, L. and E. Lunbeck, eds. (2011), *Histories of Scientific Observation*, Chicago: University of Chicago Press.

Daston, L. and K. Park (2001), *Wonders and the Order of Nature, 1150–1750*, Cambridge, MA: MIT Press.

Davidson, Clifford. (2017). *Studies in Late Medieval Wall Paintings, Manuscript Illuminations, and Texts*. Houndsmill: Palgrave.

Davidson, J. and C. Milligan (2004), "Embodying Emotion, Sensing Space: Introducing Emotional Geographies," *Social and Cultural Geography*, 5: 523–32.

Davies, R. T., ed. (1964), *Medieval English Lyrics: A Critical Anthology*, Evanston, IL: Northeastern University Press.

Dawkins, J. (1969), "Provincial Entertainment in the Renaissance: 'Le Triomphe de Diane' by Pierre de Brach," *Nottingham French Studies*, 8 (1): 3–15.

Daye, A. (2014), "The Role of *Le Balet Comique* in Forging the Stuart Masque: Part 1 the Jacobean Initiative," *Dance Research*, 32 (2): 135–207.

De Belges, J. L. (1882), "Illustrations de Gaule et Singularitez de Troyes," in J. Stecher (ed.), *Œuvres de Jean Lemaire de Belges*, 1–362, vol. 2, Leuven: Lefever.

De Bourdeille, P., Seigneur de Brantôme (1947), *Les Dames Galantes*, ed. M. Rat, Paris: Éditions Garnier Frères.

Dean, J. M., ed. (1996), *Medieval English Political Writings*, Kalamazoo: Medieval Institute Publications. Available online: http://d.lib.rochester.edu/teams/text/dean-medieval-english-political-writings-simonie (accessed September 7, 2017)

Deane, J. K. (2016), "Elastic Institutions: Beguine Communities in Early Modern Germany," in A. Weber (ed.), *Devout Laywomen in the Early Modern World*, 175–95, Abingdon: Routledge.

Delaurenti, B. (2016), *La contagion des emotions: Compassio, une énigme medieval*, Paris: Garnier.

Della Porta, G. (1586), *De humana physiognomonia libri IIII*, Vico Equense: Joseph Cacchius.

Delumeau, J. (1978), *La peur en Occident, XIVe–XVIIIe siècles*, Paris: Fayard.

Delumeau, J. (1990), *Sin and Fear: The Emergence of a Western Guilt Culture, 13th–18th. Centuries*, trans. E. Nicholson, New York: St. Martin's Press.

Deploige, J. (2005), "Studying Emotions. The Medievalist as Human Scientist?," in E. Lecuppre-Desjardin and A.-L. Van Bruaene (eds.), *Emotions in the Heart of the City (14th–16th Century)*, 3–24, Turnhout: Brepols.

Deploige, J. (2010), "Meurtre Politique, Guerre Civile et Catharsis Littéraire au XIIe siècle : Les Emotions dans l'Œuvre de Guibert de Nogent et de Galbert de Bruges," in D. Boquet and P. Nagy (eds.), *Politiques des Emotions au Moyen Âge*, Florence: Sismel.

Despars, N. (1840), *Cronijcke van den Lande Ende den Graefscepe van Vlaenderen*, ed. J. de Jonghe, vol. IV, Bruges: Noordzandstraet.

Dolan, L. (2016), *Nurture and Neglect: Childhood in Sixteenth-Century Northern England*, Abingdon: Routledge

Dolce, L. (2000), "Dialogo della Pittura (1557)," in M. Roskill (ed.), *Dolce's "Aretino" and Venetian Art Theory of the Cinquecento*, 84–218, Toronto: University of Toronto Press.

Domenico da Piacenza (n.d.), *De arte saltandj & choreas ducendj De la arte di ballare et danzare*, Paris: Bibliothèque Nationale, MS fonds it. 972.

Doniger, W. (1990), "Why the Body Is Disgusting," *New York Times*, September 23. Available online: http://www.nytimes.com/1990/09/23/books/why-the-body-is-disgusting.html?pagewanted=all&mcubz=0 (accessed June 12, 2017).

Donne, J. (2014), *The Complete Poems of John Donne*, ed. R. Robbins, London: Routledge.

Downes, S. (2015). "'Je Hé Guerre, Point Ne La Doy Prisier': Peace and the Emotions of War in the Prison Poetry of Charles d'Orléans," in S. Downes, A. Lynch, and K. O. Loughlin (eds.), *Emotion and War: Medieval to Romantic Literature*, 60–76, London: Palgrave Macmillan.

Downes, S., A. Lynch, and K. O'Loughlin, eds. (2015), *Emotion and War: Medieval to Romantic Literature*, London: Palgrave Macmillan.

Downey, C. T. (2010), "The Noble Participants in the Ballet of *la Délivrance de Renaud*," in G. Garden (ed.), *La Délivrance de Renaud: Ballet dansé par Louis XIII en 1617, Ballet Danced by Louis XIII in 1617*, 7–13, Turnhout: Brepols.

Dreier, R. P. (2010), *Der Totentanz – ein Motiv der kirchlichen Kunst als Projektionsfläche für profane Botschaften (1425–1650)*, Leiden: Printpartners Ipskamp.

Du Clercq, J. (1823), *Mémoires sur le Règne de Philippe le Bon, duc de Bourgogne*, ed. F. de Reiffenberg, vol. I, Brussels: Lacrosse.

Dubrow, H. (2008), *The Challenges of Orpheus: Lyric Poetry and Early Modern England*, Baltimore, MD: Johns Hopkins University Press.

Duby, G. (1987), "Private Power: Public Power," in G. Duby (ed.), *A History of Private Life: Revelations of the Medieval World*, 3–31, Cambridge, MA: Harvard University Press.

Duffy, E. (1992), The *Stripping of the Altars: Traditional Religion in England, 1400–1580*, New Haven, CT: Yale University Press.

Duffy, E. (2005), *The Stripping of the Altars: Traditional Religion in England, 1400–1580*, 2nd edition, New Haven, CT: Yale University Press.

Dumolyn, J. and J. Haemers, J. (2012), "A Bad Chicken was Brooding: Subversive Speech in Late Medieval Flanders," *Past and Present*, 214: 45–86.

Dunbar, W. (2004), *The Complete Works*, ed. J. Conlee, Kalamazoo, MI: Medieval Institute Publications.

Durand, É. (1617), *Discours au vray*, trans. C. T. Downey and G. Garden, in G. Garden (ed.) (2010), *La Délivrance de Renaud: Ballet dansé par Louis XIII en 1617, Ballet Danced by Louis XIII in 1617*, 244–65, Turnhout: Brepols.

Durham, L. L. (2012), "Medieval Performance Studies and Cognitive Neurosciences: Blending New Approaches," *Research Opportunities in Medieval and Renaissance Drama*, 51: 33–42.

Edgerton, S. (1985), *Pictures and Punishment: Art and Criminal Prosecution during the Florentine Renaissance*, Ithaca, NY: Cornell University Press.

Edwards, W. (2012), "Text Treatment in Motets around 1500: The Humanistic Fallacy," in T. Schmidt-Beste (ed.), *The Motet around 1500: On the Relationship of Imitation and Text Treatment?*, 113–38, Turnhout: Brepols.

Eire, C. M. N. (1986), *War Against the Idols: The Reformation of Worship from Erasmus to Calvin*, Cambridge: Cambridge University Press.

Ekman, P. (2003), *Emotions Revealed*, New York: Henry Holt.

Elias, N. (1939), *Über den Prozess der Zivilisation: Soziogenetische und Psychogenetische Untersuchungen*, vol. II, Basel: Haus zum Falken.

Eliot, T. S. (1920), "Hamlet and His Problems," in *The Sacred Wood*, 87–94, London: Methuen.

Emirbayer, M. and Goldberg, C. (2005), "Pragmatism, Bourdieu, and Collective Emotions in Contentious Politics," *Theory and Society*, 34: 469–518.

Enders, J., trans. (2011), *The Farce of the Fart and Other Ribaldries*, Philadelphia: University of Pennsylvania Press.

Enterline, L. (2012), *Shakespeare's Schoolroom: Rhetoric, Discipline, Emotion*, Philadelphia: University of Pennsylvania Press.

Erickson, R. A. (1997), *The Language of the Heart, 1600–1750*, Philadelphia: University of Pennsylvania Press.

Erikson, E. (1958), *Young Man Luther: A Study in Psychoanalysis and History*, New York: W. W. Norton & Co.

Essary, K. (2016), "Fiery Heart and Fiery Tongue: Emotion in Erasmus' *Ecclesiastes*," *Erasmus Studies*, 36, 5–34.

Essary, K. (2017), *Erasmus and Calvin on the Foolishness of God: Reason and Emotion in the Christian Philosophy*, Toronto: University of Toronto Press.

Evans, M. (1971), "Laster," in E. Kirschbaum, G. Bandmann, W. Braunfels, J. Kollwitz, W. Mrazek, A. A. Schmid, and H. Schnell (eds.), *Lexikon der Christlichen Ikonographie*, vol. 3, 15–27, Rome: Herder.

Evans, M. B. (1943), *The Passion Play of Lucerne, an Historical and Critical Introduction*, Oxford: Oxford University Press.

Falkenburg, R. L. (1995), "The Decorum of Grief: Notes on the Representation of Mary at the Cross in Late Medieval Netherlandish Literature and Painting," in M. Knapas and A. Ringbom (eds.), *Icon to Cartoon: A Tribute to Sixten Ringbom*, 65–89, Helsinki: Taidehistorian Seura.

Fallows, D. (1987), "The Contenance angloise: English Influence on Continental Composers of the Fifteenth Century," *Renaissance Studies*, 1 (2): 189–208.

Fein, Susanna Greer, ed. (1998), *Moral Love Songs and Laments*, Kalamazoo, MI: Medieval Institute Publications.

Ferrari, E. (2014), *Montaigne: Une Anthropologie des Passions*, Paris: Classiques Garnier.

Firnhaber-Baker, J. (2014), "A Son de Cloche : the Interpretation of Public Order and Legitimate Authority in Northern-France, 1355–1358," in J. Dumolyn, H. Oliva Herrer, V. Challet, and M. Antonia Carmona Ruiz (eds), *La Comunidad Medieval Como Esfera Publica*, 357–76, Sevilla: SUP.

Firnhaber-Baker, J. and D. Schoenaers, eds (2016), *The Routledge History Handbook of Medieval Revolt*, London: Routledge.

Fitzpatrick, T. (2011), *Playwright, Space and Place in Early Modern Performance: Shakespeare and Company*, Farnham: Ashgate.

Flannery, M. (2011), "A Bloody Shame: Chaucer's Honourable Women," *Review of English Studies*, 62: 337–57.

Flynn, M. (1995), "Blasphemy and the Play of Anger in Sixteenth-Century Spain," *Past and Present*, 149 (1): 29–56

Flynn, M. (1998), "Taming Anger's Daughters: New Treatments for Emotional Problems in Renaissance Spain," *Renaissance Quarterly*, 51 (3): 864–86.

Foister, S. (1981), "Paintings and Other Works of Art in Sixteenth-Century English Inventories," *Burlington Magazine*, 133 (938): 273–82.

Foxe, J. (1563), John Foxe's The Acts and Monuments Online. www.johnfoxe.org/.

Frazier, A. K. (2005), *Possible Lives: Authors and Saints in Renaissance Italy*, New York: Columbia University Press.

Freccero, J. (2009), "The Portrait of Francesca: Inferno V," *Modern Language Notes* 124 (5): Supplement, S7–36.

Freedberg, D. (1989), *The Power of Images*, Chicago: University of Chicago Press.

Freedberg, D. (2011), "Memory in Art: History and the Neuroscience of Response," in S. Nalbantian, P. M. Matthews, and J. L. McClelland (eds), *The Memory Process: Neuroscientific and Humanistic Perspectives*, 337–358, Cambridge, MA: MIT Press.

Freedman, R. (2003), "Le Jeune's "Dodecacorde" as a Site for Spiritual Meanings," *Revue de Musicologie*, 89 (2): 297–309.

French, K. (2016), "The Material Culture of Childbirth in Late Medieval London and Its Suburbs," *Journal of Women's History*, 28 (2): 126–48.

Frevert, U. (2011), *Emotions in History: Lost and Found*, Budapest: CEU Press.

Friedman, L. J. (1965), "Gradus Amoris," *Romance Philology*, 19, 167–77.

Frijda, N. (1998), "De Structuur van Emoties," in R. Stuip and C. Vellekoop (eds), *Emoties in de Middeleeuwen*, 11–17, Hilversum: Verloren.

Fris, V. (1901), *Dagboek van Gent van 1447 tot 1470, met een vervolg van 1477 tot 1515*, vol. I, Ghent: Annoot-Braeckman.

Fris, V. (1913), *Histoire de Gand*, Brussels: Van Oest.

Fuhrmann, W. (2011), "The Simplicity of Sublimity in Josquin's Psalm-Motets," in E. Jas and A. Clement (eds.), *Josquin and the Sublime: Proceedings of the International Josquin Symposium at Roosevelt Academy, Middelburg, July 12–15, 2009*, 49–71, Turnhout: Brepols.

Gagné, J. (2018), "Emotional Attachments: Prosthetic Iron Hands, their Makers, and their Wearers, 1450–1600," in S. Downes, S. Holloway, and S. Randles (eds), *Feeling Things: Objects and Emotions through History*, 133–153, Oxford: Oxford University Press.

Gammerl, B. (2012), "Emotional Styles: Concepts and Challenges in Researching Emotions," *Rethinking History*, 16: 161–75.

Garden, G. (2010a), "The *vers* and *livret* for *La Délivrance de Renaud* Compared and a *terminus ante quam* for the Publication of Durand's *Discours au vray*," in G. Garden (ed.), *La Délivrance de Renaud: Ballet dansé par Louis XIII en 1617, Ballet Danced by Louis XIII in 1617*, 15–25, Turnhout: Brepols.

Garden, G., ed. (2010b), *La Délivrance de Renaud: Ballet dansé par Louis XIII en 1617, Ballet Danced by Louis XIII in 1617*, Turnhout: Brepols.

Garrioch, D. (2003), "Sounds of the City: the Soundscape of Early modern European Towns," *Urban History*, 30: 5–25.

Gauvard, C. (1999), "Violence," in J. Le Goff and J.-C. Schmitt (eds.), *Dictionnaire Raisonné de l'Occident Médiéval*, 1208–10, Paris: Fayard.

Gawain (1967), *Sir Gawain and the Green Knight*, ed. J. R. R. Tolkien and E. V. Gordon, 2nd edition, rev. Norman Davis, Oxford: Clarendon Press.

Geremek, B. (1987), *The Margins of Society in Late Medieval Paris*, trans. J. Birrell, Cambridge: Cambridge University Press.

Gerson, J. (1998), *Early Works*, trans. B. P. McGuire, New York: Paulist Press.

Gesner, K. (1551), *Historiae animalium lib. I de quadrupedibus viuiparis*, Zurich: Christopher Froschoverum.

Gibson, A. (2001), "Malory's Reformulation of Shame," *Arthuriana*, 11 (4): 64–76.

Gilli, P. and J.-P. Guilhembet, eds. (2012), *Le Châtiment des Villes dans les Espaces Méditerranéens (Antiquité, Moyen Age, Epoque Moderne)*, Turnhout: Brepols.

Given-Wilson, C. (1987), *The English Nobility in the Late Middle Ages*, London: Routledge.

Godefroy, F. (1891), *Dictionnaire de L'ancienne Langue Française et de tous ses Dialectes du IXe jusqu'au XVe Siècle*, vol. III, Paris: Vieweg.

Goldberg, P. J. P. (1991), "The Public and the Private: Women in the Pre-Plague Economy," in P. R. Coss and S. D. Lloyd (eds.), *Thirteenth Century England III*, 75–81, Woodbridge: Boydell Press.

Goldberg, P. J. P. (1992), *Women, Work, and Life Cycle in a Medieval Economy: Women in York and Yorkshire c. 1300–1520*, Oxford: Oxford University Press.

Goldberg, P. J. P., ed. and trans. (1995), *Women in England c. 1275–1525: Documentary Sources*, Manchester: Manchester University Press.

Goldberg P. J. P. (1999), "Masters and Men in Later Medieval England," in D. M. Hadley (ed.), *Masculinity in Medieval Europe*, 56–70, London: Longman.

Goldberg, P. J. P. (2004), *Medieval England: A Social History 1250–1550*, London: Arnold.

Goldberg, P. J. P. (2006), "John Skathelok's Dick: Voyeurism and 'Pornography' in late Medieval England," in N. McDonald (ed.), *Medieval Obscenities*, 105–23, Woodbridge: York Medieval Press.

Goldberg, P. J. P. (2008a), "Childhood and Gender in Later Medieval England," *Viator*, 39 (1): 253–62.

Goldberg, P. J. P. (2008b), *Communal Discord, Child Abduction, and Rape in the Later Middle Ages*, New York: Palgrave Macmillan.

Goldberg, P. J. P. (2008c), "The Fashioning of Bourgeois Domesticity: A Material Culture Perspective," in M. Kowaleski and P. J. P. Goldberg (eds.), *Medieval Domesticity: Home, Housing and Household in Medieval England*, 124–44, Cambridge: Cambridge University Press.

Goldberg, P. J. P. (2011), "Space and Gender in the Later Medieval English House," *Viator*, 42 (2): 215.

Goldthwaite, R. A. ([1968] 2015), *Private Wealth in Renaissance Florence: A Study of Four Families*, Princeton, NJ: Princeton University Press.

Goldthwaite, R. A. (1995), *Wealth and the Demand for Art in Italy, 1300–1600*, Baltimore, MD: Johns Hopkins University Press.

Goldthwaite, R. A. (2009), *The Economy of Renaissance Florence*, Baltimore, MD: Johns Hopkins University Press.

Goodall, P. (1992), "Being Alone in Chaucer," *The Chaucer Review*, 27 (1): 1–15.

Goodland, K. (2005a), *Female Mourning and Tragedy in Medieval and Renaissance English Drama: From the Raising of Lazarus to King Lear*, Aldershot: Ashgate.

Goodland, K (2005b), "'Vs for to wepe no man may let': Accommodating Female Grief in the Medieval English Lazarus Plays," *Early Theatre*, 8 (1): 69–94.

Gordon, S. (2009), "Humour and Household Relationships: Servants in Late Medieval and Sixteenth-Century French Farce," in S. Broomhall (ed.), *Emotions in the Household, 1200–1900*, 85–102, New York: Palgrave.

Gower, J. (1902), *The Complete Works of John Gower*, Volume 5, Latin Works, ed. G. C. Macaulay, Oxford: Clarendon Press.

Gowland, A. (2006), "The Problem of Melancholy," *Past & Present*, 191 (1): 77–120.

Grace, P. (2015), *Affectionate Authorities: Fathers and Fatherly Roles in Late Medieval Basel*, Farnham: Ashgate.

Greene, R. L. (1977), *The Early English Carols*, Oxford: Clarendon Press.

Greengrass, M. (2007), *Governing Passions: Peace and Reform in the French Kingdom, 1576–1585*, Oxford: Oxford University Press.

Greengrass, M. (2014), *Christendom Destroyed: Europe 1517–1648*, Harmondsworth: Penguin.

Gregg, M. and G. J. Seigworth, eds. (2010), *The Affect Theory Reader*, Durham, NC: Duke University Press.

Grell, O. P. (1993), "Conflicting Duties: Plague and the Obligations of Early Modern Physicians towards Patients and Commonwealth in England and the Netherlands," in A. Wear, J. Greyer-Kordesch, and R. French (eds.), *Doctors and Ethics: The Earlier Historical Setting of Professional Ethics*, 131–52, Rodopi, Amsterdam.

Grenville, J. (2008), "Urban and Rural Houses and Households in the Late Middle Ages," in M. Kowaleski and P. J. P. Goldberg (eds.), *Medieval Domesticity: Home, Housing and Household in Medieval England*, 92–123, Cambridge: Cambridge University Press.

Guglielmo, Ebreo (1463), *Guilielmi Hebraei pisauriensis de practica seu arte tripudii vulgare opusculum, incipit*, Paris: Bibliothèque Nationale, MS fonds it. 973.

Guglielmo, Ebreo (n.d.), *Ghuglielmi ebrej pisauriensis de praticha seu arte tripudi vulghare opusculum, feliciter incipit*, New York: New York Public Library, Dance Collection, *MGZMB-Res. 72–254.

Gundersheimer, W. L. (1994), "Renaissance Concepts of Shame and Pocaterra's Dialoghi della Vergogna," *Renaissance Quarterly*, 47: 34–56.

Gur, Z. (2015), "Petrarch and the Ancients," in A. R. Ascoli and U. Falkeid (eds.), *The Cambridge Companion to Petrarch*, 141–53, Cambridge: Cambridge University Press.

Haar, J. (1983), "A Sixteenth-Century Attempt at Music Criticism," *The Journal of the American Musicological Society*, 36 (2): 191–209, reprinted in J. Haar, *The Science and Art of Renaissance Music*, ed. P. Corneilson, 3–19, Princeton, NJ: Princeton University Press, 1997.

Haemers, J. (2005), "A Moody Community? Emotion and Ritual in Late Medieval Urban Revolts," in E. Lecuppre-Desjardin and A.-L. Van Bruaene (eds.), *Emotions in the Heart of the City (14th–16th Century)*, 63–81, Turnhout: Brepols.

Haemers J. (2016), "Révolte et Requête: Les Gens de Métiers et les Conflits Sociaux dans les Villes de Flandre (XIIIe–XVe siècle)," *Revue Historique*, 677: 27–55.

Hamling, T. (2010), *Decorating the "Godly" Household: Religious Art in Post-Reformation Britain*, New Haven, CT: Yale University Press.

Hamling, T. (2017), "Household Objects," in S. Broomhall (ed.), *Early Modern Emotions: An Introduction*, 135–40, Abingdon: Routledge.

Hanawalt, B. A. (1986), *The Ties that Bound: Peasant Families in Medieval England*, New York: Oxford University Press.

Hanawalt, B. (2002), "Medievalists and the Study of Childhood," *Speculum*, 77: 440–60.

Hanawalt, B. (2011), "Portraits of Outlaws, Felons, and Rebels in Late Medieval England," in A. Kaufman (ed.), *British Outlaws of Literature and History: Essays on Medieval and Early Modern Figures from Robin Hood to Twm Shon Catty*, 45–64, Jefferson, NC: McFarland & Company.

Hankins, J. (2015), "Humanism and Music in Italy," in A. M. B. Berger and J. Rodin (eds.), *The Cambridge History of Fifteenth-Century Music*, 231–62, Cambridge: Cambridge University Press.

Hardison, O. B. and L. Golden, eds. (1995), *Horace for Students of Literature: The "Ars Poetica" and its Tradition*, Gainesville, FL: University of Florida Press.

Harrán, D. (1986), *Word–Tone Relations in Musical Thought: From Antiquity to the Seventeenth Century*, Neuhausen-Stuttgart, W. Germany: American Institute of Musicology: Hänssler-Verlag.

Harrán, D. (1997), "Toward a Rhetorical Code of Early Music Performance," *Journal of Musicology*, 15 (1): 19–42.

Harrington, J. F. (1995), *Reordering Marriage and Society in Reformation Germany*, Cambridge: Cambridge University Press.

Harrison, P. (2011), "Natural History," in P. Harrison, R. L. Numbers, and M. H. Shank (eds.), *Wrestling with Nature: From Omens to Science*, 117–48, Chicago: University of Chicago Press.

Harvey, K. (2017), "The Body," in S. Broomhall (ed.), *Early Modern Emotions: An Introduction*, 225–7, London: Routledge.

Haskell, Y. (2016), "Medicine and Science," in S. Broomhall (ed.), *Early Modern Emotions: An Introduction*, 257–60, London: Routledge.

Hatter, J. D. (2014), "*Musica*: Music about Music and Musicians, 1450–1530," PhD diss., McGill University.

Haug, S. and G. Messling, eds. (2014), *Fantastische Welten: Albrecht Altdorfer und das Expressive in der Kunst um 1500*, Munich: Hirmer; Frankfurt am Main: Städel Museum.

Hayum, A. (1989), *The Isenheim Altarpiece: God's Medicine and the Painter's Vision*, Princeton, NJ: Princeton University Press.

Hecker, H. (2014), "Emotionen und Politik: Gefühlsmenschen auf dem Thron," in C. Kann (ed.), *Emotionen in Mittelalter und Renaissance*, 135–56, Düsseldorf: DUP.

Henryson, R. (2010), *The Complete Works*, ed. David. J. Parkinson, Kalamazoo, MI: Medieval Institute Publications.

Herlihy, D. and C. Klapisch-Zuber (1985), *Tuscans and Their Families: A Study of the Catasto of 1427*, New Haven, CT: Yale University Press.

Higgins, P. (2007), "Lamenting 'Our Master and Good Father': Intertextuality and Creative Patrilineage in Musical Tributes by and for Johannes Ockeghem," in S. Gasch and B. Lodes (eds.), *Tod in Musik und Kultur: zum 500. Todestag Philipps des Schönen*, 277–314, Tutzing: Hans Schneider.

Hilton, R. (1989), "Révoltes Rurales et Révoltes Urbaines au Moyen Age," in *Révolte et Société*, vol. II, 25–33, Paris: Sociétés savantes.

Hobgood, A. A. (2014), *Passionate Playgoing in Early Modern England*, Cambridge: Cambridge University Press.

Hoecker, R. (1916), *Das Lehrgedicht des Karel van Mander: Text, Übersetzung und Kommentar*, The Hague: Marinus Nijhoff.

Hoegaerts, J. And T. van Osselaer (2014), "De Lichamelijkheid van Emoties," *Tijdschrift voor Geschiedenis*, 126: 452–65.

Hoffman R. C. (2014), *An Environmental History of Medieval Europe*, Cambridge: Cambridge University Press.

Hogan, P. (2002), *Cognitive Science, Literature, and the Arts: A Guide for Humanists*, New York: Routledge.

Holmes, O. (2000), *Assembling the Lyric Self: Authorship from Troubadour Song to Italian Poetry*, Minneapolis, MN: University of Minnesota Press.

Holmes, O. (2008), *Dante's Two Beloveds: Ethics and Erotics in the Divine Comedy*, New Haven, CT: Yale University Press.

Holsinger, B. (1997), "Pedagogy, Violence, and the Subject of Music: Chaucer's Prioress's Tale and the Ideologies of 'Song,'" *New Medieval Histories*, 1: 157–92.

Hotchkiss, V. R. (1999), *Clothes Make the Man: Female Cross Dressing in Medieval Europe*, London: Routledge.

Howes, L. L. (1997), *Chaucer's Gardens and the Language of Convention*, Gainesville, FL: University Press of Florida.

Hughes, M. K. and H. F. Diaz, eds. (1994), *The Medieval Warm Period*, Boston: Kluwer Academic.

Huizinga, J. (2001), *The Waning of the Middle Ages: A Study of the Forms of Life, Thought, and Art in France and the Netherlands in the Fourteenth and Fifteenth Centuries*, London: Penguin.

Hurley, E. (2010), *Theatre & Feeling*, London: Palgrave Macmillan.

Hurtado de Mendoza, A., J. M. Fernández-Dols, W. G. Parrott, and P. Carrera (2010), "Emotion Terms, Category Structure, and the Problem of Translation: The Case of Shame and Vergüenza," *Cognition and Emotion*, 24: 661–80.

Irish, B. J. (2009), "Vengeance, Variously: Revenge before Kyd in Early Elizabethan Drama," *Early Theatre*, 12 (2): 117–34

Irish, B. J. (2015), "Friendship and Frustration: Counter-Affect in the Letters of Philip Sidney and Hubert Languet," *Texas Studies in Literature and Language*, 57: 412–32.

Jaeger, S. C. (1999), *Ennobling Love: In Search of a Lost Sensibility*, Philadelphia: University of Pennsylvania Press.

Jardine, L. (1993), *Erasmus, Man of Letters: The Construction of Charisma in Print*, Princeton, NJ: Princeton University Press.

Jordan, W. C. (1996), *The Great Famine*, Princeton, NJ: Princeton University Press.

Jowett, B. ([1871] 2010), *The Dialogues of Plato: Translated into English, with Analyses and Introduction*, Cambridge: Cambridge University Press.

Jucker, M. (2006), "Negotiating and Establishing Peace between Gestures and Written Documents: the Waldmann-process in Late Medieval Zurich (1489)," in J. Van Leeuwen (ed.), *Symbolical Communication in Late Medieval Towns*, Leuven: LUP.

Judd, C. C. (2002), "Renaissance Modal Theory: Theoretical, Compositional, and Editorial Perspectives," in T. Christensen (ed.), *The Cambridge History of Western Music Theory*, 364–406. Cambridge: Cambridge University Press.

Judde de Larivière, C. (2014), *La Révolte des Boules de Neige: Murano face à Venise, 1511*, Paris: Fayard.

Judde de Larivière, C. and M. Salzberg (2013), "Le Peuple est la Cité: L'idée de Popolo et la Condition des Popolani à Venise (XVe–XVIe siècles)," *Annales: Histoire, Sciences Sociales*, 68: 1113–40.

Julian (1994), *The Shewings of Julian of Norwich*, ed. Georgia Ronan Crampton, Kalamazoo, MI: Western Michigan Publications.

Kagan, R. (1990), *Lucrecia's Dreams: Politics and Prophecy in Sixteenth-Century Spain*, Berkeley, CA: University of California Press.

Kalinke, M. E. (2011), *The Arthur of the North: The Arthurian Legend in the Norse and Rus' Realms*, Cardiff: University of Wales Press.

Karant-Nunn, S. (2010), *The Reformation of Feeling: Shaping the Religious Emotions in Early Modern Germany*, Oxford: Oxford University Press.

Kaufmann, T. DaCosta. (2010), *Visual Jokes, Natural History, and Still-Life Painting*, Chicago: University of Chicago Press.

Kemp, A. (1991), *The Estrangement of the Past: A Study in the Origins of Modern Historical Consciousness*, Oxford: Oxford University Press.

Kempis, T. à (1999), *The Imitation of Christ*, Urbana, Illinois: Project Gutenberg: http:/www.gutenberg.org/cache/epub/1653/pg1653-images.html (accessed November 21, 2016).

Kendall, G. Y. (2003), "Ornamentation and Improvisation in Sixteenth-century Dance," in T. J. McGee (ed.), *Improvisation in the Arts of the Middle Ages and Renaissance*, 170–90, Kalamazoo, MI: Medieval Institute Publications.

Kennedy, G., trans. and ed. (1991), *Aristotle, On Rhetoric: A Theory of Civic Discourse*, Oxford: Oxford University Press.

Kershaw, I. (1973), "The Great Famine and Agrarian Crisis in England, 1315–22," *Past and Present*, 59: 3–50.

Kertzer, D. (1988), *Ritual, Politics and Power*, New Haven, CT: Yale.

Kieckhefer, R. (1989), *Magic in the Middle Ages*, Cambridge: Cambridge University Press.

King, P. (2000), "Seeing and Hearing: Looking and Listening," *Early Theatre*, 3 (1): 155–66.

King, P. (2010), "Emotions in Medieval Thought," in Peter Goldie (ed.), *The Oxford Handbook of Philosophy of Emotions*, 167–87, Oxford: Oxford University Press.

Kisèry, A. (2016), *Hamlet's Moment: Drama and Political Knowledge in Early Modern England*, Oxford: Oxford University Press.

Kittsteiner, H. D. (1995), *Die Entstehung des modernen Gewissens*, Frankfurt: Suhrkamp Verlag Ag.

Klapisch-Zuber, C. (1985), *Women, Family and Ritual in Renaissance Italy*, Chicago: University of Chicago Press.

Klestinec, C. (2010), "Medical Education in Padua: Students, Faculty and Facilities," *Centres of Medical Excellence? Medical Travel and Education in Europe, 1500–1789*, ed. O. P. Grell, A. Cunningham, and J. Arrizabalaga, 193–220, Aldershot: Ashgate.

Klestinec, C. (2011), *Theaters of Anatomy: Students, Teachers, and Traditions of Dissection in Renaissance Venice*, Baltimore, MD: Johns Hopkins University Press.

Klibansky, R., E. Panofsky, and F. Saxl (1964), *Saturn and Melancholy: Studies in the History of Natural Philosophy, Religion, and Art*, London: Nelson.

Knezevic, I. (2014), "The Green Banner of La Feria: Popular Revolt and Municipal Politics in Early Sixteenth-Century Seville," in J. Dumolyn, H. Oliva Herrer, V. Challet, and M. Antonia Carmona Ruiz (eds.), *The Voices of the People in Late Medieval Europe: Communication and Popular Politics*, 167–81, Turnhout: Brepols.

Knight, A. (1983), *Aspects of Genre in Late Medieval French Drama*, Manchester: Manchester University Press.

Knorr Cetina, K. (1999), *Epistemic Cultures: How the Sciences Make Knowledge*, Cambridge MA: Harvard University Press.

Koerner, J. L. (2004), *The Reformation of the Image*, London: Reaktion.

Kristeva, J. (1982) *The Powers of Horror: An Essay on Abjection*, trans. L. S. Roudiez, New York: Columbia University Press.

Kuhn, C. (2007), "Urban Laughter as a 'Counter-Public' Sphere in Augsburg: the Case of the City Mayor, Jakob Herbrot (1490/95–1564)," *International Review of Social History*, 52: 77–93.

Kwan, N. (2012), "Woodcuts and Witches: Ulrich Molitor's *De lamiis et pythonicis mulieribus*, 1489–1669," *German History*, 30 (4): 493–527.

La Battaglia (n.d.), Florence, Biblioteca Nazionale, MS Magl. XIX, 31, 2r–5r.

La Via, S. (2013), "Alfonso Fontanelli's Cadences and the *Seconda Pratica*," *The Journal of Musicology*, 30 (1): 49–102.

Ladurie, E. LeRoy (1987), *The French Peasantry, 1450–1660*, Berkeley, CA: University of California Press

Laffan, M. and M. Weiss, eds. (2012), *Facing Fear: The History of an Emotion in Global Perspective*, Princeton, NJ: Princeton University Press.

Langland, W. (1978), *The Vision of Piers Plowman*, ed. A. V. C Schmidt, London: J. M. Dent.

Lantschner, P. (2014), "Revolts and the Political Order of Cities in the Late Middle Ages," *Past and Present*, 225: 3–46.

Lantschner, P. (2015), *The Logic of Political Conflict in Medieval Cities: Italy and the Southern Low Countries, 1370–1440*, Oxford: Oxford University Press.

Laqueur, T. W. (2003), *Solitary Sex: A Cultural History of Masturbation*, New York: Zone Books.

Larner, C. (1981), *Enemies of God: The Witch-hunt in Scotland*, London: Chatto & Windus.

Larrington, C. (2001), "The Psychology of Emotion and Study of the Medieval Period," *Early Medieval Europe*, 10: 251–6.

Larrington, C. (2015), "Learning to Feel in Old Norse Camelot?," in B. Bandlein, S. G. Eriksen, and S. Rikhardsdottir (eds.), *Arthur of the North: Histories, Emotions and Imagination*, special issue of *Scandinavian Studies*, 87 (1): 74–94.

Laslett, P. (1972), "Introduction: the History of the Family," in P. Laslett (ed.), *Household and Family in Past Time*, Cambridge: Cambridge University Press.

Leach, E. E., D. Fallows, and K. Van Orden (2015), "Recent Trends in the Study of Music of the Fourteenth, Fifteenth, and Sixteenth Centuries," *Renaissance Quarterly*, 68 (1): 187–227.

Lecuppre-Desjardin, E. (1999), "Les Lumières de la ville: Recherche sur l'Utilisation de la Lumière dans Les Cérémonies Bourguignonnes," *Revue Historique*, 123: 23–43.

Lecuppre-Desjardin, E. (2007), "L'ennemi Introuvable ou la Dérision Impossible dans les Villes des Terres du Nord," in E. Crouzet-Pavan and J. Verger (eds.), *La Dérision du Moyen Age: de la Pratique Sociale au Rituel Politique*, 143–62, Paris: PUPS.

Lederer, D. (2006), *Madness, Religion and the State in Early Modern Europe: A Bavarian Beacon*, Cambridge: Cambridge University Press.

Lederer, D. (2009) "Welfare Land: Johannes Eberlin von Günzburg and the Reformation of Folly," in M. E. Plummer and R. Barnes (eds.), *Ideas and Cultural Margins in Early Modern Germany: Essays in Honor of H.C. Erik Midelfort*, 165–81, Farnham: Ashgate.

Lederer, D. (2011), "The Myth of the All-Destructive War: Afterthoughts on German Suffering, 1618–1648," *German History*, 29 (3): 380–403.

Lefebvre, G. (1973), *The Great Fear of 1789: Rural Panic in Revolutionary France*, Princeton, NJ: Princeton University Press.

Lehmann, H. (2006), *Postdramatic Theatre*, trans. K. Jürs-Munby, London: Routledge.

Leonardo da Vinci (1956), *Treatise on Painting*, trans. A. P. McMahon, Princeton, NJ: Princeton University Press.

L'Estrange, E. (2012), *Holy Motherhood: Gender, Dynasty and Visual Culture in the Later Middle Ages*, Manchester: Manchester University Press.

Levy, R. (1975), *Mind and Experience in the Society Islands*, Chicago: University of Chicago Press.

Liddy, C. (2011), "Bill Casting and Political Communication: a Public Sphere in Late Medieval English Towns?," in J. Solorzano Telechea and B. Arizaga Bolumburu (eds.), *La Gobernanza de la Ciudad Europea en la Edad Media*, 447–61, Logrono: La Rioja.

Liddy, C. (2015), "Urban Enclosure Riots: Rising of the Commons in English Towns, 1480–1525," *Past and Present*, 226: 41–77.

Lin, E. T. (2006), "Performance Practice and Theatrical Privilege: Rethinking Weimann's Concepts of Locus and Platea," *New Theatre Quarterly*, 22 (3): 283–98.

Lind, L. R. (1975), *Studies in Pre-Vesalian Anatomy*, Philadelphia: American Philosophical Society.

Lindemann, M. (2010), *Medicine and Society in Early Modern Europe*, 2nd edition, Cambridge: Cambridge University Press.

Lomazzo, G. P. ([1584] 1974), "Trattato dell'arte della pittura, scoltura et architettura," in *Scritti sulle arti*, vol. 2, Florence: Centro Di.

Lomazzo, G. P. (1598), *A Tracte Containing the Artes of Curious Paintinge*, trans. R. Haydocke, Oxford: Ioseph Barnes for R. H.

Lord Smail, D. (1996), "Accommodating Plague in Medieval Marseille," *Continuity & Change*, 11 (1): 11–41.

Lubkin, G. (1994), *A Renaissance Court: Milan under Galeazzo Maria Sforza*, Berkeley, CA: University of California Press.

Lucas, H. S. (1930), "The Great European Famine of 1315, 1316 and 1317," *Speculum*, 5 (4): 343–77.

Luther, M. ([1517] 1915), *Disputation of Doctor Martin Luther on the Power and Efficacy of Indulgences*, Urbana, IL: Project Gutenberg: http://www.gutenberg.org/cache/epub/274/pg274-images (accessed December 12, 2016).

Luther, M. (2017), *The Annotated Luther*, Volume 5, *Christian Life in the World*, ed. Hans J. Hillerbrand, MI: Fortress Press.

Lutz, C. and G. White (1986), "The Anthropology of Emotions," *Annual Review of Anthropology*, 15: 405–36.

Lutz, C. and L. Abu-Lughod, eds. (1990), *Language and the Politics of Emotion*, Cambridge: Cambridge University Press.

Luzzaschi, L. (2003), *Complete Unaccompanied Madrigals*, ed. A. Newcomb, part 1, Middleton, WI: A-R Editions.

Lynch, A. (2015a), "Good Knights and Holy Men: Reading the Virtue of Soldier-Saints in Medieval Literary Genres," in E. von Contzen and A. Bernau (eds.), *Sanctity as Literature in Early Modern Britain*, 38–59, Manchester: Manchester University Press.

Lynch, A. (2015b), "'Another comfort': Virginity and Emotion in *Measure for Measure*," in R. S. White, K. O'Loughlin, and M. Houlahan (eds.), *Shakespeare and Emotion*, 49–58, Basingtoke: Palgrave.

Lynch, A. (2016), "'he nas but seven yeer olde': Emotions in Boy Martyr Legends of Later Medieval England," in K. Barclay, K. Reynolds, and C. Rawnsley (eds.), *Death, Emotion and Childhood in Premodern Europe*, 25–44, London: Routledge.

MacDonald, M. (1981), *Mystical Bedlam: Madness, Anxiety and Healing in Seventeenth-Century*. Cambridge: Cambridge University Press.

Macey, P. (2000), "Josquin and Musical Rhetoric: *Miserere mei, Deus* and Other Motets," in R. Sherr (ed.), *The Josquin Companion*, 485–529, Oxford: Oxford University Press.

Mackay, C. S., ed. (2009), *The Hammer of Witches: A Complete Translation of the Malleus Maleficarum*, Cambridge: Cambridge University Press.

Maclean, I. (2008), "The Medical Republic of Letters before the Thirty Years War," *Intellectual History Review*, 18 (1): 15–30.

Maddern, P. (2008), "'In myn own house': The Troubled Connections between Servant Marriages, Late-Medieval English Household Communities and Early Modern Historiography," in S. Tarbin and S. Broomhall (eds.), *Women, Identities and Communities in Early Modern Europe*, 45–60, Aldershot: Ashgate.

Maggi, A. (2005), "On Kissing and Sighing: Renaissance Homoerotic Love from Ficino's *De Amore* and *Sopra Lo Amore* to Cesare Trevisani's *L'impresa* (1569)," *Journal of Homosexuality*, 49: 315–39.

Male, E. (1986), *Religious Art in France: The Late Middle Ages. A Study of Medieval Iconography and its Sources*, ed. H. Bober, trans. Marthiel Mathews, rev. ed., Princeton, NJ: Princeton University Press.

Malory, T. (1971), *Malory, Works*. ed. Eugène Vinaver, London. Oxford University Press.

Mandressi, R. (2016), "Affected Doctors: Dead Bodies and Affective and Professional Cultures in Early Modern European Anatomy," *Osiris*, 31 (1): 119–36.

Martin, Matthew (2017), "Rituals of Love," in A. Hesson, M. Martin, and C. Zika (eds.), *Love: Art of Emotion 1400–1800*, 180–93, Melbourne: National Gallery of Victoria.

Martines, L. (2001), *Strong Words: Writing and Social Strain in the Italian Renaissance*, Baltimore, MD: Johns Hopkins University Press.

Martines, L. (2003), *April Blood: Florence and the Plot against the Medici*, Oxford: Oxford University Press.

Masschaele, J. (2002), "The Public Space of the Market Place in Medieval England," *Speculum* 77: 383–421.

Matt, S. J. (2011), "Current Emotion Research: Or, Doing History from the Inside Out," *Emotion Review*, 3 (1): 117–24.

Maus, K. E. (1995), *Inwardness and Theater in the English Renaissance*, Chicago: University of Chicago Press.

McCarthy, C. (2004), *Marriage in Medieval England: Law, Literature and Practice*. Woodbridge: Boydell Press.

McClary, S. (2004), *Modal Subjectivities: Self-Fashioning in the Italian Madrigal*, Berkeley, CA: University of California Press.

McGee, T. J. (2004), "Music, Rhetoric, and the Emperor's New Clothes," in J. Haines and R. Rosenfeld (eds.), *Music and Medieval Manuscripts, Paleography and Performance: Essays Dedicated to Andrew Hughes*, 207–59, Aldershot: Ashgate.

McGowan, M. M. (2003), "Recollections of Dancing Forms from Sixteenth-century France," *Dance Research*, 21 (1): 10–26.

McGowan, M. M. (2008a), *Dance in the Renaissance: European Fashion, French Obsession*, New Haven, CT: Yale University Press.

McGowan, M. M. (2008b), "Dance in Sixteenth- and Early Seventeenth-century France," in J. Nevile (ed.), *Dance, Spectacle, and the Body Politick, 1250–1750*, 94–113, Bloomington, IN: Indiana University Press.

McGowan, M. M. (2012), *La Danse à la Renaissance: Sources livresques et albums d'images*, Paris: Bibliothèque Nationale de France.

McGowan, M. M. (2015), "Marguerite de Valois, reine de Navarre (1553–1615): Patroness and Performer," *Early Music History*, 34: 191–206.

McIver, K. A. (2013), "Let's Eat: Kitchens and Dining in the Renaissance Palazzo and Country estate," in E. J. Campbell, S. R. Miller, and E. C. Consavari (eds.), *The Early Modern Italian Domestic Interior, 1400–1700: Objects, Spaces, Domesticities*, 159–74, Farnham: Ashgate.

McKinney, T. (2010), *Adrian Willaert and the Theory of Interval Affect: The Musica Nova Madrigals and the Novel Theories of Zarlino and Vicentino*, Farnham: Ashgate.

McNamer, S. (2007), "Feeling," in P. Strohm (ed.), *Middle English: Oxford Twentieth-Century Approaches to Literature*, 241–57, New York: Oxford University Press.

McNamer, S. (2010), *Affective Meditation and the Invention of Medieval Compassion*, Philadelphia: University of Pennsylvania Press.

McNamer, S. (2015), "The Literariness of Literature and the History of Emotion," *PMLA*, 130: 1433–42.

McSheffrey, S. (2006), *Marriage, Sex, and Civic Culture in Late Medieval London*, Philadelphia: University of Pennsylvania Press.

McTaggert, A. (2012), *Shame and Guilt in Chaucer*, New York: Palgrave Macmillan.

Meconi, H. (2007), "The Range of Mourning: Nine Questions and Some Answers," in S. Gasch and B. Lodes (eds.), *Tod in Musik und Kultur: zum 500. Todestag Philipps des Schönen*, 141–56, Tutzing: Hans Schneider, 2007.

Meek, R. and E. Sullivan, eds. (2015), *The Renaissance of Emotion: Understanding Affect in Shakespeare and His Contemporaries*, Manchester: Manchester University Press.

Meier, B. (1988), *The Modes of Classical Vocal Polyphony*, trans. E. S. Beebe, New York: Broude Brothers.

Meier, B. (1990), "Rhetorical Aspects of the Renaissance Modes," *Journal of the Royal Musical Association*, 115 (2):182–190.

Melion, W. (1991), *Shaping the Netherlandish Canon: Karel van Mander's* Schilder-Boeck, Chicago: University of Chicago Press.

Mendez de Torres, L. ([1586] 2008), *Tractado breve de la cultivation y cura de las colmenas*, Valladolid: Editorial Maxtor.

Menocal, M. R. (1987), *The Arabic Role in Medieval Literary History: A Forgotten Heritage*, Philadelphia: University of Pennsylvania Press.

Menocal, M. R. (1994), *Shards of Love: Exile and the Origins of the Lyric*, Durham, NC: Duke University Press.

Middle English Dictionary. Published electronically at https://quod.lib.umich.edu (accessed October 13, 2017)

Midelfort, H. C. E. (1999), *A History of Madness in Sixteenth Century Germany*, Stanford, CA: Stanford University Press.

Mills, D. (1985), "'Look at Me When I'm Speaking to You': The 'Behold and See' Convention in Medieval Drama," *Medieval English Theatre*, 7 (1): 4–12.

Miri Rubin, M. (2004), *Corpus Christi: The Eucharist in Late Medieval Culture*, Cambridge: Cambridge University Press.

Mitchell, P. (2007), The Purple Island *and Anatomy in Early Seventeenth-Century Literature, Philosophy and Theology*, Cranbury, NJ: Rosemont Publishing.

Mitchell, S. C. (2011), "Moral Posturing: Virtue in Christine de Pisan's *Livre de Trois Vertus*," in J. Rider and J. Freedman (eds.), *The Inner Life of Women in Medieval Romance Literature*, 85–106, New York: Palgrave Macmillan.

Monahin, N. (2011), "Reading (?into) Renaissance Dance: *misura* in the Service of Dramaturgy," in A. Buckley and C. J. Cyrus (eds.), *Music, Dance, and Society: Medieval and Renaissance Studies in Memory of Ingrid G. Brainard*, 211–30, Kalamazoo, MI: Medieval Institute Publications.

Montagut, B. de ([1619/20] 2000), *Louange de la Danse: In Praise of the Dance*, ed. and trans. Barbara Ravelhofer, Cambridge: RTM Publications.

Montaigne, M. de ([1603] 1892–3), *The Essays of Montaigne*, trans. J. Florio, ed. G. Saintsbury, London: D. Nutt.

Morgan, H. (2017), *Beds and Chambers in Late Medieval England: Readings, Representations and Realities*, Woodbridge: York Medieval Press

Morrison, S. S. (2008), *Excrement in the Late Middle Ages: Sacred Filth and Chaucer's Fecopoetics*, London: Palgrave Macmillan.

Mortensen, M., ed., "Sophie Brahe: Brev til Margrethe Brahe," *Det Kongelige Bibliotek*. Available online: https://www.google.com.au/search?q=Sophie+Brahe%3A+Brev+til+Margrethe+Brahe%2C%E2%80%9D+Det+Kongelige+Bibliotek&ie=utf-8&oe=utf-8&client=firefox-b-ab&gfe_rd=cr&dcr=0&ei=F0muWaeXE4_p8wf9pIaIBw (accessed September 5, 2017).

Moscoso, J. (2016), "Pain and Suffering," *Early Modern Emotions: An Introduction*, ed. S. Broomhall, 45–8, London: Routledge.

Moscovici, S. (1981), *L'âge des Foules: Un Traité Historique de Psychologie de Masses*, Paris: Fayard.

Mulder-Bakker, A. (2005), *Lives of the Anchoresses: The Rise of the Urban Recluse in Medieval Europe*, Philadelphia: University of Pennsylvania Press.

Munjic, S. (2008), "Leriano's Suffering Subjectivity; or, the Politics of Sentimentality in Cárcel de amor," *Revista Canadiense de Estudios Hispánicos*, 32: 203–26.

Muratori, L., ed. (1741), "Gratulatio Patavini potestatis," in *Antiquitates Italicae*, vol. 4, Milan: Mediolani.

Mustanoja, T. F., ed. (1948), *The Good Wife Taught Her Daughter, The Good Wyfe Wold a Pylgremage, The Thewis of Gud Women*, Helsinki: Suomalaisen Kirjallisuuden Scuran.

Myers, W. D. (1996), *"Poor Sinning Folk": Confession and Conscience in Counter-Reformation Germany*, Ithaca, NY: Cornell University Press.

Nagy, P. and D. Boquet (2008), "Pour une Histoire des Émotions: L'historien Face aux Questions Contemporaines," in P. Nagy and D. Boquet (eds.), *Le Sujet des Emotions au Moyen Age*, 15–51, Paris: Beauchesne.

Naphy, W. G and P. Johnson, eds. (1997), *Fear in Early Modern Society*, Manchester: Manchester University Press.

Nevile, J. (2003), "Disorder in Order: Improvisation in Italian Choreographed Dances of the Fifteenth and Sixteenth Centuries," in T. J. McGee (ed.), *Improvisation in the Arts of the Middle Ages and Renaissance*, 145–69, Kalamazoo, MI: Medieval Institute Publications.

Nevile, J. (2004), *The Eloquent Body: Dance and Humanist Culture in Fifteenth-Century Italy*, Bloomington, MI: Indiana University Press.

Nevile, J. (2008a), "Dance Performance in the Late Middle Ages: A Contested Space," in E. Gertsman (ed.), *Visualizing Medieval Performance: Perspectives, Histories, Contexts*, 295–310, Aldershot: Ashgate.

Nevile, J. (ed.) (2008b), *Dance, Spectacle, and the Body Politick, 1250–1750*, Bloomington, IN: Indiana University Press.

Newfield, T. (2009), "A Cattle Panzootic in Early Fourteenth-Century Europe," *Agricultural History Review*, 57 (2): 155–90.

Newhauser, R. G. (2010), Foreword, *The Senses and Society*, 5 (1): 5–9.

Newman, B. (2013), *Medieval Crossover: Reading the Secular against the Sacred*, Notre Dame, IN: University of Notre Dame Press.

Newman, B. (2016), *Making Love in the Twelfth Century: Letters of Two Lovers in Context*, Philadelphia: University of Pennsylvania Press.

Nicholas, D. (1997), *The Later Medieval City, 1300–1500*, London: Routledge.

Nicholson, E. (1999), "Romance as Role Model: Early Female Performances of Orlando Furioso and Gerusalemme Liberata," in V. Finucci (ed.), *Renaissance Transactions: Ariosto and Tasso*, pp. 246–69, Durham, NC: Duke University Press.

Norwich, J. J. (2011), *The Popes: A History*, London: Chatto & Windus.

O'Day, R. (2007), *Women's Agency in Early Modern Britain and the American Colonies*, Harlow: Routledge

O'Faolain, J. and L. Martines, eds. (1973), *Not in God's Image: Women in History*, London: Virago.

O'Malley, C. D. (1964), *Andreas Vesalius of Brussels, 1514–1564*, Berkeley, CA: University of California.

Oatley, K. (1999), "Why Fiction May Be Twice as True as Fact: Fiction as Cognitive and Emotional Simulation," *Review of General Pscyhology*, 3: 101–17.

Oberman, H. (1963), *The Harvest of the Middle Ages: Gabriel Biel and Late Medieval Nominalism*, Cambridge, MA: Harvard University Press.

Ogilvie, B. W. (1996), "Travel and Natural History in the Sixteenth Century," in B. W. Ogilvie, A. te Heesen, and M. Gierl (eds.), *Sammeln in der Frühen Neuzeit*, 3–28, Berlin: Max-Planck-Institut für Wissenschaftsgeschichte.

Ogilvie, B. W. (2006), *The Science of Describing: Natural History in Renaissance Europe*, Chicago: University of Chicago Press.

Oliva Herrer, R. H. (2014), "Popular Voices and Revolt : Exploring Anti-Noble Uprisings on the Eve of the War of the Communities of Castile," in J. Dumolyn, J. Haemers, H. R. Oliva Herrer, and V. Challet (eds.), *The Voices of the People in Late Medieval Europe: Communication and Popular Politics*, 49–61, Turnhout: Brepols.

Onians, J. (2008), *Neuroarthistory: From Aristotle and Pliny to Baxandall and Zeki*, London: Yale University Press.

Orlin, L. C (2007), *Locating Privacy in Tudor London*, Oxford: Oxford University Press.

Ouvrard, J.-P. (1992), "Modality and Text Expression in Sixteenth-century French Chansons: Remarks Concerning the E Mode," *Basler Jahrbuch für historische Musikpraxis*, 16: 89–116.

Oxford English Dictionary. Available online: http://www.oed.com (accessed October 13, 2017).

Ozment, S. (1985), *When Fathers Ruled: Family Life in Reformation Europe*, Cambridge, MA: Harvard University Press.

Ozment, S. (1989), *Magdalena and Balthasar: an Intimate Portrait of Life in Sixteenth-century Europe Revealed in the Letters of a Nuremberg Husband and Wife*, New Haven, CT: Yale University Press.

Page, C. (2009), "German Musicians and Their Instruments: A 14th-Century Account by Konrad of Megenberg," in T. J. McGee (ed.), *Instruments and Their Music in the Middle Ages*, 29– 37, Farnham: Ashgate. Originally published in *Early Music* 10 (2) (1982): 192–200.

Page, C. (1996), "Reading and Reminiscence: Tinctoris on the Beauty of Music," *Journal of the American Musicological Society*, 49 (1): 1–31.

Paleotti, G. (2012), *Discourse on Sacred and Profane Images*, trans. W. McCuaig, Los Angeles: Getty Publications.

Palisca, C. (1990), "Mode Ethos in the Renaissance," in L. Lockwood and E. Roesner (eds.), *Essays in Musicology: A Tribute to Alvin Johnson*, 126–39, Philadelphia: American Musicological Society.

Palisca, C. (2000), "Moving the Affections through Music: Pre-Cartesian Psycho-Physiological Theories," in P. Gozza (ed.), *Number to Sound: The Musical Way to the Scientific Revolution*, 289–308, Dordrecht: Kluwer.

Palisca, C. (2013), "The Ethos of Modes during the Renaissance," in T. Cochrane, B. Fantini, and K. R. Scherer (eds.), *The Emotional Power of Music: Multidisciplinary Perspectives on Musical Arousal, Expression, and Social Control*, Oxford: Oxford University Press.

Palissy, B. (2010), *Oeuvres completes*, ed. K. Cameron, J. Céard, M.-M. Fragonard, M.-D. Legrand, F. Lestringant, and G. Schrenk, Paris: Champion.

Panofsky, E. (1955), *The Life and Art of Albrecht Dürer*, 4th ed., Princeton, NJ: Princeton University Press.

Papal Encyclicals Online (2016), "UNAM SANCTAM: Bull of Pope Boniface VIII promulgated November 18, 1302." Available online: http://www.papalencyclicals.net/Bon08/B8unam.htm (accessed August 25, 2016).

Pappi, A. B. (1992), "Mendicant Friars and Female Pinzochere in Tuscany: From Social Marginality to Models of Sanctity," in D. Bornstein and R. Rusconi (eds.), *Women and Religion in Medieval and Renaissance Italy*, 84–103, Chicago: University of Chicago Press.

Park, K. (1988), "The Organic Soul," in C. B. Schmitt, Q. Skinner, E. Kessler, and J. Kraye (eds.), *The Cambridge History of Renaissance Philosophy*, 464–84, Cambridge: Cambridge University Press.

Park, K. (1998), "Impressed Images: Reproducing Wonders," in C. Jones and P. Galison (eds.), *Picturing Science, Producing Art*, 254–71, London: Routledge.

Parker, G. (2013), *Global Crisis: War, Climate Change and Catastrophe in the Seventeenth Century*, New Haven, CT: Yale University Press.

Parshall, P. and R. Schoch (2005), *Origins of European Printmaking: Fifteenth-Century Woodcuts and their Public*, New Haven, CT: National Gallery of Art, in association with Yale University Press.

Paster, G. (1993), *The Body Embarrassed: Drama and the Disciplines of Shame in Early Modern England*, Ithaca, NY: Cornell University Press.

Paster, G. (2004), *Humoring the Body: Emotions and the Shakespearean Stage*, Chicago: University of Chicago Press.

Paster, G. K., K. Rowe, and M. Floyd-Wilson, eds. (2004), *Reading the Early Modern Passions: Essays in the Cultural History of Emotion*, Philadelphia: University of Pennsylvania Press.

Perler, D. (2012), "Why is the Sheep Afraid of the Wolf? Medieval Debates on Animal Passions," in M. Pickavé and L. Shapiro (eds.), *Emotion and Cognitive Life in Medieval and Early Modern Philosophy*, 32–52, Oxford: Oxford University Press.

Pestalozzi, C. (1858), *Heinrich Bullinger, Leben und Ausgewählte Schriften*, Elberfeld: R. L. Friderichs.

Petrarch (1904), "Letter to a friend, 1340–1353," in J. H. Robinson, *Readings in European History*, 502, Boston: Ginn & Company. Available online: http://sourcebooks.fordham.edu/halsall/source/14Cpetrarch-pope.asp (accessed November 11, 2016).

Pirenne, H. (1903), "Les Dénombrements de la Population d'Ypres au XVe Siècle," *Vierteljahrschrift für Social- und Wirtschaftsgeschichte*, 1: 1–32.

Pizan, Christine de (1983), *The Book of the City of Ladies*, trans. E. J. Richards, London: Picador.

Plamper, J. (2009) "Fear: Soldiers and Emotion in Early Twentieth-Century Russian Military Psychology," *Slavic Review*, 68: 259–83

Plamper, J. (2015), *The History of Emotions: An Introduction*, Oxford: Oxford University Press.

Plamper, J. and B. Lazier (2012), *Fear Across the Disciplines*, Pittsburgh, PA: University of Pittsburgh Press.

Pollock, L. (1987), *A Lasting Relationship: Parents and Children over Three Centuries*, Hanover, NH: University Press of New England.

Powers, H. S. (1981), "Tonal Types and Modal Categories in Renaissance Polyphony," *Journal of the American Musicological Society*, 34 (3): 428–70.

Powers, H. S. and F. Wiering, "Mode," *Grove Music Online, Oxford Music Online*. Available online: http://www.oxfordmusiconline.com/subscriber/article/grove/music/43718 (accessed January 23, 2016).

Putter, A. (1995), *Sir Gawain and the Green Knight and French Arthurian Romance*, Oxford: Clarendon Press.

Rabkin, N. (1977), "Rabbits, Ducks, and Henry V," *Shakespeare Quarterly*, 28 (3): 279–96.

Reddy, W. M. (1997), "Against Constructionism: the Historical Ethnography of Emotions," *Current Anthropology*, 38 (3): 327–51.

Reddy, W. (2001), *The Navigation of Feeling: A Framework for the History of the Emotions*, Cambridge: Cambridge University Press.

Reddy, W. (2012), *The Making of Romantic Love: Longing and Sexuality in Europe, South Asia and Japan, 900–1200 CE*, Chicago: University of Chicago Press.

Reddy, W. (2016), "The Eurasian Origins of Empty Time and Space: Modernity as Temporality Reconsidered," *History and Theory*, 55: 325–56

Rexroth F. (2007), *Deviance and Power in late Medieval London*, Cambridge: Cambridge University Press.

Ricciardelli, F. and A. Zorzi, eds. (2015), *Emotions, Passions, and Power in Renaissance Italy*, Amsterdam: University of Amsterdam Press.

Richardson, A. (2003), "Gender and Space in English Royal Palaces c. 1160–c. 1547: A Study in Access Analysis and Imagery," *Medieval Archaeology*, 47 (1): 131–65.

Riddy, F. (1993), "'Women Talking about the Things of God': A Late Medieval Subculture," in C. M. Meale (ed.), *Women and Literature in Britain 1150–1500*, 104–27, Cambridge: Cambridge University Press.

Riddy, F. (2008), "'Burgeis' Domesticity in Late-medieval England," in M. Kowaleski and P. J. P. Goldberg (eds.), *Medieval Domesticity: Home, Housing and Household in Medieval England*, 14–36, Cambridge: Cambridge University Press.

Rider, J. and J. Friedman, eds. (2011), *The Inner Life of Women in Medieval Romance Literature: Grief, Guilt, and Hypocrisy*, New York: Palgrave Macmillan.

Ridout, N. (2006), *Stage Fright, Animals, and Other Theatrical Problems*, Cambridge: Cambridge University Press.

Roach, J. R. (1993), *The Player's Passion: Studies in the Science of Acting*, Newark, NJ: University of Delaware Press.

Robertson, A. W. (2002), *Guillaume de Machaut and Reims: Context and Meaning in His Musical Works*, Cambridge: Cambridge University Press.

Robertson, A. W. (2015), "Affective Literature and Sacred Themes in Fifteenth-Century Music," in A. M. B. Berger and J. Rodin (eds.), *The Cambridge History of Fifteenth-Century Music*, 545–60, Cambridge: Cambridge University Press.

Robinson, C. (2013), "'In One of my Body's Gardens': Hearts in Transformation in Late Medieval Iberian Passion Devotions," in S. C. Akbari and K. Mallette (eds.), *A Sea of Languages: Rethinking the Arabic Role in Medieval Literary History*, 163–81, Toronto: University of Toronto Press.

Rogerson, M. (2012), "Affective Piety: A Method for Medieval Actors in the Chester Cycle," in J. Dell, D. Klausner, and H. Ostovich (eds.), *The Chester Cycle in Context, 1555–1575*, 93–110, London: Routledge.

Rolle, R. (1988), *Richard Rolle: Prose and Verse*, ed. S. J. Ogilvie-Thomson, Oxford: Oxford University Press.

Rollo-Koster, J. and A. Holstein (2010), "Anger and Spectacle in Late Medieval Rome: Gauging Emotion in Urban Topography," in C. Goodson, A. E. Lester, and C. Symes (eds.), *Cities, Texts and Social Networks, 400–1500: Experiences and Perceptions of Medieval Urban Space*, 149–74, Farnham: Ashgate.

Roodenberg, H. (2014), "Empathy in the Making: Crafting the Believer's Emotions in the Late Medieval Low Countries," *BMGN: Low Countries Historical Review*, 129 (2): 42–62.

Roodenburg, H. and C. Santing (2014), "Batavian Phlegm? The Dutch and Their Emotions in Pre-modern Times," *Low Countries Historical Review*, 129: 7–19.

Roper, L. (1991), *The Holy Household: Women and Morals in Reformation Augsburg*, Oxford: Clarendon Press.

Roper, L. (1994), *Oedipus and the Devil: Witchcraft, Religion and Sexuality in Early Modern Europe*, London: Routledge.

Roper, L. (2004), *Witchcraze: Terror and Fantasy in Baroque Germany*, New Haven, CT: Yale University Press.

Roper, L. (2016), *Martin Luther: Renegade and Prophet*. London: Bodley Head.

Rose, C. M. and G. L. Greco (2009), *The Good Wife's Guide (Le Ménagier de Paris): A Medieval Household Book*, Ithaca, NY: Cornell University Press.

Rosenfeld, J. (2011), *Ethics and Enjoyment in Late Medieval Poetry: Love After Aristotle*, Cambridge: Cambridge University Press.

Rosenwein, B. (1998), "Controlling Paradigms," in B. Rosenwein (ed.), *Anger's Past: The Social Uses of an Emotion in the Middle Ages*, 233–45, London: Cornell.

Rosenwein, B. (2002), "Worrying about Emotions in History," *American Historical Review*, 107 (3): 821–45.

Rosenwein, B. (2006), *Emotional Communities in the Early Middle Ages*, Ithaca, NY: Cornell University Press.

Rosenwein, B. (2016), *Generations of Feeling: A History of Emotions, 600–1700*, Cambridge: Cambridge University Press.

Rubin, M. (2009), *Emotion and Devotion: The Meaning of Mary in Medieval Religious Cultures*, Budapest: Central European University Press.

Ruggiero, G. (1993), *Binding Passions: Tales of Magic, Marriage, and Power at the End of the Renaissance*, Oxford: Oxford University Press.

Russell, N. and H. Visentin (2007), "The Multilayered Production of Meaning in Sixteenth-century French Ceremonial Entries," in N. Russell and H. Visentin (eds.), *French Ceremonial Entries in the Sixteenth Century: Event, Image, Text*, 15–27, Toronto: Centre for Reformation and Renaissance Studies.

Ryrie, A. (2013), *Being Protestant in Reformation Britain*, Oxford: Oxford University Press.

Salih, S. (2011), "Unpleasures of the Flesh: Medieval Marriage, Masochism, and the History of Sexuality," *Studies in the Age of Chaucer*, 33: 125–47.

Salmon, J. H. M. (1975), *Society in Crisis: France in the Sixteenth Century*, London: E. Benn.

Salzberg, R. and M. Rospocher (2012), "Street Singers in Italian Renaissance Urban Culture and Communication," *Cultural and Social History*, 9: 9–26.

Sánchez y Sánchez, S. (2010), "Death Gets Personal: Inventing Early Modern Grief in 15th Century Spain," *Celestinesca*, 34: 145–78.

Sarti, R. (2002), *Europe at Home: Family and Material Culture 1500–1800*, New Haven, CT: Yale University Press.

Saunders, C. (2009), "The Affective Body: Love, Virtue and Vision in English Medieval Literature," in C. Saunders, U. Maude, and J. McNaughton (eds.), *The Body and the Arts*, New York: Palgrave.

Saupe, K., ed. (1997), *Middle English Marian Lyrics*, Kalamazoo, MI: Medieval Institute Publications.

Scaglione, A. (1991), *Knights at Court: Courtliness, Chivalry, and Courtesy from Ottonian Germany to the Italian Renaissance*, Berkeley, CA: University of California Press.

Scheer, M. (2012), "Are Emotions a Kind of Practice (and Is That What Makes Them Have a History)? A Bourdieuian Approach to Understanding Emotion," *History and Theory*, 51: 193–220.

Schiller, G. (1971–2), *Iconography of Christian Art*, trans. J. Seligman, Greenwich, CT: New York Graphic Society.

Schmidt, S. K. (2011), *Altered and Adorned: Using Renaissance Prints in Daily Life*, Chicago: Art Institute of Chicago.

Schofield, J. and A. Vince (2003), *Medieval Towns: The Archaeology of British Towns in the European Setting*, London: A & C Black.

Schuler, C. (1992), "The Seven Sorrows of the Virgin: Popular Culture and Cultic Imagery in Pre-Reformation Europe," *Simiolus*, 21 (1/2): 5–28.

Schwerhoff, G. (1998), "Zivilisationsprozeß und Geschichtswissenschaft: Norbert Elias Forschungsparadigma in historischer Sicht," *Historische Zeitschrift*, 266: 561–605.

Scott, J. (2004). *Understanding Dante*, Notre Dame, IN: University of Notre Dame Press.
Scribner, R. (1981), *For the Sake of Simple Folk: Popular Propaganda for the German Reformation*, Cambridge: Cambridge University Press.
Scribner, R. (1994), *For the Sake of Simple Folk: Popular Propaganda for the German Reformation*, 2nd rev. ed., Oxford: Clarendon Press.
Scribner, R. (1998), "Ways of Seeing in the Age of Dürer," in D. Eichberger and C. Zika (eds.), *Dürer and His Culture*, 93–117, Cambridge: Cambridge University Press.
Scribner, R. (2001), *Religion and Culture in Germany (1400–1800)*, ed. L. Roper, Leiden: Brill.
Seitz, J. (2011), *Witchcraft and Inquisition in Early Modern Venice*, Cambridge: Cambridge University Press.
Serres, O. de (1599), *La cueillette de la soye*, Paris: Jamet Mettayer.
Shakespeare, W. (1992), The Poems, ed. John Roe, Cambridge: Cambridge University Press.
Shakespeare, W. (2013a), "Hamlet," ed. H. Jenkins, in A. Thompson and D. S. Kastan (eds.), *Arden Complete Works of William Shakespeare*, rev. ed., 291–332, London: Bloomsbury.
Shakespeare, W. (2013b), "King Henry V," ed. T. W. Craik, in A. Thompson and D. S. Kastan (eds.), *Arden Complete Works of William Shakespeare*, rev. ed., 429–62, London: Bloomsbury.
Shank, J. B. (2008), "Crisis: A Useful Category of Post–Social Scientific Historical Analysis?," *American Historical Review*, 113 (4): 1090–9.
Shapin, S. (2010), *Never Pure: Historical Studies of Science as if it was Produced by People with Bodies, Situated in Time, Space, Culture, and Society, and Struggling for Credibility and Authority*, Baltimore, MD: Johns Hopkins University Press.
Sharpe, K. and S. N. Zwicker (2003), "Introduction: Discovering the Renaissance Reader," in Sharpe and Zwicker (eds.), *Reading Society and Politics in Early Modern England*, 1–37, Cambridge: Cambridge University Press.
Shuger, D. (1990), *Habits of Thought in the English Renaissance*, Berkeley, CA: University of California Press.
Sidney, P. (1988), *An Apology For Poetry (Or The Defence Of Poesy)*, ed. G. Shepherd, 3rd edition, rev. R. W. Maslen, Manchester: Manchester University Press.
Simon, E., ed. (1991), *The Theatre of Medieval Europe: New Research in Early Drama*, Cambridge, Cambridge University Press.
Simon, E. (2008), "German Medieval Theatre: Tenth Century to 1600," in S. Williams and M. Hamburger (eds.), *A History of German Theatre*, 8–37, Cambridge: Cambridge University Press.
Simons, P. (2011a), *The Sex of Men in Premodern Europe: A Cultural History*, Cambridge: Cambridge University Press.
Simons, P. (2011b), "Gender, Sight and Scandal in Renaissance France," in H. Roberts, G. Peureux, and L. Wajeman (eds.), *Obscénités Renaissantes*, 113–26, Geneva: Droz.
Simons, P. (2015), "Salience and the Snail: Liminality and Incarnation in Francesco del Cossa's *Annunciation* (c. 1470)," in J. Spinks and D. Eichberger (eds.), *Religion, the Supernatural and Visual Culture in Early Modern Europe: An Album Amicorum for Charles Zika*, 305–29, Leiden: Brill.
Simons, P. (2017a), "Emotion," in S. Broomhall (ed.), *Early Modern Emotions: An Introduction*, 36–9, London: Routledge.
Simons, P. (2017b), "Dicks and Stones: Double–Sided Humour in a Maiolica Dish of 1536," in F. Alberti and D. Bodart (eds.), *Rire en Images à la Renaissance*, Turnhout: Brepols.
Simons, W. (2001), *Cities of Ladies: Beguine Communities in the Medieval Low Countries, 1200–1565*, Philadelphia: University of Pennsylvania Press.

Simpson, J. (2004), *Reform and Cultural Revolution*, Oxford: Oxford University Press.
Skinner, Q. (1999), "Ambrogio Lorenzetti's *Buon Governo* Frescoes: Two Old Questions, Two New Answers," *Journal of the Warburg and Courtauld Institutes*, 62: 1–28.
Skoda, H. (2013), *Medieval Violence. Physical Brutality in Northern France, 1270–1330*, Oxford: Oxford University Press.
Slone, L. L. (2008), "'I'll watch him tame and talk him out of patience': The Curtain Lecture and Shakespeare's *Othello*," in M. E. Lamb and K. Bamford (eds.), *Oral Traditions and Gender in Early Modern Literary Texts*, 85–101, Aldershot: Ashgate.
Sluhovsky, M. (2007), *Believe Not Every Spirit: Possession, Mysticism, and Discernment in Early Modern Catholicism*, Chicago: University of Chicago Press.
Smagghe, L. (2012), *Les Émotions du Prince: Émotion et Discours Politique dans l'Espace Bourguignon*, Paris: Garnier.
Smail, D. (2012), "Violence and Predation in Late Medieval Mediterranean Europe," *Comparative Studies in Society and History*, 54: 7–34.
Smith, A. (1992), "Willaert Motets and Mode," *Basler Jahrbuch für Muiskpraxis*, 16: 117–65.
Smith, B. R. (2004), "Hearing Green," in G. K. Paster, K. Rowe, and M. Floyd-Wilson (eds.), *Reading the Early Modern Passions: Essays in the Cultural History of Emotion*, 147–68, Philadelphia: University of Pennsylvania Press.
Smith, B. R. (2009), *The Key of Green: Passion and Perception in Renaissance Culture*, Chicago: University of Chicago Press.
Smith, J. C. (1994), *German Sculpture of the Later Renaissance c. 1520–1580: Art in the Age of Uncertainty*, Princeton, NJ: Princeton University Press.
Smith, J. C. (2002), *Sensuous Worship: Jesuits and the Art of the Early Catholic Reformation in Germany*, Princeton, NJ: Princeton University Press.
Smith, M. (1976) *Prudentius' "Psychomachia": A Reexamination*, Princeton, NJ: Princeton University Press.
Sneyd, Charlotte Augusta, ed. and trans. (1847), *A Relation . . . of the Island of England . . . About the Year 1500*, London: Camden Society.
Solga, K. (2009), *Violence Against Women in Early Modern Drama: Invisible Acts*, London: Palgrave Macmillan.
Solorzano Telechea, J. (2014), "The Politics of the Urban Commons in Northern Atlantic Spain in the Later Middle Ages," *Urban History*, 41: 183–203.
Somerset, F. (2014), *Feeling Like Saints: Lollard Writings after Wyclif*, Ithaca, NY: Cornell University Press.
Sommers, S. (1988), "Understanding Emotions: Some Interdisciplinary Considerations," in C. Stearns and P. Stearns (eds.), *Emotion and Social Change: Toward a New Psychohistory*, 23–38, New York: Holmes & Meier.
Spearing, A. C. (2005), *Textual Subjectivity: The Encoding of Subjectivity in Medieval Narratives and Lyrics*, Oxford: Oxford University Press.
Spenser, E. (1965), *Books I and II of The Faerie Queene*, ed. R. Kellogg and O. Steele, Indianapolis, IN: Odyssey.
Staley, L., ed. (1996), *The Book of Margery Kempe*, Kalamazoo, MI: Medieval Institute Publications.
States, B. O. (1985), *Great Reckonings in Little Rooms: On the Phenomenology of Theater*, Berkeley, CA: University of California Press.
Stearns, P. (2006), *American Fear: The Causes and Consequences of High Anxiety*, New York: Routledge, 2006.

Steinhoff, J. (2012), "Weeping Women: Social Roles and Images in Fourteenth-Century Tuscany," in E. Gertsman (ed.), *Crying in the Middle Ages: Tears of History*, 35–52, London: Routledge.

Stell, P. M., ed. (2006), *Probate Inventories of the York Diocese*, York: York Archaeological Trust.

Stella, A. (1993), *La Révolte des Ciompi: Les Hommes, les Lieux, le Travail*, Paris: EHESS.

Stevenson, J. (2010), *Performance, Cognitive Theory, and Devotional Culture: Sensual Piety in Late Medieval York*, London: Palgrave Macmillan.

Stewart, A. (1993), "Paper Festivals and Popular Entertainment: The Kermis Woodcuts of Sebald Beham in Reformation Nuremberg," *Sixteenth Century Journal*, 24 (2): 301–50.

Stoessel, J. (2015), "*Con lagreme bagnandome el viso*: Mourning and Music in Late Medieval Padua," *Plainsong and Medieval Music*, 24 (1): 71–89.

Stone, G. B. (2015), "Animals are from Venus, Human Beings are from Mars: Averroës's Artistotle and the Rationality of Emotion in Guido Cavalcanti's 'Donna me prega,'" *PMLA*, 130: 1269–84.

Strier, R. (2004), "'Against the Rule of Reason: Praise of Passion from Petrarch to Luther to Shakespeare to Herbert," in G. K. Paster, K. Rowe, and M. Floyd-Wilson (eds.), *Reading the Early Modern Passions: Essays in the Cultural History of Emotion*, Pennsylvania: University of Pennsylvania Press

Strohm, R. (2015), "Fifteenth-Century Humanism and Music outside Italy,' in A. M. B. Berger and J. Rodin (eds.), *The Cambridge History of Fifteenth-Century Music*, 263–80, Cambridge: Cambridge University Press.

Strong, R. (1979), *The Renaissance Garden in England*, London: Thames & Hudson.

Strype, John (ed.) (1822), *Ecclesiastical Memorials: Relating Chiefly to Religion*, Volume 3, Oxford: Clarendon Press.

Sturgis, A. (2001), "Expression and Gesture," in H. Brigstocke (ed.), *The Oxford Companion to Western Art*, Oxford: Oxford University Press. Available online: http:www.oxfordartonline.com (accessed July 17, 2016).

Sturm-Maddox, Sara (1992), *Petrarch's Laurels*, University Park, PA: Pennsylvania State University Press.

Sylvius, J. (1551), *Vaesani cuiusdam calumniarum in Hippocratis Galenique rem anatomicam depulsio*, Paris: Apud Catharinam Barbé viduam Jacobi Gazelli.

Taddei, I. (2012), "Recalling the Affront: Rituals of War in Italy in the Age of the Communes," in S. Cohn and F. Ricciardelli (eds.), *The Culture of Violence in Renaissance Italy*, 81–97, Florence: Le Lettere.

Tagliacozzi, G. (1996), *De curtorum chirurgia per insitionem*, ed. and trans. J. H. Thomas, New York: Gryphon Editions.

Talvacchia, B. (1999), *Taking Positions: On the Erotic in Renaissance Culture*, Princeton, NJ: Princeton University Press.

Tamalio, Raffaele (1994), *Federico Gonzaga alla corte di Francesco I di Franco nel carteggio privato con Mantova (1515–1517)*, Paris: Honoré Champion.

Tambling, J. (1997), "Dante and the Modern Subject: Overcoming Anger in the Purgatorio," *New Literary History*, 28: 401–20.

Tanon, L. (1883), *Histoire des Justices des Anciennes Eglises et Communautés Monastiques de Paris*, Paris: Larose et Forcel.

Tarbin, S. (2008), "Good Friendship in the Household: Illicit Sexuality, Emotions and Women's Relationships in Late Sixteenth-Century England," in S. Broomhall (ed.), *Emotions in the Household, 1200–1900*, 135–52, Basingstoke: Palgrave Macmillan.

Tarbin, S. (2015), "Raising Girls and Boys: Fear, Awe and Dread in the Early Modern Household," in S. Broomhall (ed.), *Authority, Gender and Emotions in Late Medieval and Early Modern England*, 106–30, Basingstoke: Palgrave Macmillan.

Tasso, T. (1961), *Opere di Torquato Tasso*, ed. G. Petrocchi, Milan: Mursia.

Taylor, C., ed. and trans. (2006), *Joan of Arc: La Pucelle*, Manchester: Manchester University Press.

Tentler, T. (1977), *Sin and Confession on the Eve of the Reformation*, Princeton, NJ: Princeton University Press.

Throop, S. and P. Hyams, eds. (2010), *Vengeance in the Middle Ages: Emotions, Religion and Feud*, Farnham: Ashgate.

Thürlemann, F. (2011), "The Paradoxical Rhetoric of Tears: Looking at the Madrid *Descent from the Cross*," in E. Gertsman (ed.), *Crying in the Middle Ages: Tears of History*, 53–75, London: Routledge.

Tilly, C. (2006), *Regimes and Repertoires*, Chicago: University of Chicago Press.

Tinagli, P. and M. Rogers (1997), *Women in Italian Renaissance Art: Gender, Representation, Identity*, Manchester: Manchester University Press.

Toft, R. (1984), "'Musicke a Sister to Poetrie': Rhetorical Artifice in the Passionate Airs of John Dowland," *Early Music*, 12 (2): 190–9.

Tomlinson, G. (1993), *Music in Renaissance Magic: Toward a Historiography of Others*, Chicago: University of Chicago Press.

Topsell, E. (1658), *The History of Four-Footed Beasts and Serpents*, London: E. Cotes.

Touati, F.-O. (1990), "Révolte et Société: l'Exemple du Moyen Âge," in *Violence et Contestation au Moyen Âge*, 7–16, Paris: CTHS.

Tournier, M. (2004), "Émotion Populaire: Petite Note Lexicologique," *Mots. Les Langages du Politique*, 75: 121–5.

Trexler, R. (1980), *Pubic Life in Renaissance Florence*, New York: Academic Press.

Trexler, R. (1984a), "Correre la Terra: Collective Insults in the Late Middle Ages," *Mélanges de l'Ecole Française de Rome: Moyen Age, Temps Modernes*, 96: 872–91.

Trexler, R. (1984b), "Follow the Flag: the Ciompi Revolt Seen from the Streets," *Bibliothèque d'Humanisme et Renaissance*, 46: 357–92.

Trigg, S. (2012), *Shame and Honor: A Vulgar History of the Order of the Garter*, Philadelphia: University of Pennsylvania Press.

Trigg, S. (2014), "Introduction: Emotional Histories – Beyond the Personalization of the Past and the Abstraction of Affect Theory," *Exemplaria*, 26: 3–15.

Trigg, S. (2017), "Affect Theory," in S. Broomhall (ed.), *Early Modern Emotions*, 10–13, London: Routledge.

Turner, H. S., ed. (2013), *Early Modern Theatricality*, Oxford: Oxford University Press.

Turner, J. G. (2017), *Eros Visible: Art, Sexuality and Antiquity in Renaissance Italy*, London: Yale University Press.

Tusser, T. (1570), *A Hundreth Good Pointes of Husbandry Lately Maried Vnto a Hundreth Good Poynts of Huswifery*, London.

Van Diest, Peter (1496), *Den Spieghel der Salicheit van Elckerlijc*, Delft: Snellaert.

Van Miert, D. (2014), "What was the Republic of Letters? A Brief Introduction to a Long History (1417–2008)," *Groniek*, 204 (5): 269–87.

Van Uytven, R. (1998), "Flämische Belfriede und Südniederländische Städtische Bauwerke im Mittelalter: Symbol und Mythos," in A. Haverkamp (ed.), *Information, Kommunikation und Selbstdarstellung in Mittelalterlichen Gemeinden*, 129–43, Munich: Oldenbourg.

Varchi, B. (1549), *Due lezzioni*, Florence: Lorenzo Torrentino.

Varela, F. J., E. Thompson, and E. Rosch (1991), *The Embodied Mind: Cognitive Science and Human Experience*, Cambridge, MA: MIT Press.

Vasari, G. (1912) *Lives of the Most Eminent Painters, Sculptors and Architects*, 10 vols., Vol. 2, *Berna to Michelozzo* Michelozzi, trans. Gaston du C. de Vere, London: Macmillan.

Vaught, J. C. and L. D. Bruckner, eds. (2003), *Grief and Gender, 700–1700*, Basingstoke: Palgrave Macmillan.

Vesalius, A. (2007), *On the Fabric of the Human Body. Book V: The Organs of Nutrition and Generation*, trans. W. F. Richardson in collaboration with J. B. Carman, Novato, CA: Norman Publishing.

Villon, F. (1955), *I Laugh through Tears*, trans. G. P. Cuttino, New York: Philosophical Library.

von Wartburg, W. (1949), *Französisches Etymologisches Wörterbuch: eine Darstellung galloromanischen Sprachschatzes*, vol. III, Basel: Zbinden.

Waite, G. K. (2000), *Reformers on Stage: Popular Drama and Religious Propaganda in the Low Countries of Charles V, 1515–1556*, Toronto: University of Toronto Press.

Walker, K. (2014), "Spectatorship and Vision in the York Corpus Christi Plays," *Comitatus*, 45: 169–89.

Walker-Bynum, C. (1987), *Holy Feast and Holy Fast: The Religious Significance of Food to Medieval Women*, Berkeley, CA: University of California Press.

Walsham, A. (2006), *Charitable Hatred: Tolerance and Intolerance in England, 1500–1700*, Manchester: Manchester University Press.

Watkins, R. N. (1972), "Petrarch and the Black Death: From Fear to Monuments," *Studies in the Renaissance*, 19: 196–223.

Watt, J. R. (1992), *The Making of Modern Marriage: Matrimonial Control and the Rise of Sentiment in Neuchâtel, 1550–1800*, Ithaca, NY: Cornell University Press.

Wear, A. (2000), *Knowledge and Practice in English Medicine, 1550–1680*, Cambridge: Cambridge University Press.

Wegman, R. C. (2002), "'Musical Understanding' in the 15th Century," *Early Music*, 30 (1): 46–66.

Wegman, R. C. (2003), "New Music for a World Grown Old: Martin Le Franc and the 'Contenance Angloise,'" *Acta Musicologica*, 75 (2): 201–41.

Weimann, R. (1978), *Shakespeare and the Popular Tradition in the Theatre*, Baltimore, MD: Johns Hopkins University Press.

Weiss-Krejci, E. (2010), "Heart Burial in Medieval and Early Post-Medieval Central Europe," in K. Rebay-Salisbury, M. L. Stig Sørensen, and J. Hughes (eds.), *Body Parts and Bodies Whole*, 119–34, Oxford: Oxbow Books.

Wells, R. H. (1985), "John Dowland and Elizabethan Melancholy," *Early Music*, 13 (4): 514–28.

Wells, S. (2004), "Manners Maketh a Man: Living, Dining and Becoming a Man in the Later Middle Ages," in N. McDonald and W. M. Ormrod (eds.), *Rites of Passage: Cultures of Transition in the Fourteenth Century*, 67–82, Woodbridge: York Medieval Press.

Weston, R. L. (2015), "Medical Effects and Affects: The Expression of Emotions in Early Modern Patient–Physician Correspondence," in S. Broomhall (ed.), *Ordering Emotions in Europe, 1100–1800*, 105–8, Leiden: Brill.

White Jr, L. (1969), "Kyeser's "Bellifortis": The First Technological Treatise of the Fifteenth Century," *Technology and Culture*, 10 (3): 436–41.

White, R. S., M. Houlahan and K. O'Loughlin, eds. (2015), *Shakespeare and Emotions: Inheritances, Enactments, Legacies*, London: Palgrave Macmillan.

White, S. (1998), "The Politics of Anger," in B. Rosenwein (ed.), *Anger's Past: The Social Uses of an Emotion in the Middle Ages*, Ithaca: Cornell University Press, 127–52.

Wickerstrom, J. B. (2000), "Carthusians," in W. M. Johnson (ed.), *Encyclopedia of Monasticism*, vol. 1, 244–7, Chicago: University of Chicago Press.

Wickham, G. (1959), *Early English Stages* 1300–1660, vol. 1, London: Routledge & Kegan Paul.

Wierzbicka, A. (1999), *Emotions across Languages and Cultures: Diversity and Universals*, Cambridge: Cambridge University Press.

Wiesner-Hanks, M. (1986), *Working Women in Renaissance Germany*, New Brunswick, NJ: Rutgers University Press.

Wilhite, V. (2005), "The Loss of Love's Emotions: The Urban Consistori and the Reconceptualization of the Court's Love Lyric," in E. Lecuppre-Desjardin and A.-L. van Bruaene (eds.), *Emotions in the Heart of the City: Les émotions au coeur de la ville (XIVe–XVIe siècle)*, 203–22, Turnhout: Brepols.

William A. Christian (1981), *Apparitions in Late Medieval Spain*, Princeton, NJ: Princeton University Press.

Williams, C. J. (2015), "Modes and Manipulation: Music, the State, and Emotion," in Susan Broomhall (ed.), *Ordering Emotions in Europe, 1100–1800*, 48–68. Leiden: Brill.

Williams R. (1960), *Culture and Society 1780–1950*, New York: Doubleday.

Williams, R. (1961), *The Long Revolution*, London: Chatto & Windus.

Wood, A. (2013), *The Memory of the People: Custom and Popular Senses of the Past in Early-Modern England*, Cambridge: Cambridge University Press.

Wood, C. (1993), *Albrecht Altdorfer and the Origins of Landscape*, Chicago: University of Chicago Press.

Woolgar, C. M. (1999), *The Great Household in Late Medieval England*, New Haven, CT: Yale University Press.

Woolgar, C. M. (2006), *The Senses in Late Medieval England*, New Haven, CT: Yale University Press.

Worsley, L. (2011), *If Walls Could Talk: An Intimate History of the Home*, London: Faber and Faber.

Wuidar, L. (2013), "Control and the Science of Affect: Music and Power in the Medieval and Renaissance Periods," in T. Cochrane, B. Fantini, and K. R. Scherer (eds.), trans. K. G. Jafflin *The Emotional Power of Music: Multidisciplinary Perspectives on Musical Arousal, Expression, and Social Control*, Oxford: Oxford University Press.

Wyatt, T. (1969), *Collected Poems of Sir Thomas Wyatt*, ed. K. Muir and P. Thomson, Liverpool: Liverpool University Press.

Yarnall, J. (1994), *Transformations of Circe: The History of an Enchantress*, Urbana, IL: University of Illinois Press.

Yoshikawa, N. K. (2009), "Holy Medicine and Diseases of the Soul: Henry of Lancaster and Le Livre de Seyntz Medicines," *Medical History*, 53 (3): 397–414.

Zeeberg, P. (1994), "Alchemy, Astrology and Ovid: A Love Poem by Tycho Brahe," in A. Moss, P. Dust, P. G. Schmidt, J. Chamarat, and F. Tateo (eds.), *Acta Conventus Neo-Latini Hafniensis*, 997–1007, New York: Medieval and Renaissance Texts and Studies.

Zemon Davis, N. (1975), *Society and Culture in Early Modern France*, London: Duckworth.

Ziegler, J. (1998), *Medicine and Religion, c. 1300: The Case of Arnau de Vilanova*, Oxford, Oxford University Press.

Zika, C. (2014), "Visual Signs of Imminent Disaster in the Sixteenth-Century Zurich Archive of Johann Jakob Wick," in M. Juneja and G. J. Schenk (eds.), *Disaster as Image: Iconographies and Media Strategies across Europe and Asia*, 43–53, 217–220, Regensburg: Schnell und Steiner.

Zika, C. (2017), "The Cruelty of Witchcraft: The Drawings of Jacques de Gheyn the Younger," in L. Kounine and M. Ostling (eds.), *Emotions in the History of Witchcraft*, 27–56, London: Palgrave Macmillan.

Zimmerman, M. and I. Veith (1993), *Great Ideas in the History of Surgery*, San Francisco, CA: Norman Publishing.

Zupka, D. (2014), "Communication in a Town: Urban Rituals and Literacy in the Medieval Kingdom of Hungaria," in M. Mostert and A. Adamska (eds.), *Uses of the Written Word in Medieval Towns: Medieval Urban Literacy II*, 341–73, Turnhout: Brepols.

INDEX

Italic numbers are used for illustrations.

Académie de Poésie et de Musique 58
Acosta, José de 9
actor's dilemma in drama 79–80
actors' emotions 76
adlocutio gesture 90
affect theory 110–11, 112–14
affective meditations 116–17
affective piety
   in drama 78, 81–2
   of the reformed church 46–7
affetti 85, 88, 90
Agramont, Jacme d' 27–8
Alberti, Leon Battista 88, 89–90, 92, 93–4, 97, 104
Album de chansons (Margaret of Austria) 52
Alfonso d'Avalos addressing his troops 7(Titian) 90
allegory, use of
   in art 34–5, 37, 87, 97, 98, 100, 102, 104–6
   in drama 77–8
   in text 35, 37, 43–5
Allegory with Venus and Cupid (Bronzino) 97, *98*, 102, 104
Altdorfer, Albrecht 99–100, *99*
Althoff, Gerd 151
Americas, attitudes towards 9
amorous imagery 103–6
amusing images 101–3
Anatomica methodus (Laguna) 21
anatomical knowledge 15
anchorholds 124
anger 100–1, 111–12, 126, 144–5, 146–9, 151–3
   See also divine wrath
Anger, Jane 10
animals, allegories for vices 100
animals, emotions of 22–3, 24, 27
anti-Jewish sentiment 116
anti-masque dances 64, 66
Aphrodite (Praxiteles) 105

Apologie of Jhon Philpot. Written for spittyng on an Aryan 10
Apostle spoons 135
Arbeau, Thoinot 60
Arcadelt, Jacques 52
Arcimboldo, Giuseppe 103
Areford, David 95
Arellano, Pietro Francesco 28
Arena Chapel, Padua 34–6, *34–5*, 90, *91*, 94
Aristotle 6, 20, 53, 82, 88, 111
Arnau de Vilanova 21
Ars d'amour, de vertu et de boneurté 6
Ars Moriendi 37, *38*
Ars Poetica (Horace) 82, 90
Arthurian literature 3, 5, 8, 119
artistic patrons 36
Ascent of Mount Ventoux (Petrarch) 33
Aspertini, Amico 55, *56*
audiences for drama 77, 82
Augsburg insults (1552) 150
Augustinianism 32
Avignon Papacy 33, 37
awe 14, 60, 88

Baker, Deborah Lesko 109–10
Bakhtin, Mikhail 83
Bale, Anthony 116
ballads 149, 150
balletto La Battaglia 66
ballo Gelosia (Domenico da Piacenza) 62
ballo Pizochara 66
ballo Santomera (Ebreo) 62–3
Barasch, Moshe 89
Barolsky, Paul 101
Basochiens 73
Battle for the Soul (*Psychomachia*) (Prudentius) 35
Baxter, Margery 132
bed chambers 129–30, 130–1, 132–3, *133*
beds, sharing of 128, 129, 130
bees 23
beggars 39

Beguines 40, 124
Behaim, Magdalena 11
Beham, Sebald 102
Bellifortis (Kyeser) 19, *19*
bells, use and abuse of 148
Bent, Margaret 54
Berengario da Carpi, Jacopo 22
Berger, Christian 51–2
Berger, K. 54
Berot, Jacques 11
Beza, Theodore 25
bill-posting campaigns 150–1
Binchois, Gilles 55
Black Death 26, 26, 36
Bloom, Harold 75
bodily functions 79, 129
bodily symptoms of emotions 6
body language in art 89–93
body, management of 20–1
body, metaphor for Christian society 31–2
body, privacy of 128–9
Boniface VIII, pope 32
books
    conduct guides 58, 118
    illustrated 5, 95
    of medicine and science 17–20
    misogynistic 10
    printed 2, 42–3
    religious 132
    See also literature; reading
boredom 14
Bosch, Hieronymus 101
botany 14
Botticelli, Sandro 97, 105
Bourdieu, Pierre 75
Bouts, Dieric 104
boy martyrs 115–16
Brach, Pierre de 57, 66
Brahe, Sophie 16
Brahe, Tycho 16, 18
brain 88
Brainard, Ingrid 60
Brandolino, Raffaele 53
Brandsma, Frank 119–20
Brant, Sebastian 43–4, *44*
Brantôme, Pierre 61, 104
brawls 152
Bronzino, Agnolo 97, 98, 102, 104
Brown, H. M. 55
Bruegel the Elder, Pieter 98
Bruges revolt (1488) 148, 153
Bruto, Giovanni 125–6

Bucer, Martin 86
Bullinger, Heinrich 25
Burckhardt, J. 36
Burger, Glenn 112–13, 118
Burke, Peter 144

Cadesby, John 131
Calvin, Jean 5, 9, 47
Campin, Robert 94, 134, *135*
Canzoniere (Petrarch) 6, 109
Caraglio, Jacopo 104
Caravaggio 101
Cardsharps (Caravaggio) 101
caricatures 101–2
Caroso, Fabritio 60
Carracci, Agostino 104
Carrera, Elena 117
Carthusians 124
Cary, Elizabeth 132
catharsis in drama 82
Catherine of Siena 40
Celestine V, pope 32
Cellini, Benvenuto 86
Certaldo, Paolo da 138
chansons 43, 52
chanting by crowds 149
charitable love 125, 134, *135*
charity 25, 28, 39, 123
Charles V, Holy Roman Emperor 153
Charles IX, King of France 61
Charles the Bold, Duke of Burgundy 148
Chaucer, Geoffrey 6, 8, 116
children
    beds, sharing of 128, 130
    death of 115–16
    emotional expression of 137
    pleasure in 11
    service of 122–7
choreographies 58, 60–1, 62, 66
Christ. *See* Jesus
Christ on the Mount of Olives (Altdorfer) 99–100, *99*
Christine de Pizan 9–10, 42, 118, 128
chronicles 26, 27, 141–2, 143
Chrysoloras, Manuel 88
Cicero 90, 101, 110
Ciconia, Johannes 53
Clement V, pope 33
clerical marriage 46
Clericis Laicos (papal bull) 33
climactic changes 25
Clyfland, Joan 132

INDEX

Cockcroft, Robert 73
Coëffeteau, Nicolas 21–2
Cohen Hanegbi, Naama 20
Cohn Jr., Samuel K. 28
collective emotions 143, 145–7
color, use of in art 97, 113
Columbo, Realdo 24
comic dances 62
Commedia (Dante) 10, 109, 112
communal living 40–1, 125, 136–7
composers, laments for 55
composition of art 98
Con lagreme (Ciconia) 53
conceptual blending of drama 76–9
Concert Champêtre (Titian) 99
conduct books 58, 118
confession 41, 117
Conjuror (Bosch) 101
Consistori de la subregaya companhia del Gai Saber 109
consultations, medical 14–15
Cook, Amy 77
Cooper, Helen 8
Coornhert, Dirck Volckertsz 98
Corpus Christi plays 76
Corpus Christi processions 63–4
Corpus Christianum 31–3
Cortesi, Paolo 53
Corti, Matteo 22
cosmos, order of 61, 62
counter-affect in letters 110
Counter-Reformation 9, 46
court life 9, 118–19
Coventry enclosure riots (1525) 146
craft guilds 125
Cranach, Lucas 96, 97
Crane, Susan 118–19
criminal activities 39
crises, emotions during 25–8
critical theory 112
Crocker, Holly 112–13
cross-dressing 62
Crucifixion, with Lamentation (Grünewald) 92, 93, 97, 98
crying. *See* mourning; weeping
cultural context of drama 75
Cuneus, Gabriel 15
Cysat, Renward 72

dance 57–66
  as communal activity 57, 61
  impact of behavior and emotions 58, 60
  manipulation of steps and music 66
  methods of investigation 58–61
  negative emotions 64
  personal level 61–4
  state level 64–6
dance masters 60, 66
dancing, in art 102
Danse Macabre 37, 38
Dante Alighieri 8, 10, 12, 32, 33, 109, 112, 119
Das Feldbuch der Wundarzney (Gersdoff) 14
Davis, Natalie Zemon 132, 149
De cardinalate (Cortesi) 53
De corporis humanii fabrica (Vesalius) 15, 17, 17–18, 24
De Curtorun Chirurgia per insitionem (Tagliacozzi) 22
De Lamiis et Pythonicis Mulieribus (Molitor) 43
De Monarchia (Dante) 33
De musica (Brandolino) 53
Deadly Sins (Dell) 100–1
death
  art of dying 37, 38
  of children 115–16
  fear of 37, 149
  in *Hamlet* 73–4, 80
  in morality plays 79
  Thomas à Kempis meditations on 41
Death of Actaeon (Titian) 97
Death of the Virgin (Bruegel) 98
defecation 79
Defence of Poetry (Sidney) 5
Dell the Elder, Peter 100–1
Della Porta, Giovanni 94
Delumeau, J. 32
demonology 43
Den Spieghel der Salicheit van Elckerlijc (The Mirror of Bliss of Everyman) 75, 78
denial 41
Descent from the Cross (Weyden) 88, 89, 94
desire
  in art 100–1, 105
  in dance 62, 64
  green, the color of 113
  in literature 110, 119
  and love magic 43
D'Esparvans, Jeannot 128
deviant behaviors 43–4
Devotio Moderna 40–1
devotional literature 5, 116–17, 132
devotional movements 40–1, 124–5

devotional spaces, domestic 130–1, *131*, 135
difference, fear of 9
Dinant protest (1466) 148
dining 134–5
disgust 10, 79–80, 82, 104
dismay 95–6
dissection 15
distraction 14, 100
Ditié de Jehanne d'Arc (Christine de Pizan) 42
diversity, origins of 9
divine wrath 27, 34, 36
Dodecacorde (Le Jeune) 51
dogs, emotions of 24
Dolce, Lodovico 94, 97, 104
Domenico da Piacenza 62
Donne, John 6
double coding in literature 4–5
Dowland, John 55
drama 69–83
   actor's dilemma 79–80
   affective piety and pathopoeia 81–2
   conceptual blending 76–9
   emotional communities 75–6
   emotional practices 73–5
   female characters in 120
   mobilizing and regulating emotions 82–3
   sacred and secular spaces 70–3
drawings 99–100, 99, 101
Du Clercq, Jacques 141
Dubois, Jacques (Jacobius Sylvius) 15
Due Dialogi della Vergogna 114
Duenas revolt (1520) 147
Dunbar, William 4
Durand, Étienne 58, 60, 64
Dürer, Albrecht 87, *87*, 93

eating, shared 134–5
Ebreo, Guglielmo 60, 62–3, 64
ecstatic marriage to Christ 40
educational settings 120
Edwards, Warwick 53
efficacious resemblance 88
Eiximenis, Francesc 117
Ekman, Paul 83
elephants 23
Eliot, T. S. 82
Elizabeth of York, Queen of England 132
emotion, etymological origin of 141
emotional communities 57, 75–6, 109, 125, 144
emotional practices of drama 73–5
emotions, types of 85–7

emotive realism in art 92, *92*
empathy 86–7, 94
enactivism and emotional experience 31
enclosure riots 146
enemies of God 8–9
engravings 71, 87, *87*, 98, 100, 104
Enterline, Lynn 120
entertaining in the home 135–6
Entombment (Campin) 94
envy 100, 152
epidemics 26–8, *26*, 36
Erasmus 5, 32, 45
Erikson, Erik 46
erotic art 103–6
eruption of the Real in drama 79
Ewich, Johann von 28
excrement 79
executions 146, 152–3
experiments on animals 24
expressions 22, 94
Eye, Simon 27
eyes 22, 88, 94–5, 105

Fabrizi d'Acquapendente 22
facial expressions 22, 94
Falcucci, Nicolò 14
Fallows, David 49
family groups 125–7
family ties and dance 65
famine 25–6
fantasmata (pause) in dance 66
farces 71, 79–80, 82
Fazio, Bartolomeo 88, 102–3
fear
   in art 88, 95, 97
   during crises 28, 32
   of death 37, 149
   of difference 9
   and love 6
   spread of 148, 151
   of witches 43
   of women 9–10
Ficino, Marsilio 55
Filelfo, Mario 58
first-person singular in the history of emotions 110
Fitzpatrick, Tim 72–3
flags, use of 148–9
Florence insults (1440) 150
Florence, political disputes 152
folly 43–5
forgiveness of sin 45

Foxe, John 2–3
Freccero, J. 119
Freedman, Richard 51
French, Katherine 133
frescoes 34–6, *35*
friendships, same-sex 110
Fris, Victor 143
Fuhrmann, Wolfgang 53–4

Gaetani, Benedetto 32
Galen 15
gall bladder 22
Garden, Greer 58
gardens 61, 137–8
Gauvard, Claude 145
gavottes 62
gender differences in emotional display 118
gentil love 109
geometric patterns in dance 61, 62–3
Gersdoff, Hans von 14
Gerson, Jean 41, 42, 128
Gerusalemme Liberata (Tasso) 10
Gesner, Conrad 23
Ghent revolt (1437) 154
Ghent revolt (1452) 141, 143, 145
Ghirlandaio, Domenico 96
giaranzana dances 65
Giotto 34–6, *34–5*, 90, 94, 97
gluttony 101
go-betweens 119
Goodland, Katharine 81
Goodly Bryfe Treatyse of the Pestylence (Phayre) 27
Gower, John 8
grace of rulers 153–4
graffiti 150
grammar schools 120
Great Bovine Pestilence (1319) 27
Great Famine (1315–22) 25
great masters of art 2
Greenham, Richard 131
Gregory of Rimini 23
grief 6, 55, 81–2, 90, 94–7, 114–16
Grünewald, Matthias 92, *93*, 97, 98
Gui de Chauliac 26
guilds of craftspeople 125
Guillaume de Machaut 52–3
guilt 28, 32, 36, 41, 46, 47

Haarlem, Cornelis van 96
habitus of Shakespeare 75

hall furnishings 134–6
halls 125, 134, 137
Hamlet (Shakespeare) 73–4, 81–2
Hamling, Tara 135
Hammer of Witches (Kramer/Institoris) 43
Hanawalt, Barbara 116, 138
Hankins, James 53
happiness 10–12, 28, 61, 97, 116
Harew, Angela 137
harmonies 54
Harrán, Don 54
Harrison, Peter 15
Haskell, Yasmin 14
hatred 8–9, 36, 152
Havée, Perrette la 129
heart as seat of emotion 7, 21–2, 88
Hecuba 81–2
Heemskerck, Maerten van 104
Henerus, Renatus 16
Henry V (Shakespeare) 77, 78–9, 80
heraldic devices 132
Herbrot, Jacob 150
Heseler, Baldassar 22
heterogeneous cultural products 11
Heyden, Pieter van der 102, *103*
Hilton, Rodney 145
Hippolytus gesture 90
historians, treatment of emotions 143
historical phenomenology 113
historical time 2–3
homosexual desire 110
Horace 82, 90
Hôtel-Dieu, Paris, France 128
households 125–8
Huerta, Jean de la 94
Huizinga, J. 32, 33
humanism and music 53–4
humiliation, public 148
humor, visual 101–4
Hus, Jan 37
hypocognized emotions 32, 47

"I" in the history of emotions 110
I modi (Romano and Raimondi) 104
idolatry 9
Il bianco e dolce cigno (Arcadelt) 52
Ill-Matched Lovers (Matsys) 101
Imitation of Christ (Kempis) 41
In Praise of Folly (Erasmus) 45
individualism 139
indulgences 33, 37, 45
Inferno (Dante) 32, 119

inner life in drama 74–5
instrumental music 55, *56*
insults 148, 150
Irish, Bradley 110
Isagogae breves (Berengario da Carpi) 22
Italian Relation 127

Jane Anger Her Protection for Women 10
Jardine, Lisa 18–19
jealousy 62, 97, 100
Jeanne d'Arc 42
Jesus 33–4, *34*, 91–3, *92*, 95
Jews 8, 27, 36, 116
Joan of Arc 42
John XXIII, pope 37
John the Baptist 92, *93*
John the Evangelist 90, *92*, 94
Josquin des Prez 53–4, *55*
joy 10–12, 65, 101–3
joy, amusement and laughter 101–3
Judd, Cristle Collins 50
Julian of Norwich 12

Karlstadt, Andreas 86
Keller, Samuele 22
Kempe, Margery 130
Kempis, Thomas à 41
King, Pamela 76
kinship groups 125
kissing in dance 62
Kittsteiner, H. D. 41
Knight, Alan 70–1
Knorr Cetina, Karin 13
knowledge and emotions 13–20
Konrad of Megenberg 55
Kramer, Heinrich (Institoris) 43
Kristeva, Julia 79
Kyeser, Konrad 19–20, *19*

La Délivrance de Renaud (Durand) 58, 60, 64
La Institutione di una Fanciulla (Bruto) 125–6
La Noue, François de 9
Labé, Louise 109–10
Laguna, Andrés de 21
Lamentation of Christ (Giotto) *34*, 90, 94, 97
laments for dead composers 55
Lanchals, Pieter 153
Landino, Cristoforo 18
landscape painting 99
Langland, William 123
Languet, Hubert 110
Larner, C. 43

Larrington, Carolyne 119–20
Lascivie (Carracci) 104
Last Judgment (Giotto) 35–6, *35*
Last Judgment (Traini) 95
laughter 62, 83, 101–3, 104, 150
Le gratie d'amore (Negri) 58
Le Jeune, Claude 51
Le Moiturier, Antoine 94
Le Morte Darthur (Malory) 8
Leach, Elizabeth Eva 49
Lehmann, Hans-Thies 78
Leland, John 2
Leonardo da Vinci 88, 101, 102, 104, 105
L'Estrange, Elizabeth 132
letters 11, 16–17, 110–11
lighting in art 97
Lin, Erika 70
Lindemann, Mary 6
Lipsius, Justus 32
listening to music 54–5
literature 107–21
    affect theory 112–14
    anger 111–12
    love 108–11
    performing emotion 116–21
    source for the history of emotion 114–16
Livre de Trois Vertus (Christine de Pizan) 118
Livre des tournois (René d'Anjou) 5
Livre du Corps de Policie (Christine de Pizan) 118
Livre du cuer d'amours espris (René d'Anjou) 5
Lomazzo, Gian Paolo 85, 86, 90, 97
London revolts (1316) 151
Louis XI, King of France 153
Louis XIII, King of France 58, 60
love
    in art 104–6
    charitable 125, 134, 135
    and dances 58
    of the divine 3–4
    and fear 6
    at first sight 105
    of humans 8
    invention of 3
    in literature 108–11
    magic for 43
    neighborly 23, 45, 46
    parental 127
    physical nature of 6
    and salvation 40
    of surgeons for patients 14
love-gifts 11, *11*

Loves of the Gods (Caraglio) 104
Lucerne Passion Play 72
lust 100–1, 105
    See also desire
Luther, Martin 8, 28, 32, 45–6, 51, *51*
Luzzaschi, Luzzasco 52
Lynch, Andrew 115–16
Lyon protests (1551) 149

Macey, Patrick 54
madrigals 52
magic for love 43
Malleus Maleficarum (Kramer/Institoris) 43
Malory, Thomas 8
Man of Sorrows 95, 96
Man Tricked by Gypsies (Leonardo) 101
Mandressi, Rafael 15
Mannerism 100
Margaret of Austria 52
Marguerite de Valois 62
marriage
    to Christ 10, 40
    clerical 46
    emotional closeness in 130
marriage contracts 137
martyrs 10, 115–16
Mary, mother of Jesus 6, 81, 91, 92–3, *92*, *93*, 94–5
Mary Magdalene 92, *92*, 93, *93*, 94
Masaccio 2, 7
Masque of Queens 64, 66
masquerades 57
Massacre of the Innocents, paintings of 95–7
Master of the Stötteritz Altarpiece 94
masturbation 41
Matsys, Quentin 101
Mayerne, Théodore Turquet de 14–15
McClary, Susan 52
McGee, Timothy 54
McKinney, Timothy 49
meals, sharing of 134–6
medical and scientific understanding 13–29
    emotions during crises 25–8
    the production of knowledge 13–20
    theories of emotions 20–4
medical practitioners 14–15, 26–8
Meier, Bernhard 50
melancholy
    in art 93, 97
    as cause of ill-health 21, 28
    and music 52, 55
    origins of 14

Melencolia I (Dürer) 87, *87*, 93
Ménagier de Paris 125, 130, 131, 134
Mendez de Torres, Luis 23
Mérode Altarpiece (Campin) 134, *135*
military victories and dance 65
Miraculous Victory of the Maid (Gerson) 42
mirror characters 120
Mirror of Bliss of Everyman, The 75, 78
Mirror of Simple Souls (Porete) 40
Miserere mei, Deus (Josquin) 54
misogyny 10
Mitchell, Sharon 118
Modern Devotion movement 40–1
modes in music 50–2
modesty 128–9
Molitor, Heinrich 43
Mona Lisa (Leonardo) 102
monastic orders 124, 125
Mondeville, Henri de 14
Montagut, Barthélemy de 60
Montaigne, Michel de 23
morality plays 71, 76, 79
More, Sir Thomas 45, 137
Morelli, Giovanni 86
Mort tu as navré/Miserere (Ockeghem) 55
Moscovici, Serge 145
motets 52–3
Mother of Sorrows (Master of the Stötteritz Altarpiece) 94
mourning 6, 55, 81–2, 90, 94–7, 114–16
movement, in art 99
Murano protest (1511) 146
music 49–57
    humanism, influence of 53–4
    instrumental music 55, *56*
    laments for dead composers 55
    modes 50–2
    study of emotions 49–50, 52–3
mystery plays 70, 76, 81
mysticism 39–40, 41, 42

nakedness in the home 128–9
Natural and Moral History of the Indies (Acosta) 9
natural disasters 25
natural history scholars 14
naturalism and emotion in art 88
negative emotions in dance 64
Negri, Cesare 58, *63*
Nesfeld, Thomas 126
neurological research 120
Newe, Roger 138

Niccolò dell'Arca 91, 92, 93
Nicodemus 91, 92
nightwear 128, 129
Ninety-Five Theses (Luther) 45
Nobiltà di dame (Caroso) 60
Notke, Bert 38
Noves, Laura de 36
Nymphes des bois/Requiem (Josquin) 55

O magnum mysterium (Willaert) 52
obedience of women 125–6
Ockeghem, Johannes 55
Ogilvie, Brian W. 14
Old Testament 3, 100
On the Confession of Masturbation (Gerson) 41
On the Evil Times of Edward II 25–6
On Witches and Women Soothsayers (Molitor) 43
order of the cosmos 61, 62
Orlin, Lena 128
Orvieto revolt (1345) 149
outdoor dramatic performances 70, 71, 72, 76
outdoors, private activities in the 129, 137
Ouvrard, Jean-Pierre 52

pageant wagons 70, 71, 76
pain 21, 28, 95
paintings 88–90, 89, 91, 92–9, 93, 102, 104–5
    See also frescoes
Paleotti, Gabriele 86, 101, 103
Palisca, Claude 50
Palissy, Bernard 23
Paris brawl (1288) 152
Passe, Crispin de 100
pathopoeia 81
patrons of the arts 36
Paumgartner, Balthasar 11
Pearl 116
peasant festivities 136, *136*
Peasant Wedding Dance (Heyden) 102, *103*
Peasants' Revolt (1381) 8
penance 41
Penne, Ralph 137
performance of emotions 14, 35, 116–21, 151
Perseus (Cellini) 86
petitions 151
Petrarch 2, 6, 33, 36–7, 109
Phayre, Thomas 27
Philip IV, King of France 32–3

Philip the Good, Duke of Burgundy 141, 154
physical experiences and emotions 6
Piers Plowman (Langland) 123
Pietà (Niccolò dell'Arca) 91, 92, 93
Pisanello 102–3
Pizan, Christine de 9–10, 42, 118, 128
place-and-scaffold staging 70–2, 76
places and emotions 146
plagues 26–8, *26*, 36
plants, feelings of 23–4
Plato 82
pleasure of music and drama 54, 55, 61, 82
Plour dames (Guillaume de Machaut) 52
Poetics (Aristotle) 82
poetry 5–6, 39
Polk, K. 55
popes, abuses by 45–6
popes, struggle with France 32–3
Porete, Marguerite 40
posada (pause) in dance 66
poverty, responses to 39
Pozzo, Francesco dal 15
practice theory 117
Praxiteles 105
prayers 3–4, 117, 131
Primavera (Botticelli) 105
prints 95, 101–2
privacy, concept of 124, 128–9, 137–9
private emotional experience 11
private life 123–39
    beds and sleeping arrangements 128–33
    families and households 125–8
    meals and dining 133–6
    monastic and secluded life 124–5
    privacy 124, 137–8
    women and the home 138–9
privies 129
procession of shame 153
processions 149
Protestant Reformation 9, 45–6, 86
Prudentius 35
psalms 51, 53–4
psychoanalytic theory 120
Psychomachia (Prudentius) 35
public life 141–55
    collective emotions, rituals and space 145–7
    historians, sources and emotions 142–4
    violence, shame and forgiveness 151–4
    words, bells and flags 147–51
publishing of medicine and science 17–20
Purgatorio (Dante) 112

Rabkin, Norman 77
Rabus, Johann Wolfango 22
Raimondi, Marcantonio 104
Rape of Lucrece (Shakespeare) 6–7
reading 4, 132
reality and fiction in drama 70–1
reconstructive facial surgery 22
Reddy, William M. 3, 110
reformation of religion 2, 9, 43, 45–7, 86
Regimen for Protection against Epidemics (Agramont) 27–8
religion and spirituality 31–47
   Avignon papacy 33, 37
   communal spirituality 5
   emotion in art 33–6
   mysticism 40–2
   plagues and pestilence, responses to 36–7
   poverty, responses to 39
   reformation of religion 45–7
   satire 43–5
   struggle with France 32–3
   waning of church 37
   witches and magic 43
religious experience of dance 61, 63–4
religious images 9, 86, 135
religious orders 124–5
remission by rulers 153–4
René d'Anjou 5
representation in literature 114–15
Republic (Plato) 82
revolts 8, 141–2, 143, 145–51
rhetoric and art 90
rhetoric and drama 73–4, 76
rhetoric and music 54
Rhetoric (Aristotle) 111
Richard III (Shakespeare) 81
Riddy, F. 138
riding of animals in art 100
Rienzo, Cola di 146
Rime sparse (Petrarch) 109
rituals 64–5, 145
Roach, Joseph 76
Robert, Stephen 137
Robertson, Anne Walters 52–3
Robinson, Cynthia 117
Rolle, Richard 3, 6, 131
Rolleston, Joan de 129
Roman de la Rose (Romance of the Rose) 5
romances 3, 5, 8, 119
Romano, Giulio 104
romantic love 108–10
Rome, execution of Cola Rienzo, (1355) 146

Romeo and Juliet (Shakespeare) 124
Roodenberg, Herman 81
Roper, Lyndal 8, 46
Roper, William 137
Rosenwein, Barbara 7, 10, 31, 57, 69, 144
Rouclif, Alice de 128
royal entries and dance 65–6
Ryrie, Alec 131

sacred and secular spaces of drama 70–3
Salih, Sarah 130
same-sex desire 110
San Vicente de la Barquera guild petition (1496) 151
sarcasm 45
satire 43–5, 101–2
Scandinavian literature 119–20
Scharp, Joan 134
Scheer, Monique 69, 75, 117–18, 144
Schism in the Western Church 37
schools 120
scientific understanding. *See* medical and scientific understanding
Sclavus, Martin 153
scorn and censure 87
sculpture 90–1, 92, 97, 100–1
sectarianism, rise of 32
self-control 41, 45, 86
self-pollution 41
Serres, Oliver de 23
servants 126–7, 130, 134
Seville protest (1521) 148–9
sexual desire 62, 64, 105, 110
sexual intimacy 129, 130
Sforza, Anna 128
Shakespeare, William 6, 73–5, 77, 78–9, 80, 81–2, 124
shame 114, 153
Shapin, Simon 13
Ship of Fools (Brant) 43, *44*
shouting of crowds 146–7
Sidney, Sir Philip 5, 110
Siena revolt (1355) 149
sight 88, 104–5
   See also eyes
silkworms 23
Simon, Eckehard 69, 70
Simpson, James 2
singing 55, 56, 149
sins 34–5, 41, 45, 100–1, 111–12
Sir Gawain and the Green Knight 5
Skoda, Hannah 151

sleeping 128
slogans 146–7
sloth 14, 93
Smail, Daniel 26, 153
Smith, Anne 52
Smith, Bruce R. 113–14
social disturbances 141–2
social order and dance 64–5
sociétés joyeuses 82
Solga, Kim 83
soliloquy in drama 73–5
solitude, views of 124
Somerset, Fiona 117
Somonyng of Everyman 75–6, 77–8
Song of Songs 3
soul 20, 21, 22, 35, 37, 88
sound, implied in art 97–8, 105, 113
sources for the history of emotion 114–16
spaces for dramatic performances 70–3
spectacles, danced 58, 60
Spenser, Edmund 10
spiritual decay and art 33–4
St. Paul (Swabian) Neidhart Play 79
Standing Venus (Botticelli) 97
States, Bert O. 78
Stevenson, Jill 78
Stoessel, Jason 53
Stone, Gregory 109
Strozzi, Filippo 18
Strozzi, Pierre 62
suffering 21, 81, 95, 96
Summoner's Tale (Chaucer) 116
sweetness of music 54–5
Sylvius, Jacobius (Jacques Dubois) 15
sympathy 87, 90
synesthesia 113

Tagliacozzi, Gaspare 22
Talkan, Robert 134
Tambling, Jeremy 112
Tasso, Torquato 10
Taylor, John 61
tears 94
textual insincerity of drama 69
theater, definition of 69
theatrical performances 70
theology and medicine 21
theories of emotions 20–4, 87–8
Tilly, Charles 145
Tinctoris, Johannes 54, 55
Titian 90, 97, 99, 105, *106*
Toft, Robert 55

toilets 129
Topsell, Edward 23
Touati, François Olivier 145
Tractado breve de la cultivation y cura de las colmenas (Mendez de Torres) 23
Traini, Francesco 95
Traité sur l'Oraison Dominicale (Melot) 132
trees, feelings of 23–4
Trigg, Stephanie 112
tripudium dances 65
troubadour songs 109
truth, attitudes toward 8–9
Tusser, Thomas 134

Unam Sanctam (papal bull) 33
universities 15
Urania Titani (Brahe) 16
urban communities 109
urban nuisance cases 129, 138
urination 129
Utopia (More) 45
Utopianism 45

Valenciennes violence (1562) 152
Van Orden, Kate 49
Vasari, Giorgio 2, 105
Venus, Cupid and an Organist (Titian) *106*
vernacular drama 69–70
Verrocchio 97
Vesalius, Andreas 15, 17, *17*–18, 22, 24, *24*
vices 34–5, 64, 100–1
Villeveyrac, France 146
Villon, François 39
violence
   in art 96
   in crowds 147–8, 151–3
virtues, depictions of 34–5
virtuous hypocrisies 118
visual arts 85–106
   amorous imagery 103–6
   facial expressions 94
   grief, loss, pain, despair and fear 94–7
   joy, amusement and laughter 101–3
   other visual means 97–100
   religious art 33–6
   theories of emotions 87–8
   types of emotion 85–7
   vices and sins 100–1
   visualization of emotions 89–93
vivisection 24

vocabularies of emotion 113–14
vocal music 55, 56, 149
voyeurism in art 105

wagons for pageants 70, 71, 76
Waldmann, Hans 145, 152–3
Walker-Bynum, C. 40
Walsham, Alexandra 9
wapening 145
war and emotions 117–18
Waryn, Robert 131
watching of dance 57, 61–2
Wear, Andrew 28
weather, changes in 25
wedding celebrations and dance 65
weeping 81, 83, 94
    See also mourning
Wegman, Rob 54–5
Weimann, Robert 70
welfare 39, 46
Weyden, Rogier van der 88, 89, 94
Wickham, Glynne 70
widowhood 127
Wilhite, Valerie 109
Willaert, Adrian 52
Williams, Raymond 1–2
Winchester College, England 128
witchcraft 43
witches 10, 94

women
    challenges to role of 42
    dancing of 62, 65
    and dining 134
    in drama 83, 120
    fear of 9–10
    and the home 138–9
    household roles 126, 127, 130, 132
    mourning of 81–2
    mysticism of 39–40
    obedience of 125–7
    positive images of women 10
    and reading 132
    secluded devotion of 124
    witches 43
wonder 14
woodcuts 43, 44, 95, 96, 101–2, *102*, 104
words and popular emotion 147–8
Worstede, Richard de 138
wrath of god 27, 34, 36
Wuidar, Laurence 50
Wyatt, Sir Thomas 9

Yconomica (Konrad of Megenberg) 55
York bill-posting campaign (1536) 150–1
York Corpus Christi Plays 76

Zürich revolt (1489) 145, 152–3
Zwingli, Ulrich 86